Computers in translation

Researchers have been attempting to develop systems to emulate the human translation process for some forty years. What is it about natural language that makes this such a daunting challenge? While other software applications have achieved rapid and lasting success, machine translation has failed to penetrate the worldwide market to any appreciable extent. Does this merely reflect a reluctance to adopt it, or does it signal a more fundamental and intractable problem?

Computers in translation is a comprehensive guide to the practical issues surrounding machine translation and computer-based translation tools. Translators, system designers, system operators and researchers present the facts about machine translation: its history, its successes, its limitations and its potential. Three chapters deal with actual machine translation applications, discussing installations including the METEO system, used in Canada to translate weather bulletins and weather reports, and the system used in the Foreign Technology Department of the US Air Force. As a guide for non-specialists seeking to broaden their knowledge of the practicalities of machine translation, it will be of particular interest to translators, technical authors, technical publications managers, students and lecturers in languages and linguistics.

John Newton, a Senior Lecturer in the Department of Languages at Manchester Polytechnic, also runs his own consultancy business, providing translation services and distributing linguistic software. He has undertaken translation-related international consultancy assignments and has given talks and presentations on machine translation throughout Europe. He has also supervised a number of machine translation installations, and is the author of several articles on machine translation and related topics.

Computers in translation

A practical appraisal

Edited by
John Newton

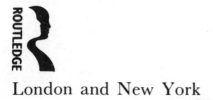

London and New York

First published 1992
by Routledge
11 New Fetter Lane, London EC4P 4EE

Simultaneously published in the USA and Canada
by Routledge
a division of Routledge, Chapman and Hall, Inc.
29 West 35th Street, New York, NY 10001

© 1992 John Newton

Typeset in Baskerville by
Columns Design and Production Services Ltd, Reading
Printed in Great Britain by Biddles Ltd, Guildford and King's Lynn

A catalogue record for this book is available from the British Library.

ISBN 0–415–05432–X

Library of Congress Cataloging-in-Publication Data

Computers in translation : a practical appraisal / edited by John
  Newton.
    Includes bibliographical references and index.
    ISBN 0–415–05432–X
    1. Machine translating. I. Newton, John, 1944–
P308.C67 1992
418′.02′0285—dc20   91–41614
                                                        CIP

This book is dedicated to the expertise and
wisdom of its contributors and to
the marvel of natural language.

Contents

Figures

Contributors

Dale A. Bostad is a technical adviser in the Directorate of Translations at the Foreign Technology Division, US Air Force, Dayton, Ohio. Originally a traditional translator from Russian into English, he became involved in machine translation in 1976 and has found the latter career considerably more challenging. Currently he is studying Japanese, Arabic and Chinese.

John Chandioux is the founder and President of John Chandioux Consultants Inc., which specializes in research and development in the field of computational linguistics. He is the owner and designer of the famed machine-translation system METEO and has developed his own proprietary programming language known as GramR. He is also the author of a number of spelling checkers incorporated into French versions of word-processing programs, including the initial dictionary sold with WordPerfect 5.0. His most recent activities include the launching of a family of French-language spelling and grammar checkers in Europe and North America under the generic name GramR.

Annette Grimaila, originally a programmer-analyst in the finance industry, has been associated with John Chandioux Consultants Inc. for some four years. She was project leader and principal programmer of the General TAO system.

Alex Gross served as a literary adviser to the Royal Shakespeare Company during the 1960s, and his translations of Dürrenmatt and Peter Weiss have been produced in London and elsewhere. He was awarded a two-year fellowship as writer-in-residence by the Berliner Künstler-Programm, and one of his plays has been produced in several German cities. Having spent twelve years in

Europe, he is fluent in French, German, Italian and Spanish. He has published works related to the translation of traditional Chinese medicine and is planning further work in this field. Two more recent play translations were commissioned and produced by UBU Repertory Company in New York, one of them as part of the official American celebration of the French Revolutionary Bicentennial in 1989. Published play translations are *The Investigation* (Peter Weiss, 1986, London: Calder & Boyars) and *Enough is Enough* (Protais Asseng, 1985, NYC: UBU Repertory Co.). His translation experience has also encompassed journalistic, diplomatic and commerical texts, and he has taught translation as part of NYU's translation certificate programme. Over the last few years a number of his articles on computers, translation and linguistics have appeared in the United Kingdom, the Netherlands and the United States. He is chairperson of the Machine Translation Committee of the New York Circle of Translators, is also an active member of the American Translators Association and has been involved in the presentations and publications of both groups.

Alan Melby is Associate Professor of Linguistics at Brigham Young University (Provo, Utah, USA), where he also chairs the Translation Research Group (BYU-TRG). He is also Director of Research and Development at LinguaTech International (Orem, Utah), where he designed MTX(tm), one of the first micro-computer-based terminology management systems. He has done research in a number of areas of natural language processing, including machine translation, speech processing, translator tools and full-text electronic dictionaries. During February 1990, he was Visiting Professor at the Collège de France, one of the most prestigious academic institutions in France, where he delivered a series of lectures on linguistic theory. He believes that the difference between lexical and terminological units is more fundamental than was previously suspected. His favourite living philosophers are J.-M. Zemb and E. Levinas.

John Newton is a Senior Lecturer in the Department of Languages at Manchester Polytechnic. His experience of the practical aspects of machine translation and translation tools is long and varied. He was the founding managing director of

Weidner Translation (Europe) Limited, and also served as operations director of another major international translation company. More recently, he has concentrated on importing and distributing linguistic software via his own consultancy company, Mentor Documentation Services Limited. He has undertaken a number of international translation-related consultancy assignments and has given talks and presentations on machine translation throughout Europe. He has also been involved in operational research for translation tools developers and has made many presentations of such products to commercial, industrial, institutional and academic audiences. At WTE, he played a leading role in devising training programmes and in introducing the MicroCat system to the UK higher education sector. He also supervised a number of industrial machine translation installations. Mr Newton, who has had a number of articles published on machine translation and related topics, is a former member of the Institute of Linguists' Council and was Chairman of the Institute's Central Southern Regional Society from 1987–91.

Jeanette Pugh worked at UMIST in the Department of Language and Linguistics from 1985–91. Throughout this period, she was closely involved with the EUROTRA machine translation programme, and played a major role in the planning and co-ordination of the work of the British EUROTRA team. She was a member of EUROTRA's central management committee (liaison group) and regularly attended its meetings at the European Commission in Luxembourg. She was also appointed to EUROTRA's central planning committee which worked on the formulation of proposals for the content of the 1991–2 EUROTRA transition programme. Dr Pugh was a co-author of *Multilingual Aspects of Information Technology* (1986, Gower Press), and recently co-authored an article on machine translation in Europe which is to appear in *The Encyclopaedia of Language and Linguistics* published by Pergamon Press.

Klaus Schubert studied general linguistics, Nordic philology and Slavic philology at the universities of Kiel (Germany) and Uppsala (Sweden). He obtained a doctor's degree from the University of Kiel in 1982 where he also carried out sociolinguistic research for several years. Since 1985, he has been with the software company *Buro voor Systeemontwikkeling* (BSO) in Utrecht, the Netherlands. He participated in the DLT machine translation project at BSO/

Research as a computational linguist and later became a linguistic system designer and project manager. At present, he is attached to BSO/Language Technology in Baarn, the Netherlands, a department which provides software services in the fields of natural language processing, machine-aided translation and linguistic knowledge engineering. Klaus Schubert's major publications include *Anredeforschung* (Braun, Kohz, Schubert, 1986, Tübingen: Narr), *Metataxis. Contrastive dependency syntax for machine translation* (Schubert, 1987, Dordrecht/Providence: Foris), *Interlinguistics. Aspects of the science of planned languages* (Schubert (ed.), 1989, Berlin/New York: Mouton de Gruyter). He is also European editor of the scholarly journal *Language Problems and Language Planning* (Amsterdam/Philadelphia: Benjamins), and, in August 1992, will be moving to Flensburg, Germany, to take up a position as a professor of computational linguistics and technical translation at the Institut für Übersetzen of the Fachhochschule.

Harold L. Somers is a Senior Lecturer in the Department of Language and Linguistics and in the Centre for Computational Linguistics at the University of Manchester Institute of Science and Technology (UMIST). He is involved in teaching and research in the field of machine translation (MT). Teaching activities include lecturing to undergraduate students on the department's BSc course in computational linguistics, and to postgraduates on the MSc course in MT, both courses unique and innovatory when they began in 1978 and 1987 respectively. In addition, he is frequently invited to give guest lectures on MT and natural language processing (NLP) to linguistics and computer science students elsewhere in the UK and in Europe. His research interests are all aspects of MT, and more narrowly syntax and semantics in NLP. He is the author of *Case and Valency in Computational Linguistics* (1987, Edinburgh University Press), and is co-author, with John Hutchins, of a textbook on machine translation published by Academic Press. A Prolog and NLP textbook aimed at linguistics students is also in preparation. He has worked on several MT projects, including the EC's EUROTRA system, and various other MT projects at UMIST. In 1988–9 he was a visiting research fellow at Toshiba Corporation's R&D Centre in Japan. Since his return to the UK, his main research interests have been dialogue-based MT and example-based MT, in both cases involving Japanese as well as European languages.

Patricia Thomas has made a career using languages, particularly French, as translator and teacher, in addition to being involved in the editing of learned scientific books and journals. After gaining an MPhil at the University of Surrey in 1983, she followed terminology training at Infoterm, the international terminology organization in Vienna. She has been instrumental in creating a multilingual terminology data bank in specialized subject domains at the University of Surrey, for which some of the input resulted from her supervision of MA students in translation studies who were interested in pursuing computational methods of terminology for their final dissertations. This led naturally to her becoming involved, while at Surrey, in producing terminology for a project sponsored by the European Commission's ESPRIT II programme to develop a multilingual translator's workbench (project no. 2315). A number of invited papers have been given at international meetings and she has co-authored publications on terminology and term banks. She has also participated in the work of international nomenclature and taxonomy organizations in the biological sciences. She is a member of ISO TC 37 Working Group (vocabulary of terminology), editor for the International Institute for Terminology Research (IITR), Vienna, regional editor for Southern England for Infoterm, Vienna, and is a Fellow of the Institute of Linguists. She is currently doing research for her PhD.

Muriel Vasconcellos holds a BS degree in languages and a Master's and PhD in linguistics from Georgetown University. She has devoted her entire career to translation, including twenty years specifically to machine translation. Since 1977, she has been responsible for the development and implementation of MT at the Pan American Health Organization, Regional Office for the Americas of the World Health Organization.

Yorick Wilks is Director of the Computing Research Laboratory at New Mexico State University, a centre of excellence for research in artificial intelligence and its applications. He received his doctorate from Cambridge University in 1968 for work in computer programs that understand written English in terms of a theory later called 'preference semantics': the claim that language is to be understood by means of a search for semantic 'gists', combined with a coherence function over such structures that minimizes effort in the analyser. This has continued as the focus of his work, and has applications in the areas of machine translation, the use of English as a 'front end' for users of databases and the computation of belief structures. He has published five books and numerous articles in this area of artificial intelligence and, before going to

New Mexico, was Professor of Computer Science and Linguistics at the University of Essex (UK).

Preface

Machine translation (MT) clearly arouses considerable interest beyond the ranks of those directly concerned with developing systems or operating them. When I was involved in supplying and installing translation software, I was frequently asked to recommend a book with a practical focus that would serve as a general introduction to the field. This proved to be difficult, as most existing publications were aimed at a specialist readership and assumed a prior knowledge of the subject's technical aspects that the general reader was unlikely to possess. The idea of presenting a collection of practical accounts from researchers, system developers, system operators and translators, together with an appraisal of MT's position in the world today and an outline of the main avenues of current research, grew out of this experience.

As opinions voiced on MT vary from the wildly optimistic to the fiercely negative, we have attemped to place the matter in perspective by describing the conditions under which MT systems are likely to produce optimum results and by making some general statements on their current limitations.

Any assessment of the computer's contribution in the sphere of natural-language translation should recognize the importance of so-called 'lower level' computerized translation tools. Unlike MT systems, which can only be gainfully employed under certain conditions, computerized tools offer tangible benefits in almost every area of written translation. Products in this category have therefore been given due consideration in this volume.

Our aim of providing a broad practical introduction to the field clearly demanded contributions from authors representing as many strands of opinion and as many allied disciplines as was practicable in a work this size. I therefore invited a number of leading authorities in Europe and North America each to provide a chapter dealing with their own specialism and was fortunate enough to receive their enthusiastic support.

It would, of course, be impossible to deal with our subject exhaustively in a work of any size, let alone within the confines of this volume. We believe, however, that our policy of selecting practical topics and providing sufficient space for an in-depth treatment of each has yielded a collection which goes some way towards meeting the needs of readers seeking information in an accessible and (dare I say it?!) 'user-friendly' form.

I extend my warmest thanks to all the contributors and to Routledge for turning this idea into a reality.

John Newton

Abbreviations and acronyms

AFNOR	Association française de normalisation (French standards organization)
ACH	Association for Computing in the Humanities
ACL	Association for Computational Linguistics
AI	Artificial Intelligence
ALLC	Association for Literary and Linguistic Computing
ALPAC	Automatic Language Processing Advisory Committee
ASCII	American Standard Code for Information Interchange
Aslib	Association for Information Management (Association of Special Libraries and Information Bureaux)
ATA	American Translators Association
ATR	Automated Telephony Research
BSO	Buro voor Systeemontwikkeling
BT	British Telecom
CAT	Computer-Assisted (-Aided) Translation
CCL	Centre for Computational Linguistics (at UMIST)
CCRIT	Centre Canadien de Recherche en Informatisation du Travail
CD-ROM	Compact Disc Read Only Memory
CEC	Commission of the European Communities
CFE	Caterpillar Fundamental English
CICC	Center for International Cultural Cooperation (Japan)
CL	Computational Linguistics
CLL	Centre for Computational Linguistics
CMU	Carnegie Mellon University
COLING	(International Conference on) Computational Linguistics

CPU	Central Processing Unit
DARPA	Defense Advanced Research Projects Agency
DIN	Deutsches Institut für Normung
DLT	Distributed Language Translation
DOS	Disk Operating System
DTP	Desk-Top Publishing
EC	European Community
ECHO	European Commission Host Organisation
EDR	Electronic Dictionary Research (Project)
EEC	European Economic Community
ENGSPAN	English to Spanish MT system (at PAHO)
EURATOM	European Atomic Energy Authority
EUSIDIC	European Association of Scientific Information Dissemination Centres
FAHQT	Fully Automated High Quality Translation
FTD	Foreign Technology Division (US Air Force)
GETA	Groupe d'études pour la traduction automatique
GUI	Graphical User Interface
HPSG	Head-Driven Phrase Structure Grammar
HAMT	Human-Assisted (-Aided) Machine Translation
HT	Human Translation
IBM	International Business Machines
ICCL	International Conference on Computational Linguistics (COLING)
ILSAM	International Language for Service and Maintenance
IPSS	International Packet Switch Stream
ISSCO	Institut Dalle Molle pour les études sémantiques et cognitives
JEIDA	Japanese Electronic Industry Development Association
JICST	Japan's Information Centre of Science and Technology
Kb	Kilobyte
KBMT	Knowledge-Based Machine Translation
LCD	Liquid Crystal Display
LFG	Lexical Functional Grammar
LIDIA	Large Internationalisation of Documents by Interacting with their Authors
LSP	Language for Special Purposes

MAHT	Machine-Assisted (-Aided) Human Translation
MATER	Magnetic Tape Exchange Format (for Terminological/Lexicographical Records)
MicroMATER	Magnetic Tape Exchange Format (for microcomputers)
MIT	Massachusetts Institute of Technology
MITI	(Japanese) Ministry of International Trade and Industry
MAT	Machine-Assisted (-Aided) Translation
MT	Machine Translation
NLP	Natural Language Processing
NMSU	New Mexico State University
NSF	(US) National Science Foundation
NYU	New York University
OCR	Optical Character Reader, Optical Character Recognition
PACE	Perkins Approved Clear English
PAHO	Pan American Health Organization
PC	Personal Computer
PECOF	Post-Editor's Correction Feedback
PSS	Packet Switch Stream
RAM	Random Access Memory
SGML	Standard Generalized Markup Language
SL	Source Language
SPANAM	Spanish to American (English) MT system (at PAHO)
SUSY	Saarbrücker ÜbersetzungsSYstem
TAO	Traduction assistée par ordinateur
TAUM	Traduction Automatique de l'Université de Montréal
TEAM	Terminology Evaluation and Management
TEI	Text Encoding Initiative
TL	Target Language
UMIST	University of Manchester Institute of Science and Technology
WYSIWYG	What You See Is What You Get

Chapter 1

Introduction and overview

John Newton

A BRIEF HISTORICAL PERSPECTIVE

Translation, a *sine qua non* for the comprehension of a text by a reader unfamiliar with the language in which it was first written, has doubtless been practised in one form or another for several millennia; yet, until modern times, translators possessed little in the way of tools, apart from manual writing implements, erasers and hard–copy reference sources.

Present-day translators are major beneficiaries of the technological revolution in office practice which was born with the advent of the typewriter in the nineteenth century and which led to today's proliferation of personal computers (PCs) and their associated peripherals. Most professional translators now regard word processing as the normal method of creating a target text, while those who prefer to use dictation machines invariably resort to it for transcription.

Modern technology has transposed some of the translator's traditional tools to a new and more flexible medium: more and more dictionaries (monolingual, bilingual, multilingual) are becoming available in machine–readable form. These utilities are accessible from a text file, via windows, and allow selected translation equivalents to be 'pasted' directly into the text at the cursor position; some also permit the user to make new entries and modify existing entries.

Facsimile machines and electronic mail systems have brought similarly significant benefits, eliminating delays in receiving and transmitting texts, and making suitably equipped translators globally and instantly accessible, irrespective of their base location.

Although of great benefit to translators, the systems and devices mentioned so far were designed to meet a broad range of general needs outside of translation. The chapters which follow discuss and describe systems that were conceived specifically to facilitate, or even perform, translation.

The products that we are concerned with come under two headings: machine translation systems, and translation tools.

Systems which perform a syntactic analysis of a source text and then generate a target language rendering thereof which seeks to preserve and reconstitute its semantic and stylistic elements are described as 'machine translation' (MT) systems, while those designed to facilitate human translation through providing a terminology management system, instant access to on–line dictionaries, and other utilities are referred to as 'translation tools'. Despite this distinction, it is important to emphasize the essentially auxiliary role of MT in most of its applications.

A typical translation tools package has two main constituents: a text analyser, which furnishes input for various wordlists and bilingual glossaries; and a terminology database, which provides a flexible framework for storage and retrieval. These systems are used to create bilingual 'document' dictionaries containing all the lexical items – except articles, conjunctions and prepositions – found in a specified source text, along with their translation equivalents. They also perform morphological reductions to generate lists of base forms (i.e. for English, all verbal, plural and possessive inflections are removed) to simplify dictionary updating. In common with the off-the-shelf dictionary products, most translation tools packages offer automatic look-up and 'paste-in'.

Translation tools and machine-readable dictionaries have to be integrated into whatever combination of hardware and software the translator happens to be using and this often results in an assemblage of disparate elements that do not form a congruous whole. Recognition of this problem led some researchers to adopt a holistic approach in the 1980s. The translator workstation or translator's workbench (see Chapter 8: Patricia Thomas; and Chapter 9: Alan Melby) combines any or all of the functions and facilities mentioned above in an ergonomically designed unit aimed at creating greater efficiency, greater productivity, and greater translator satisfaction and well-being.

Of course, if texts are to be machine processed, they have to be available in a compatible magnetic format, or they need to be entered via an optical character reader (OCR). Extensive use of word processing, together with the availability of media conversion and budget-priced OCR systems, has made the bulk of today's commercially translated text accessible to MT and translation tools.

Compared with translation tools, MT has a relatively long and chequered history (see Chapter 2: Jeanette Pugh). Despite its acknowledged success in a number of well-publicized restricted domain or restricted input environments, only a small proportion of today's worldwide translation workload is processed using MT, and the commercially available systems' ability to handle general (i.e. unrestricted) text will need to improve significantly before the installed base shows any substantial growth.

The difficulties inherent in tackling the kaleidoscopic and cognitive aspects of natural language constitute a daunting challenge for system developers which has led to many different and ingenious approaches. In Chapter 11, Harold Somers provides a detailed outline of the main strands of current MT research, including some radical new concepts, and in Chapter 6 Klaus Schubert gives us an in-depth account of his experience with the BSO DLT system and explains the rationale behind the choice of Esperanto as an intermediate language.

At first sight, it may seem surprising that MT projects should have existed several decades before anyone tackled the less ambitious task of developing translation tools and translator workstations. However, this appears less remarkable if one considers that such products only became practically feasible and commercially viable when the price of PCs had dropped sufficiently to encourage their widespread use among translators (see Chapter 9).

MT VERSUS HUMAN TRANSLATION

What, then, is the status of MT? If we accept that translation demands total sensitivity to the cognitive aspects of a source text, it follows that a computer would need to understand language and assimilate facts in the way that humans do in order to resolve textual ambiguity and create a version that paid due regard to semantic content and register. For example, an awareness of context is essential for the correct interpretation of a sentence such as *visiting European dignitaries can be a nuisance*. In translating this sentence, a human translator would take into account the sentences which preceded and followed, as well as the general context, the overall theme of the text and any relevant social, economic or cultural factors. However, a computer's inability to acquire, comprehend and rationally apply real-world knowledge in this way does not render MT useless as a production tool. Raw MT output does not need to be perfect in order to be useful. With the exception of a few specific applications (e.g. unedited raw translation used for *information only* purposes), it is rarely regarded as a finished product; like other raw materials, it is converted into a finished product only through human agency (i.e. post-editing). Direct comparisons between a system's raw output and human translation are therefore pointless; as MT is a production tool, its capacity to increase or speed up production, within acceptable cost parameters, is the only valid measure of its effectiveness. If its use can be shown to increase productivity and/or reduce costs, it is clearly advantageous; if it fails to do either, it is a white elephant.

In Chapter 10, Yorick Wilks presents for the first time a detailed description of the methodology he used in 1979–80 when conducting an evaluation of the SYSTRAN Russian to English MT system for the US Air Force. After explaining the rationale behind the test and enumerating his evaluation criteria, he gives a full account of the implementation procedures and follows this with an analysis and discussion of the results obtained. This document should prove invaluable to anyone seeking a blueprint for MT evaluation.

Contrary to a view sometimes expressed by people remote from the translation process, a source text lexical item does not necessarily have just one 'correct' target language equivalent. If this is true at the word or term level, it applies even more at the level of the clause or the sentence. The notion that there is always a unique and obvious way to translate any combination of words from one natural language to another is fallacious in the extreme. The number of word combinations possible in any natural language is unquantifiable and infinitely expandable, yet humans usually manage to infer intended meanings from context. The headline 'Navy bases are safe', which appeared in a Hampshire (UK) newspaper in February 1991, illustrates the importance of context. Anyone unfamiliar with the local scene could have assumed that terrorist threats had been made against naval bases, or that there had been fears of radiation or some other form of contamination. The headline was, in reality, aimed at dispelling rumours of closures and consequent job losses. Anyone who had followed the controversy surrounding the bases would have grasped the intended meaning immediately, and those without such prior knowledge would have been fully enlightened by the first paragraph of the article, which read: 'The Royal Navy is set to expand its bases in the Solent . . . fears that bases could be closed . . . were unfounded'.

Nevertheless, the human's ability to infer meaning does not always present translators with clear-cut solutions to translation problems. Producing a translation which may need to convey concepts, attitudes and physical realities alien to the target-language culture demands considerable resourcefulness and creativity. Several acceptable renderings of a sentence may be proposed but the adoption of one in preference to the others must ultimately be based on subjective criteria. No human translator can claim to render the semantic content and stylistic features of any source text with total fidelity, and it is unlikely that any two translators would ever produce identical renderings of anything but the shortest and simplest document. It is equally unlikely that a single human translator would produce identical versions if asked to translate a text of any substance on more than one occasion. These points are made here solely to dispel any notion that translation is a straightforward process involving clear choices.

Having stated that human translators usually score over MT systems in the areas of interpretation and preservation of register, it is important to stress that when it comes to spelling and terminological consistency the computer invariably outperforms the human. In these areas, it simply cannot make mistakes; all spelling anomalies in its output are attributable to human error in dictionary compilation or updating; likewise, it cannot deviate from the translation equivalents that are entered (see Chapter 4 for a description of dictionary entry in a batch-processing MT system). Consumers of translation sometimes attempt to overcome the problem of terminological inconsistency in human translation by distributing glossaries – or document dictionaries, as described above – to translators but this does not, in itself, ensure that the prescribed terminology will be used exclusively and consistently throughout a translation.

Computers can handle any number of variant spellings, provided the dictionary entries and rules allow for them (e.g. British and American variants 'sceptical'/'skeptical'; other variants such as 'time frame'/'time-frame'/'timeframe' or 'judgement'/'judgment'), and render them with a single target language equivalent, if this is desired. Nevertheless, systems are usually designed to deal only with standard syntax and grammar. This means that they are unable to compensate for human errors and ideolectal deviations in the form of non-standard syntax, usage and punctuation, or inadvertently missed or repeated words. Moreover, they obviously lack the capacity to comprehend what an author intends to convey when he/she deliberately deviates from the established conventions in a very personal way. In all of these cases, a human translator will invariably deduce the author's intended meaning and produce a translation which is more coherent than the source text. However, the ability to exercise judgement in interpretation does not guarantee consistent use of terminology, and it is not unknown for a human translator to render recurrent sentences in different ways within a single text. This does not imply that one rendering is 'wrong' and the others 'right', or even that one is necessarily 'better' than the others. Such stylistic variation may be prized in some forms of writing but in technical manuals and user instructions it can be disorientating and is generally frowned upon. The problem of human inconsistency is particularly acute when a text has to be divided between a number of translators in order to meet a delivery deadline or on account of its sheer volume. These cases highlight collective as well as individual inconsistency and editing is generally needed to achieve an acceptable level of homogeneity.

Spelling mistakes and typing errors are not at all unusual in human-translated output, nor are serious errors of usage and grammar (is anyone infallible in all of these areas?). Computers can help here, of course, but many people who have spell checkers and grammar checkers fail to use them (complacency, or pressure of work?). When considering the merits or demerits of MT, we should not therefore labour under the false notion that human translation, or even edited human translation, is always perfect. The very fact of being human creates a potential for error, and instances of whole sentences, paragraphs or even pages being 'skipped' in translation are by no means uncommon, nor are mistranslations. I have seen warnings on technical products translated in a way that makes them say the opposite of what the source text said. How can this happen? It is quite simply the human factor at work. The world knowledge and life experience of human translators can help them to grasp the precise meaning of a sentence or passage but it can also cause them to make assumptions which are wrong. A translator who has been translating all day can easily fail to spot a deviation from what appears to be a uniform sequence of messages as the working day draws to a close. If 'never' occurs just once in a list of safety instructions beginning 'always', it is not difficult to imagine how an error could creep in. In large organisations where translations are routinely proofread by other translators or editors, errors of this kind would normally be discovered and corrected but many translators have to work without this safety net.

As stated above, MT systems cannot deviate from the translation equivalents that figure in the dictionary or dictionaries specified for any particular task. However, if the human-supplied dictionary input is wrong, the system will consistently reproduce errors in raw translation until the entry is corrected. Fortunately, most MT output is post-edited, and a post-editor, like the proofreader of human translation, can be expected to notice problems of this kind and take corrective measures in the text and in the dictionary. Moreover, MT does not carry the risk of lines, paragraphs or pages being unintentionally 'skipped' in translation.

WHERE CAN MT BE USED TO ADVANTAGE?

The suitability of MT for any particular task depends on the nature of the source text and the intended purpose of the translation; several contributors to this book make this point (Chandioux, Gross, Melby, Newton). Poetry and industrial parts lists represent two extremes in this regard, for while it would be absurd to contemplate using MT for the former, one could reasonably expect a perfect result (requiring no editing) for the latter; provided, of course, that all the relevant nomenclature was in the system's dictionaries.

It is clear then that machine translation cannot be used indiscriminately. Many source texts have to be excluded from MT on the grounds that their text typology precludes anything but the attention of a skilled and highly specialized human translator. Literary works are obvious candidates for exclusion, as are all kinds of advertising and promotional text. Indeed, for the latter category, translation alone will not suffice; a complete adaptation is needed to take account of the native aspirations, susceptibilities and prejudices of the target market.

Notwithstanding the large volume of text that it would be impractical or imprudent to submit to MT, there remains a substantial and growing body of technical and scientific text that can be handled efficiently and profitably using computers if the requisite operational conditions exist, as is exemplified by the applications described in Chapters 3, 4 and 5 of this volume. It would, nonetheless, be unrealistic to expect any system to perform well with source texts drawn randomly from a wide range of subject areas and text typologies.

I have stated above that an MT system's raw output – 'raw translation' – is not usually regarded as a finished product. This reflects the fact that most users practise post-editing to some degree. The techniques applied range from rapid post-editing, for information-only purposes, to comprehensive 'polishing' aimed at making the finished product indistinguishable from human translation. Most MT systems have a synchronized split-screen editing mode which enables the post-editor to view and scroll the raw translation in tandem with the corresponding section of source text. Quality control rests with the post-editor and must be assumed to be as rigorous as that applied to human translation produced for similar purposes.

Syntax errors in raw translation are only a problem if they are so numerous that post-editing requires as much effort as normal human translation (see Chapter 3: Annette Grimaila and John Chandioux). It is always advisable to conduct tests to ascertain whether MT is suited to a particular environment before incurring the expense of purchasing a system, but if such tests are to be fair to the prospective purchaser and to the system, they should involve a substantial volume of truly typical text and the requisite level of dictionary updating. Anything less than this is unlikely to yield an accurate picture.

THE HUMAN FACTOR IN MT

If MT is to be used to maximum advantage, those responsible for operating the system must be receptive to its introduction. It would be unwise and unfair to impose MT on translators who had not been consulted and given an opportunity to express their highly relevant views on a proposal which has such momentous implications for them. In common with other major computer applications, MT systems demand a considerable learning effort from their operators; it would therefore be unrealistic to expect translators to maintain their normal workload while getting to grips with MT. Moreover, a system can only be fully exploited if users are trained in all aspects of its operation and feel generally comfortable with it; thus, any attempt to take shortcuts in the area of training would be likely to have a very deleterious effect on the results obtained and on the translators' attitude to MT.

In Chapter 7, Alex Gross makes the point that MT demands special skills of a very high order on the part of the operator. Introducing it into a department which may lack the requisite aptitude or commitment is therefore unlikely to produce optimum results. While some translators take to MT like the proverbial duck to water, others find the prospect of adapting to it extremely daunting. My experience of training groups of translators to use MT systems suggests that a good translator does not necessarily make a good MT operator; although I did find that most translators – including some who were nearing retirement – were able and willing to make the necessary adjustment.

There should be no conflict of interest between human translators and MT. The latter has proved beneficial to some translators through opening up a new and challenging career, and the publicity MT receives does, at least, bring discussion of translation into the broader public domain. Furthermore, the presence of an MT system, in a clearly subordinate role, serves to highlight the skills of the human translator/post-editor. As one MT provider accurately described it, 'the system takes care of the donkey work, while the human translator concentrates on fine-tuning the dictionaries and polishing the raw output'. We should also recognize that some of the tasks assigned to MT, e.g. information-only translation (as discussed by Muriel Vasconcellos and Dale Bostad in Chapter 5), and translation of time-sensitive restricted domain texts (as described in Chapter 3), would probably not be performed at all if MT were not available.

ATTITUDES TO MT

There are a number of (largely apocryphal) stories in circulation about bizarre computer renderings of well-known phrases and idioms; the most notorious of these is probably 'out of sight, out of mind', allegedly rendered as 'invisible idiot'. It calls to mind an occasion when I was invited to demonstrate a French–English MT system on television. It was clear from the outset that the presenter wanted to maximize the entertainment value of the situation. After an introduction which made exaggerated claims for the system, he gleefully produced a piece of paper bearing the words, *Plongeur dans un restaurant, il avait du mal à gagner sa vie* and asked me to enter the sentence and translate it. Given the fact that the only translation for *plongeur* in my dictionary was *diver*, the desired comic effect was achieved. Fortunately, I had time to create another entry for *plongeur*, in a different dictionary, giving *washer-up* as its translation, and I retranslated the sentence using a different dictionary look-up sequence. This enabled me to demonstate that, with MT, vocabulary and terminology are totally controllable. So stories about 'hydraulic rams' being machine translated as 'water goats' should be treated with the contempt they deserve, because they are evidence not of an MT system's inability to handle vocabulary but of a raconteur's lack of familiarity with the workings of an MT system.

Much criticism of MT is unjustly directed towards its inability to perform tasks it was never designed to tackle (e.g. literary translation). On the other hand, the extravagant accuracy claims sometimes made for it by salesmen do nothing to enhance its image among the better informed. Alex Gross (see Chapter 7) points out the absurdity of attempting to quantify translation accuracy in percentage terms, and also notes the ambivalence displayed by some laymen who expect perfect results from MT, but who are nevertheless among the first to chuckle at its alleged bizarre renderings. In the same vein, I have met people who refused to heed warnings about the unsuitability of MT for a particular application, only to become indignant and disillusioned when tests they had insisted on conducting proved this to be the case.

Over the past two or three years, numerous cheap hand-held 'translation' devices have been promoted through mailings and off-the-page advertisements. Although they are little more than electronic dictionaries with very limited vocabularies, they have helped to spread the notion that automatic translation is routine and commonplace. Even the *Collins English Dictionary* (second edition 1986) encourages this assumption by defining 'translator' as 'a person or machine that translates speech or writing'.

Another misconception concerning MT stems from a false

analogy drawn between the unrestrained and flexible nature of natural language and the exactitude and precision of mathematics. Because computers can cope with the intricacies of a spreadsheet, it is assumed that they can be made to produce flawless on-demand translations of any source text. If each word in a language had one – and only one – clearly circumscribed value, and if the total value of a group of words could be ascertained by adding together their individual values, this analogy might have some merit. The reality, however, is very different and those who propound this theory would do well to ponder natural language a little more intently.

Translators who have had direct involvement with MT tend to have a realistic and positive attitude towards it; they know what it can do and they are aware of its limitations. Some find working with a system far more challenging and fulfilling than traditional translation methods. However, as working environments which lend themselves to MT are so rare, relatively few translators have the opportunity to familiarize themselves with the workings of a system. Some translators no doubt feel that MT is so remote from their own activities, or that it accounts for so small a portion of translated text, that it is irrelevant; however, most of those I have spoken to expressed a keen desire for more information and it is hoped that the present volume will go some way towards meeting their needs.

CONCLUSIONS

Along with other writers, translators were quick to realize the benefits of computers. Word processing is now used almost universally among translators and translation tools and computerized dictionaries are steadily gaining ground.

Commercially-available MT systems are often designed to meet wide-ranging needs. The fact that potential users tend to have very specific needs renders a large proportion of an off-the-shelf system's capability superfluous in most applications. It would therefore seem desirable to extend the principle of subject specialization, as practised by human translators, to MT. Bespoke systems (as described in Chapter 3) undoubtedly maximize the potential for success. At some future time, it may even be possible to assemble systems from 'bolt-on' modules, selected or adapted to cope with specified features of a particular text type; for instance, in an

English–French context it would be useful to be able to choose how the negative imperative should be handled. If this idea does become a reality one day, what is left out (for any single application) will be every bit as important as what is included.

The fact that MT is already making a valuable contribution in some areas is amply evidenced by the first-hand accounts provided in the present volume. Nevertheless, it is important to bear in mind that these successes are the fruit of a substantial amount of preparation and the deployment of considerable human, physical and financial resources. Moreover, putting in place the elements needed for implementation does not in itself ensure success. Many text types simply do not lend themselves to MT. Before embarking on any new MT installation it is therefore imperative that tests be conducted to determine its feasibility.

MT's much-publicized propensity for producing the occasional amusing rendering (e.g. *engine views* translated into French as *le moteur regarde* or *traffic jam* as *confiture de circulation*) is irrelevant if post-editing its output results in totally acceptable versions being produced more quickly and/or at lower cost than with other processing methods. In any event, repetition of such mistranslations is easily avoided through dictionary updating, and once the appropriate translation equivalents have been entered, the system will use them unfailingly; it is worth restating that (given a translation task of any magnitude) MT should always have the edge over the human translator as far as terminological consistency is concerned.

The emergence, in recent years, of international networks of translation companies, and of translation companies specializing in one or more (invariably high-tech) domains, is a strategic response to changes in the pattern and nature of translation demand. These developments, creating as they do larger pools of translators – either on-site, or via on-line link-ups – tend to favour the spread of translation tools and translator workstations. At the same time, the standardization of formats for multilingual terminology databases (see Chapter 8) should encourage translators to make greater use of them.

It is, perhaps, regrettable that translation tools do not attract the same level of media coverage as MT, for unlike the latter, they can be used by any translator for almost any text type (subject to the requisite language pairs or modules being available). Translator workstations are similarly broad in their appeal and in the range of their applications; when a standard specification emerges, it will no doubt be warmly received.

The diverse interests and activities of the contributors to this volume give an indication of the potential that computers have to offer in the field of natural language translation. There can be little doubt that the balance of the 1990s will witness an increase in the number of commercial MT installations, along with significant growth in the use of translation tools.

Chapter 2

The story so far: an evaluation of machine translation in the world today

Jeanette Pugh

INTRODUCTION

This chapter presents an assessment of the position of machine translation (MT) in the world today. In this assessment I address questions such as: how was the current situation of MT arrived at? What does MT mean today? How is MT perceived in different parts of the world and by different sectors of society? What contribution does MT have to make now and in the future?

It is assumed that the reader is familiar with the general background to MT, and only a very brief historical survey of the field is given. The emphasis throughout the chapter is on the contemporary position and status of MT; hence, the origins and development of the field to date are considered only to the extent that they may shed light on modern attitudes and perspectives.

To circumscribe the domain under examination, a short overview of the kinds of activities that make up 'machine translation' today and how these relate to other associated disciplines and domains is given. The purpose of this overview is to situate MT in a scientific sense, and to give the reader a feel for the divergences in breadth and depth of MT-related activities in different parts of the world (Western Europe, Eastern Europe, the United States, Japan, etc.), and among different sectors (academic research, the public sector, commercial research and development, international initiatives, etc.).

In the main body of the chapter, I present an analysis of the present position of machine translation and explore the reasons for the divergences identified earlier. Obviously, a thorough, in-depth analysis of all the elements which emerge would be beyond the scope of this chapter. What I will aim at, then, is rather a broad review of possible factors underlying such differences as those in national and governmental attitudes, funding priorities, variations in levels of 'intellectual' commitment, etc. In addition, I will pay attention to issues of public awareness: popular perceptions – and misconceptions – about MT, and how these also vary.

My analysis will be performed not only from a geographical viewpoint, looking at the different situations in different parts of the world, but also from the point of view of different groups of individuals within and across countries. Such groups include, for example, MT and natural language processing (NLP) researchers, end-users, customers, industry, etc. I will examine attitudes, usage and beliefs about the actual and expected benefits of MT-related activities and products.

I will conclude with a brief look to the future, speculating on possible shifts that may occur in the position and standing of MT. References to sources of further information are also provided.

HISTORICAL PERSPECTIVE

The origins and development of machine translation have been well documented and I wil not give yet another detailed historical account here (the interested reader is invited to consult Hutchins 1986 which is an excellent source). However, while the historical facts are amply recorded, their significance today and, in particular, the extent to which they have shaped modern attitudes to and within MT, have been paid relatively little attention. In this part of the chapter, I review the history of MT from a contemporary perspective.

While the concept of mechanical translation can be traced back as far as the seventeenth century, the enabling technology for the present-day concept of 'machine translation' appeared less than fifty years ago. The electronic digital computer made its first impact in the Second World War. In the immediate post-War period, there was a natural move to explore its potential capabilities, and the translation of languages was soon identified as one of the obvious candidates for exploitation.

These early explorations reached a watershed in 1949 with the famous Weaver memorandum, which 'in effect . . . launched machine translation . . . in the United States and subsequently elsewhere' (Hutchins 1986: 28). The significance of the Weaver memorandum is undeniable. Interestingly, it focused on the general strategies and long-term objectives of machine translation rather than on the concrete technical problems which had thus far emerged. Weaver raised four points: the problem of multiple meaning and the resolution of ambiguity, the logical basis of language, the application of communication theory and cryptographic techniques, and the possibilities of language universals. He thus identified many of the fundamental problems of MT which remain a challenge today.

Weaver's memorandum sparked off a wave of interest not only in the United States but also across the Atlantic in Britain. The first MT conference was held at the Massachusetts Institute of Technology (MIT) in 1952. Of the eighteen participants, seventeen were US and one was British. Four years later, the first real international conference on MT was held, again in the United States, but this time with US, British and Canadian delegates, and with contributions from the Soviet Union which by then had also established a research basis in the field. From 1956 onwards, activity in MT flourished in many different parts of the world. In the United States, it was given increasingly substantial financial support from the government and from military and private sources. In 1966, however, the bubble burst, with the publication of the Automatic Language Processing Advisory Committee (ALPAC) report (ALPAC 1966) which recommended the cessation of all MT funding. The mood had changed from enthusiastic optimism to fatalistic condemnation in less than a decade.

Viewed from today's perspective, the English-speaking origins of MT in the light of the subsequent fortunes of MT in the United States are perhaps ironic. In a sense, then, the present apparent resurgence of interest in American MT (see below) marks the return of a 'prodigal son' to the fold.

The strong military influence in the emergence of MT is also interesting in retrospect. A prime area for MT application remains that of defence and related concerns today, and MT research is conducted or supported by a number of military establishments, so this aspect of MT has persisted. However, more important from a scientific point of view is the original association of MT with cryptography, which was very largely reponsible for the adoption of over-simplistic techniques that ultimately proved flawed and led, eventually, to the ALPAC condemnation.

While the ALPAC report was specifically directed towards an assessment of the value of MT R&D in the United States, it had a far-reaching negative impact and caused the virtual cessation of MT funding in the United Kingdom and a severe slow-down in funding in France and the Federal Republic of Germany, all of which had by that time established MT research groups. The fortunes of MT activities in Eastern Europe, where research groups existed in Hungary, Czechoslovakia and the Soviet Union, were relatively unaffected by ALPAC and flourished in the next decade, despite technological disadvantages. In Western Europe, activities also continued, albeit in a subdued atmosphere, and in 1967 the Commission of the European Communities (CEC) started its first tentative research on MT at its EURATOM establishment in Italy. Considerable progress was made in the years up to the late 1970s, which in retrospect can be seen as a period of reflection, learning and of gathering strength.

The late 1970s saw a dynamic new impetus for MT in Western Europe with the launch in 1978 of the ambitious EUROTRA initiative. The Commission of the European Communities, after initial abortive attempts to expand the imported American SYSTRAN system to meet its multilingual needs, decided to start its own R&D programme in MT. This decision proved revitalizing for European MT and led to the expansion and consolidation of existing MT research centres and to the establishment of new centres in other countries, many of which had no previous experience in the field. While MT in Europe cannot be uniquely identified with EUROTRA (see below), its contribution to the emergence of an integrated MT community with an established communications infrastructure – which contrasts sharply with the fragmentation of expertise and resources in the United States – should not be ignored.

The progress of MT in the 1980s was marked by Japan's arrival on the scene. In the years which have followed, Japan has shown a commitment to MT hitherto unparalleled in any country. During that decade, MT activities continued to thrive in Europe, while in the United States involvement was relatively much more limited. The 1990s and beyond seem to herald a greater internationalization of MT efforts, and there is reason to hope that the ghost of ALPAC will finally be laid to rest.

THE SCOPE OF MT TODAY

Originally, the concept of machine translation was more exclusive – and more uncompromising – than it is generally held to be today. The goal of fully automated high quality translation (FAHQT) was the aspiration of most MT researchers in the period up to the early 1980s. By that time, however, the elusiveness of this objective had become all too apparent, and today FAHQT is more of a dream than an ambition.

While the horizon may have receded, however, the breadth of the goals of MT and the realism of those involved in it have expanded. Computer technology – the engineering *sine qua non* of MT – which was at first greeted as a liberating panacea, has over the years come to be regarded by MT researchers as a tool which is not only enabling but also constraining. The limitations of the available technology have helped researchers to shape their ideas about the process of translation, and forced them to adopt a disciplined, scientific approach to linguistic problems, with the accent on formal rigour and computability. In this way, the field of MT has acquired enhanced respectability and has evolved as an independent area of activity, although with close associations with other, related fields such as computer science, artificial intelligence (AI), theoretical linguistics and NLP.

The range of protagonists in MT has also expanded considerably since its inception. It has extended beyond the domain of academic research to include private industry (most notably software houses) and national governments. In recent years, there has also been an increasing internationalization of MT activities with established international conferences and publications, and transnational project collaboration.

The expansion of the concept of machine translation has been mirrored by the appearance of a range of acronyms denoting different levels of automation and human intervention. Thus, we speak of MAHT (machine-assisted human translation), where the major translating effort comes from a human user, as opposed to HAMT (human-assisted machine translation), where the machine performs the basic translation process and the human operator's intervention is restricted to pre- or post-editing texts. The trend in recent years – which is continuing today – is a move away from large-scale systems towards an increasing variety of automatic aids for translation, including on-line dictionary facilities, multilingual word-processing packages, interactive editing facilities, etc. (Vasconcellos 1988: Section III). It is these sorts of aids which have proved most susceptible to commercialization, although larger systems can also be found on the market. From the human translator's perspective, MT has gradually become more of an ally than a threat.

I thus take a very broad view of MT which, I feel, is in line with the way in which the field has developed and is continuing to evolve. In my survey of the state of MT activities in different parts of the world, I focus on those projects where the degree of intended automation of the translation process is greatest, but I have also tried to make room for MAHT and HAMT as this is where, I believe, the future thrust of expansion will occur. (For an overview of the technical state of the art, see Chapter 11: Harold Somers.)

MT IN EUROPE

In Europe, the impact of the ALPAC report was initially dramatic, but it took little more than a decade for its effects to disappear. As we have seen, the late 1970s witnessed a veritable explosion of MT activity in Europe, the most notable initiative being the launch by the CEC of the EUROTRA programme which has received sustained high-level funding from both the European Commission and the national authorities of all EC member states. It has involved all twelve EC countries, working on all nine official EC languages, with some twenty individual research sites and, at its peak, about two hundred participants (Raw *et al.* 1989; Steiner (ed.) 1991). At the time of writing, the EUROTRA programme has taken a new and exciting turn, with the move to a two-year transition programme in which both the scope of its activities and the range of participants will be much more diversified. The primary aim of this two-year programme is to prepare the transition from EUROTRA's pre-operational prototype to an industrialization of the system. This will involve the active participation of European industry which, it is hoped, will invest not only manpower but also financial resources. The EUROTRA stage has thus become much wider and the range and roles of its actors more varied (EEC 1990).

Although EUROTRA has dominated the European MT scene by virtue of its sheer size, it is by no means the sole MT effort in Europe. There are also a number of national MT programmes which testify to significant public-sector commitment, as well as substantial involvement by the private sector.

France, Germany and the United Kingdom have the longest traditions in MT in Western Europe. The famous French centre,

Groupe d'études pour la traduction automatique (GETA), is one of the oldest MT research groups in the world, and is renowned for its development of the ARIANE system. Recently, France's largest technical documentation company, SITE, took on ARIANE and, with public- and private-sector support, will collaborate with GETA to move towards the eventual commercialization of the system. Meanwhile, GETA continues to remain in the forefront of European MT with new work on the development of interactive MT systems or 'dialogue-based MT', where translation is performed via a natural dialogue between the user and the system.

The largest university-based MT centre in Germany is at Saarbrücken where the SUSY system was developed (Maas 1987), with financial support from the Federal German government from 1972–86. MT activities at Saarbrücken have not been confined to work on SUSY, however, and it has been involved in a number of other projects, including EUROTRA, and some recent work on 'text-oriented MT'. There are also active MT centres in Stuttgart, Berlin and Bonn. The German government has an admirable record of supplying financial backing to MT endeavours, to the extent that one American observer was prompted to remark recently that 'German government funding for MT R&D alone, not counting EEC sponsorship, is presently about ten times the entire United States government R&D funding for MT' (Carbonell 1990: 120). Germany also has significant private-sector involvement in MT R&D, the most notable example being Siemens' development of the METAL system (Thurmair 1990) which was judged at the 1989 MT summit in Munich to be among the most impressive demonstrated. There is also a substantial MT user community in Germany, and a sizeable domestic market for MT-related products.

The United Kingdom, consistent with its early influential role in the field, continues to have a strong MT presence. While several of its universities are active in NLP in general, the most specialized MT centre is that in Manchester (UMIST) at the Centre for Computational Linguistics (CCL) which, in addition to being involved in EUROTRA (together with the University of Essex), participates in several MT projects. One of the earliest was NTRAN, which was publicly funded from 1984–7 from the national Alvey programme in information technology. NTRAN was a document-processing and English–Japanese translation system which was innovative in being designed for use by *monolingual* technical writers

(Whitelock *et al.* 1986). The prototype was successfully demonstrated but implementation was stopped due to lack of further public or industrial funding. Since 1987, CCL has been involved in a number of other MT projects with British and, notably, Japanese industrial backing.

In the UK private sector, there is a certain amount of activity in MT-related R&D. British Telecom Research Laboratories are carrying out their own research on automatic speech translation (Steer and Stentiford 1989). Such industrial involvement in MT in the UK is rare, however, and in general the level of commitment is limited, and is certainly less than is to be found among its continental European counterparts where large companies such as Siemens, Philips and IBM-Europe are all making a significant investment in this area. The extent to which this relative lack of commitment can be attributed to the oft-cited British linguistic chauvinism is a matter for debate, but as a possible contributory factor it cannot be dismissed out of hand.

Elsewhere in Europe, industrial and public-sector interest in MT is also in evidence, in addition to the multinational investment in the EUROTRA programme, which I have already mentioned. The distributed language translation (DLT) project is a good example of a national MT effort with combined sponsorship. A multilingual MT project, DLT is located in Baarn at the software house Buro voor Systeemontwikkeling (BSO). It is currently in a seven-year R&D period (1985–92), jointly funded by BSO and the Netherlands Ministry of Economic Affairs (see Chapter 6, this volume and Pappegaaij *et al.* 1986). Interestingly, the Netherlands is also home to another major MT project with private-sector backing in the form of the Rosetta project, which is based at Philips Research Laboratories at Eindhoven (Landsbergen 1987).

In Switzerland, MT has also become an established activity. The main MT centre is ISSCO, a research institute in Geneva which is privately owned but which has had administrative links with the university. There, work is under way on three main projects (King 1989). The first is in the area of text generation of avalanche warnings; the second involves the development of a prototype MT system; and the third concerns the evaluation of MT systems, which is one of the current 'hot topics' in the field.

Industrial involvement in European MT has led in recent years to a proliferation of MT and MT-related products. The main commercial companies which have marketed such products in Europe are Gachot, Logos, ALPNET, Globalink and the London and Tel Aviv-based Tovna. The oldest commercialized system is SYSTRAN, which has been available now for well over a decade. SYSTRAN was originally based in La Jolla (California) but was taken over in 1988 by the French company Gachot. Its main user is the European Commission in Luxembourg to whom the SYSTRAN system was sold under special licence. For general commercial purposes, Gachot sells SYSTRAN output, rather than the system itself, on diskettes, via modem or even over the French public telecommunications system, Minitel (Trabulsi 1989).

Other available systems and translation aids include those marketed by Logos, which has a European base in Germany (but whose headquarters are in New Jersey in the United States) and Globalink, which is again based in the USA. Until recently, another American company, ALPNET, also marketed its products in Europe from a base in Switzerland. It offered arguably the most sophisticated system on the European market, with a suite of translation tools ranging from on-line dictionary facilities to fully interactive translation, although it covered a more restricted number of language pairs than some of its competitors. Ironically, however, some translators find its interactive translation facilities (TransActive) cumbersome.

The commercial systems I have mentioned here are probably the largest and best known but they do not account for the entire European market in MT-related products. These cover a whole gamut of applications ranging from multilingual word-processing packages and sophisticated desk-top publishing (DTP) facilities to multilingual dictionaries and term banks and multilingual OCR software (for an illustrative catalogue of such products, see the 'Multilingual Wordworker's Resource Guide' in *LT/Electric Word*, 13/1989).

Some further observations are worth making here. First, it is ironic that the most commercially successful systems in Europe all have US connections. Second, while Western Europe represents a huge multilingual community, the MT products available for the most part deal with bilingual translation only, a situation which may perhaps change as a result of the EUROTRA transition programme. Finally, although the quality of the available systems is in many cases far from ideal, and is largely based on outdated technology, the systems do sell. The market is substantial and is continuing to grow. Indeed, demand probably exceeds supply – which may account for the apparent customer satisfaction with low-quality products.

Before moving on, let us look briefly at the public profile of MT in Western Europe. Over recent years, some 'popular' journals (e.g. *Electric Word*) have appeared, although generally they have been rather too specialized to sustain broad commercial success. Typically, such publications carry publicity for commercially available products and 'layman' articles on aspects of MT and related activities (multilingual word processing, speech analysis, etc.). They are thus aimed at a narrow sector of the industrial market. MT also receives attention from time to time in computing publications (e.g. *PC World, Computing*, etc.), again targeting a specialized audience. Occasionally, interest is shown by the general media but while such exposure undoubtedly serves to heighten public awareness, it is by no means clear that it improves public understanding of the issues involved, and the time-worn recourse by journalists to examples of 'amusing' mistranslations is still very much apparent.

Finally, we should not neglect to mention Eastern Europe where there is a thriving MT community, notably in Czechoslovakia, Hungary, Bulgaria and the republics of the former Soviet Union. Efforts have been fairly static since the mid 1980s but the opening up of Europe seems likely to lead to a revitalization of activities.

CANADIAN MT – A SPECIAL CASE

Canada is a noteworthy example of a country with an enlightened approach to machine translation. Canadian public-sector interest in MT stems from its commitment to bilingualism, and Canada has the claim to fame of being the first country in which an MT system (METEO) was put to widespread public use. The METEO system was originally developed at the University of Montreal and translates meteorological bulletins from English to French (Chandioux 1989). (See Chapter 3, this volume) While its development was carried out with government sponsorship, in 1984 the system was taken into private ownership and a more efficient reimplementation of it was developed. The Canadian government has remained committed to the use of this high-quality system and now pays for the service. Moreover, METEO is not the only example of the Canadian government's interest in MT. In addition, it has sponsored several wide-ranging surveys of available systems conducted by its large translation department.

MT work is also being carried out at the Centre Canadien de Recherche en Informatisation du Travail (CCRIT) in Montreal (Isabelle 1989), and at the University of Ottawa.

As a result, no doubt, of its particular linguistic circumstances, Canada has always shown a keen awareness of the value of good-quality translation. With its commitment to MT, it has also exhibited a willingness to experiment and to develop an advanced approach to its translation problems. That such commitment should exist in the public sector is indeed enlightened, and stands in stark contrast to the attitudes which have been displayed by its North American neighbour.

THE STATE OF AMERICAN MT

In the United States, perhaps not surprisingly, the damning effects of the ALPAC report have proved more difficult to shake off than in Europe. ALPAC hit American MT very hard. The twenty-five years which followed have been referred to as the 'dark ages' of American MT and while this assessment is perhaps an unfair reflection on the quite substantial research activities which have survived in the USA despite ALPAC, it certainly does seem an appropriate epithet when one compares the situation with the progress of events in Europe and Japan. However, it is now widely believed that the United States is at long last starting to emerge from the 'dark ages', so that the 1990s could very well become the Renaissance of American MT, leading perhaps – who knows? – to a Golden Age in the next century.

At present, there are relatively few active MT research centres in the United States. The largest is the Center for Machine Translation at Carnegie Mellon University (CMU), whose work is primarily supported by private funding, over half of which comes from abroad (Nirenburg 1989). New Mexico State University (NMSU) (Farwell and Wilks 1990) and the University of Texas at Austin (Bennett and Slocum 1985) also have major MT groups, and there are smaller efforts at New York University (NYU), Brigham Young and Georgetown. The US National Science Foundation (NSF) provides some $350,000 per year to CMU,

NMSU and NYU, and it is hoped that a DARPA initiative will boost this with another million. 'The total amount, however, would still be significantly inferior to the budget of a single well-sponsored Japanese MT laboratory' (Carbonell 1990: 120). The Pan American Health Organization (PAHO) has also developed MT systems but the only large industrial company with a serious MT effort in the USA is IBM.

The preceding overview illustrates the limited scale of MT activity in the United States. It has been suggested that this is, at least in part, attributable to the fact that Americans generally regard translation as a low-status profession, an attitude which differs sharply from that in Europe and Canada where 'translation is a fact of life rather than an oddity' (Slocum 1984: 546).

Despite such entrenched attitudes, there is evidence to suggest that American MT is about to enjoy a new lease of life. Moreover, the resurgence of interest is not confined to the private sector looking to jump on the bandwagon of Japanese and European successes but is also increasingly apparent within the US government. In December 1989, the US Department of Commerce sponsored a national conference on Japanese–English machine translation at the National Academy of Sciences (Valentine 1990: 167–213), at which the keynote speaker was the foremost Japanese MT expert, Makoto Nagao. It is widely believed that this event did much to stimulate the US community. Subsequently, a US task force organized a study team to visit Japan to review the state of the art of Japanese MT and to prepare for specific cooperative projects.

The reasons for the renewal of interest and activity in American MT are many and diverse. In a recent hearing (itself a milestone in recent American MT history) before the Subcommittee on Science, Research and Technology of the Committee on Science, Space and Technology in the US House of Representatives, the Assistant Secretary for Technology Policy in the US Department of Commerce put forward her suggested reasons for the revival. A major factor identified is economic: the massive fall in the cost of computing, and the parallel rise in the costs of human translation, especially for non-Roman-alphabet languages, notably Japanese. This greater economic facilitation of MT R&D is reinforced by the very considerable progress which has been made over the last quarter of a century in computational linguistics (CL) and in language theory in general. Moreover, the increasing number of available translation software products and tools like large automated dictionaries demonstrate the practical feasibility of MT, reinforced by the emergence in Europe and Japan of a market for MT and MT-related products. Furthermore, the central role of Japan in recent technological advances makes the need for speedy access to translated Japanese documentation crucial. Finally, machine translation has emerged as an important test-bed for the larger fields of computational linguistics, NLP and AI in which the US has sustained a high level of research activity. From this point of view, therefore, MT is not only an end in itself but an important means to other objectives.

The apparent revival of interest in MT in the USA within government, the private sector, the academic community and even the Amerian public appears to stem from a mixture of motives ranging from economic necessity through technological chauvinism to scientific aspiration. As I have indicated, the main focus of the new interest in the United States appears to be on translation from Japanese to English, which is scarcely surprising given the economic motivations. The prioritization of this language pair (and direction) seems bound to have important consequences for MT not only at national level within the USA but also on an international scale, leading to more specific collaboration between the USA and Japan.

As a footnote, it is interesting to note that Washington DC was chosen as the venue of the third MT summit in 1991. The previous summits were held in Japan (1988) and Germany (1989), and the decision to hold the third in the United States was itself illustrative of the return to centre stage of American MT.

MT IN JAPAN

Although the future prospects for MT in the United States look better now than at any other time in the post-ALPAC period, the current situation still compares poorly with that in Japan. There, MT enjoys a privileged status and is a highly valued, high-priority activity in which an enormous investment of public and private financial and human resources has been made. Every major Japanese computer or electronics firm has invested considerable effort in MT R&D, and many claim to have developed operational systems.

Moreover, this investment is not confined to the private sector. A major, long-term initiative in MT R&D was launched by the Ministry of International Trade and Industry (MITI) which sponsored MT activity involving the Electrotechnical Laboratory, the Science and Technology Agency's Japan Information Centre of Science and Technology (JICST) and Kyoto University (Nagao *et al.* 1985). The ten-year electronic dictionary research (EDR) project, launched in 1987, is conducted by MITI in connection with the fifth generation computer project, and aims at the development of a detailed dictionary with over 200,000 words and multiple usages (Uchida and Kakizaki 1989). At Advanced Telephony Research (ATR) laboratories, research is under way on telephone dialogue translation (Iida 1989), with the support of the Ministry of Post and Telecommunications. Recently, MITI initiated the Center for International Cultural Cooperation (CICC) project to assist neighbouring countries to develop an MT research programme for multilingual translation of Chinese, Thai, Malaysian and Indonesian, as well as English and Japanese (Tsujii 1989).

The very solid commitment to MT R&D which thus exists in Japan rests on basic attitudes which appear to differ fundamentally from those in the United States. Undoubtedly, the quite different situations of the two countries' languages are significant in this respect and account for greater importance being attached in Japan to translation in general. Yet this does not provide a full explanation of the contrast in attitudes. At both public- and private-sector level, Japan demonstrates a strongly held belief in the long-term benefits of MT, not only as a means to more efficient translation but also as an essential part of the future development of an information-based society. Of course, economic considerations also come into play. A recent study by the Japanese Electronic Industry Development Association (JEIDA 1989) estimated that the annual market for translation in 1988 was some 800 million yen, with Japanese–English and English–Japanese reportedly accounting for 90 per cent of this figure. However, experts have noted that perceived commercial advantage is not necessarily the primary motivation for large Japanese companies (including Mitsubishi Electric, NEC, Fujitsu, Sharp, Toshiba, Hitachi and Sanyo Electric, to name but a few) working on MT. Rather, they regard machine translation as a learning tool which will give them general insights into NLP which they consider will be a key technology in the next century. As we have seen, this far-sightedness is shared by the Japanese government which has backed up its beliefs with massive, long-term financial investment.

Where MT activity has survived in the USA, it has been in the main oriented towards theoretical research, and little attention has been paid to development work. In contrast, MT workers in Japan have by and large adopted a pragmatic, 'problem-solving' approach and have concentrated on building working, eventually commercializable, systems. An obvious consequence of this is that, while there are many high-quality American research papers, few operational systems have been produced, and, conversely, while there are many working MT systems in Japan, the extent to which they are the result of sound theoretical research is unclear.

MT IN THE FUTURE

In this chapter, I have sought to give the reader a 'snapshot' view of the current status of MT in different parts of the world, focusing on the contrast in attitudes between public and private sectors, and on the varying policies of national governments. One fact which clearly emerges is that MT is today a recognized international scientific field with a worldwide community of researchers. Yet, while its international status is now firmly established, the standing which it enjoys at national level is by no means uniform across the globe. Japan's perception of MT as a key element in the future development of an information-based society and its consequent long-term commitment to MT activities lies at the extreme end of the spectrum of national attitudes. In Europe, there is a solid tradition of MT, and the EUROTRA programme has done much to improve collaboration and to consolidate and expand expertise. It is to be hoped – and expected – that future European research programmes will ensure that ample place is given to MT and related issues. As for the United States, the signs are very encouraging and we can expect that, following the enlightened example of Canada, the USA will come to play a leading role in the future of MT.

There are also signs that involvement in MT will continue to spread to include countries which have little experience in the field so far. Recent developments in South Korea, for instance, indicate that the private sector there is set to follow the example of its

Japanese counterpart with large-scale investment in MT R&D. It is thus likely that a strong MT community will emerge in the Far East which will set a challenge for the United States and Europe in an area where the technological and economic stakes are likely to be high, at least in the long term.

It also seems probable that the MT user community will grow in the future. As the field has evolved, there has been increasing emphasis on the development of viable MT-related products, and an ever-widening market for these products has emerged. In an age characterized by greater internationalization of commercial activity, and with an expanding volume of documentation, companies large and small are finding the need for efficient translation ever more pressing. Human translators, whether working in-house or freelance, have gradually come to abandon their initial trepidations and, in general, no longer see their role threatened by MT. Indeed, they are likely to be demanding an even greater variety of automated translation aids. Small-scale MT systems or computerized translation tools could become commonplace, as Hutchins foresees:

> It is reasonable to predict that in another twenty years MT and/ or MAT in various forms and packages will be normal and accepted facilities in nearly every office and laboratory.
>
> (Hutchins 1988: 238)

Work on the basic research issues underlying MT will continue to be given attention by academic researchers but it is to be hoped – expected even – that there will eventually be a synergy of MT efforts in the academic and industrial spheres, so that the combined advantages of each can work to produce high-quality products and systems which are efficient and which are based on solid theoretical foundations. One would also hope that progress will be made towards the development of a theory of machine translation.

Similarly, we expect that the recent trend towards increasing internationalization of MT efforts will continue with more and more collaborative projects. The specific cooperative efforts of the United States and Japan are a particularly exciting area and it will be interesting to watch the progress in that direction.

Finally, there is little doubt that a major focus of future MT activity will be the field of evaluation and standards. So far, relatively little work has been done on the assessment of MT systems but it has come to be recognized as an area vital to future progress.

BIBLIOGRAPHY

Abbou, A. (ed.) (1989) *Traduction Assistée par Ordinateur: Perspectives technologiques, industrielles et économiques envisageables à l'horizon 1990: l'offre, la demande, les marchés et les évolutions en cours*, Actes du Séminaire international (Paris, March 1988), Paris: DAICADIF.

ALPAC (1966) *Language and Machines: Computers in Translation and Linguistics* (Report by the Automatic Language Processing Advisory Committee, Division of Behavioral Sciences, National Research Council), Washington, DC: National Academy of Sciences.

Bennett, W.S. and Slocum, J. (1985) 'The LRC machine translation system', in *Computational Linguistics* 11: 111–21; reprinted in J. Slocum (ed.) *Machine Translation Systems*, Cambridge: Cambridge University Press, 1988, 111–40.

Boitet, Ch. (1990) 'Towards personal MT: general design, dialogue structure, potential role of speech', in H. Karlgren (ed.) *COLING–90: Papers presented to the 13th International Conference on Computational Linguistics*, Helsinki: Yliopistopaino, vol. 3, 30–5.

Carbonell, J.G. (1990) 'Machine translation technology: status and recommendations', in T. Valentine (ed.) (1990) 'Status of machine translation (MT) technology: Hearing before the Subcommittee on Science, Research and Technology of the Committee on Science, Space and Technology, US House of Representatives, 101st Congress, Second Session, September 11, 1990', [no. 153], Chairman: Rep. T. Valentine, Washington: US Government Printing Office, 119–31.

Chandioux, J. (1989) 'METEO: 100 million words later', in ATA conference proceedings, 449–53.

EEC (1990) 'Council decision of 26 November 1990 adopting a specific programme concerning the preparation of the development of an operational EUROTRA system', *Official Journal of the European Communities*, no. L 358/84, EEC/664/90, 21.12.90.

Farwell, D. and Wilks, Y. (1990) 'Ultra: a multilingual machine translator', Research Report MCCS-90-202, Computing Research Laboratory, New Mexico State University, Las Cruces, New Mexico.

Hammond, D.L. (ed.) (1989) *Coming of Age and the proceedings of the Thirtieth Annual Conference of the American Translators Association, October 11–15 1989, Washington D.C.*, Medford, New Jersey: Learned Information.

Hutchins, W.J. (1986) *Machine Translation: Past, Present, Future*, Chichester: Ellis Horwood.

—— (1988) 'Future perspectives in translation technologies', in M. Vasconcellos (ed.) *Technology as Translation Strategy* (American Translators Association, Scholarly Monograph Series, vol. II, Binghamton, New York: State University of New York Press, 223–40.

Iida, H. (1989) 'Advanced dialogue translation techniques: plan-based, memory-based and parallel approaches', in *ATR Symposium on Basic*

Research for Telephone Interpretation, Kyoto, Japan, Proceedings 8/7–8/8.

Isabelle, P. (1989) 'Bilan et perspectives de la traduction assistée par ordinateur au Canada', in A. Abbou (ed.) *Traduction Assistée par Ordinateur: Perspectives technologiques, industrielles et économiques envisageables à l'horizon 1990: l'offre, la demande, les marchés et les évolutions en cours*, Actes du séminaire international (Paris, March 1988), Paris: DAICADIF, 153–8.

JEIDA (1989) 'A Japanese view of machine translation in light of the considerations and recommendations reported by ALPAC, USA', Tokyo: JEIDA.

King, M. (1989) 'Perspectives, recherches, besoins, marchés et projets en Suisse', in A. Abbou (ed.) *Traduction Assistée par Ordinateur: Perspectives technologiques, industrielles et économiques envisageables à l'horizon 1990: l'offre, la demande, les marchés et les évolutions en cours*, Actes du séminaire international (Paris, March 1988), Paris: DAICADIF, 177–9.

Landsbergen, J. (1987) 'Isomorphic grammars and their use in the ROSETTA translation system', in M. King (ed.) *Machine Translation Today: the state of the art*, Edinburgh: Edinburgh University Press, 351–72.

Maas, D. (1987) 'The Saarbrücken automatic translation system (SUSY)', in *Overcoming the language barrier*, Commission of the European Communities, Munich: Verlag Dokumentation, vol. 1: 585–92.

Nagao, M., Tsujii, J. and Nakamura, J. (1985) 'The Japanese government project for machine translation', *Computational Linguistics* 11: 91–110.

Nirenburg, S. (1989) 'Knowledge-based machine translation', *Machine Translation*, 4: 5–24.

Papegaaij, B.C., Sadler, V. and Witkam, A.P.M. (eds) (1986) *Word Expert Semantics: an Interlingual Knowledge-based Approach*, (Distributed Language Translation 1), Dordrecht: Foris.

Pogson, G. (1989) 'The LT/Electric Word multilingual wordworker's resource guide', *LT/Electric Word* 13, Amsterdam: Language Technology BV.

Raw, A., van Eynde, F., ten Hacken, P., Hoekstra, H. and Vandecapelle, B. (1989) 'An introduction to the Eurotra machine translation system', Working Papers in Natural Language Processing 1, TAAL Technologie, Utrecht and Katholieke Universiteit Leuven.

Slocum, J. (1984) 'Machine translation: its history, current status, and future prospects', in *10th International Conference on Computational Linguistics*, Proceedings of COLING–84, Stanford, California, 546–61.

Steer, M.G. and Stentiford, F.W.M. (1989) 'Speech language translation', in J. Peckham (ed.) *Recent Developments and Applications of Natural Language Processing*, London: Kogan Page, 129–40.

Steiner, E. (ed.) (1991) 'Special issue on Eurotra', *Machine Translation* 6.2–3.

Thurmair, G. (1990) 'Complex lexical transfer in METAL', in *Third International Conference on Theoretical and Methodological Issues in Machine Translation of Natural Languages*, Austin, Texas, 91–107.

Trabulsi, S. (1989) 'Le système SYSTRAN', in A. Abbou (ed.) *Traduction Assistée par Ordinateur: Perspectives technologiques, industrielles et économiques envisageables à l'horizon 1990: l'offre, la demande, les marchés et les évolutions en cours*, Actes du séminaire international (Paris, March 1988), Paris: DAICADIF, 15–27.

Tsujii, J. (1989) 'Machine translation with Japan's neighboring countries', in M. Nagao (ed.) *Machine Translation Summit*, Tokyo: Ohmsha, 50–3.

Uchida, H. and Kakizaki, T. (1989) 'Electronic dictionary project', in M. Nagao (ed.) *Machine Translation Summit*, Tokyo: Ohmsha, 83–7.

Valentine, T. (1990) 'Status of machine translation (MT) technology: Hearing before the Subcommittee on Science, Research and Technology of the Committee on Science, Space and Technology, US House of Representatives, 101st Congress, Second Session, September 11, 1990 [no. 153], Chairman: Rep. T. Valentine. Washington: US Government Printing Office.

Vasconcellos, M. (ed.) (1988) *Technology as Translation Strategy* (American Translators Association Scholarly Monograph Series, vol. II), Binghamton, New York: State University of New York.

Whitelock, P.J., Wood, M.MacG., Chandler, B.J., Holden, N. and Horsfall, H.J. (1986) 'Strategies for interactive machine translation: the experience and implications of the UMIST Japanese project', in *11th International Conference on Computational Linguistics*, Proceedings of COLING–86, Bonn, 329–34.

Chapter 3

Made to measure solutions

Annette Grimaila in collaboration with
John Chandioux

Let us separate the machine from the translation and remember that it is the machine that serves the translation and not the other way round.

In all real-world applications of MT, the translator is not replaced. In fact, he or she is the one person who must be consulted, considered and helped by the application. If the machine output is of such low quality or if its manipulation is so complex that the translator wastes more time revising the results than he or she would spend translating a source text, then the usefulness of the system is seriously in doubt.

There is one world-renowned MT system which has been in continuous use since the early 1980s: METEO and the Canadian government's use of it to translate public weather forecasts from English to French (and from French to English since early 1989) have been well publicized but its creator's views on the subject have seldom been sought out or clearly understood.

JOHN CHANDIOUX AND THE METEO SYSTEM

John Chandioux started out as an English-language specialist who moved from France in 1973 to undertake further studies and research with the Traduction Automatique de l'Université de Montréal (TAUM) group. The late Professor Bernard Vauquois, then director of the Groupe d'études pour la traduction automatique (GETA) of the University of Grenoble, France, had been instrumental in setting up the TAUM group and over the years continued to show an interest in its progress. TAUM's most famous project was a prototype of a mainframe machine-translation system for the government of Canada which became

known as TAUM-METEO. What is less clear from the literature
is that the prototype developed in 1975–6 was never put into
operation by the TAUM group which thereafter concentrated its
research on another project: TAUM-AVIATION.

The Canadian government had practically shelved the METEO
project when Chandioux, who had by then left the university, came
to them with a proposal to resume development of the prototype.
What a shock when the first results showed that only 40 percent of
the sentences in the weather bulletins were adequately translated!
In fact, the prototype had been developed on a non-representative
corpus of texts which was too small and did not include all of the
weather regions for which the system was destined. The Canadian
weather is so diverse that it took a full year of analysis,
development and adjustments to ensure an 80 per cent success
rate.

METEO-1 finally reached this goal in 1978. It ran on a Cyber-
7600 mainframe, required 1.6 megabytes of random access memory
and translated some 7,000 words per day.

Concurrently with his work on METEO, Chandioux had
undertaken the development of a programming language specifically designed for linguistics. He wasn't satisfied with what could
be done with traditional programming tools like PROLOG or
LISP, and even Q-SYSTEMS, with which METEO had been
developed, had had to be substantially rewritten in order to
eliminate a certain number of inconsistencies and unpredictable
bugs.

Chandioux had always been considered a visionary by the
computer experts at the University of Montreal. When he
explained what he wanted done, no one thought it was possible.

In 1976, Alain Colmerauer, a computer specialist who had been
the first to implement PROLOG as a programming language,
returned to Montreal to visit the TAUM group which he had
directed for some years and where he had written Q-SYSTEMS.
Discussions with Colmerauer, who considered the project feasible,
convinced Chandioux that the future of computing and of his new
language lay in the smaller machines that would come to be known
as microcomputers. In 1977, Chandioux met with Professor
Vauquois who, also agreeing with Chandioux's vision, took the
time to detail what he would have done differently with GETA's
machine translation projects were he to start all over again.

As no one at the University was willing to get involved, Chandioux set out to write the compiler and run-time engine himself. By 1982, GramR was operating on a microcomputer and being used in a prototype MT system to translate computer and software manuals. This fourth-generation language is a deterministic labelled-tree transducer, technically in the same family as Q-SYSTEMS, but avoids combinatorial explosions thus making it an effective development tool whereas Q-SYSTEMS, which is not deterministic, is most useful as a research tool.

If GramR could translate computer jargon, why not weather bulletins? After a year's non-subsidized development and a three-month comparative trial in 1983, METEO-2 beat METEO-1 on performance, cost, reliability and user-friendliness. METEO-2 has been in continuous use since 10 October 1984, rented by the Canadian government's translation bureau on a turnkey basis from John Chandioux Consultants Inc. A software and hardware service is provided twenty-four hours a day, seven days a week, with a guarantee that full service is restored within four hours of a service call. The principal component, like its fail-safe double, is a 68000 CPU microcomputer from Cromemco, under a Unix-like operating system.

This workhorse is linked to a translator's workstation as well as to a Tandem communications node of the Canadian weather forecast network. The Tandem directly feeds the weather bulletins to the Cromemco from all of the eight weather centres: Gander, Halifax, Montreal, Toronto, Winnipeg, Edmonton, Vancouver and the Yukon. The Cromemco then sorts the English and French bulletins, since those from the Province of Quebec are written in French, and translates them into the target language. The translator's workstation then displays the bulletin's code number to indicate that it is ready for revision. This revision is mandated by law, due to the nature of the information, with sea transport and the coastguard, among other essential services, dependent on its accuracy. Control is resumed by the Cromemco for transmission back to the Tandem at 9600 baud.

As at December 1990, less than 4 percent of the machine's total output required editing, turnaround time was less than 20 minutes and the volume had risen from 7,000 words per day to 45,000. The hardware is now operating near its physical limits and its successor, METEO-3, is being developed to move the application to 80386-based machines.

The secrets of success

What is METEO's secret? How is it possible to reach and maintain such a degree of accuracy in machine translation? There are three principal reasons.

First, there is the nature of the problem itself. Machine translation in its present state is far from capable of translating general texts. Human language is much too ambiguous for a simple machine to treat correctly and all attempts to date have been horrendously expensive if not also totally laughable. Weather bulletins, even the detailed ones prepared by meteorologists, are at least less ambiguous: their subject is the weather, and only the weather. Some of the remaining ambiguities can be circumvented by careful programming but constant adjustments are required to keep up with non-standard formulations in the source texts which are composed by human meteorologists. Moreover, the useful life of weather bulletins (approximately six hours) and their volume make them excellent candidates for an automated system.

GramR, the language, is the second reason. Typical of second-generation techniques which, as completely as possible, separate the linguistics from the programming, this special tool is easily accessible to a linguist or translator and allows him or her to compose a set of transformational rules, compile these rules into an executable program and test it on a chosen sample. Extremely reliable – its last known bug was corrected in 1987 – GramR lends itself to any number of linguistic applications from MT to automatic accentuation of French texts, to spelling and grammar checkers. GramR's appeal to linguists can be compared to the impact that spreadsheet programs had on people who needed to perform financial analysis in the early days of microcomputers.

The third, and not the least important, factor is the continuous feedback and involvement of the translators who work with the METEO system. They are constantly solicited for their input on the system, for error detection in the output and for suggestions as to possible improvements. Most of the staff assigned to the group have been there for a number of years. Some even remember pre-computer days when weather bulletins came in over telex lines, were translated on an ordinary typewriter and then handed back personally to a communicator who retyped the bulletin in the outgoing telex machine. Of course, the volume of text was much more limited in those days. Today, 80 percent of their workload is machine translated and requires them to assume their role of revisers with the computer looking after the routines of receiving, translating and transmitting. The remaining 20 percent of their workload takes up half of their working hours even though terminals and other microcomputers allow them quicker access to the bulletins and the other tools which simplify their job.

Clearing up a misconception

It has often been said that the METEO system works because weather bulletins use a simplified syntax, because the vocabulary is limited or because the texts are so repetitive that there is no challenge.

In reality, the syntax is not at all controlled at the input level: the meteorologists are only required to respect certain semantic controls, such as 'strong winds' being limited to velocities between 'x' and 'y' kilometers per hour. The recommended style resembles telegraphic texts, with little if any punctuation or other syntactical points of reference to help the translation process. The vocabulary, excluding place names which are also translated, totals some 2,000 words. Repetition? Yes, the texts can be repetitive but not predictably so. The eight meteorological centres across Canada each reflect regional differences and diverging styles as well as meteorological realities as diverse as the country is vast.

The following is an extract of a weather bulletin submitted to the METEO system on 31 January 1991:

METRO TORONTO.
TODAY . . . MAINLY CLOUDY AND COLD WITH
OCCASIONAL FLURRIES. BRISK WESTERLY WINDS
TO 50 KM/H. HIGH NEAR MINUS 7.
TONIGHT . . . VARIABLE CLOUDINESS. ISOLATED
FLURRIES. DIMINISHING WINDS. LOW NEAR MINUS
15.
FRIDAY . . . VARIABLE CLOUDINESS. HIGH NEAR
MINUS 6.
PROBABILITY OF PRECIPITATION IN PERCENT 60
TODAY. 30 TONIGHT. 20 FRIDAY.
WATERLOO-WELLINGTON-DUFFERIN
BARRIE-HURONIA
GREY-BRUCE

HURON-PERTH
. . . SNOWSQUALL WARNING IN EFFECT . . .
TODAY . . . SNOW AND LOCAL SNOWSQUALLS. BRISK
WESTERLY WINDS TO 50 KM/H CAUSING REDUCED
VISIBILITIES IN BLOWING AND DRIFTING SNOW.
ACCUMULATIONS OF 15 TO 25 CM EXCEPT LOCALLY
UP TO 35 CM IN HEAVIER SQUALLS. HIGH NEAR
MINUS 9.
TONIGHT . . . FLURRIES AND LOCAL SNOWSQUALLS
CONTINUING. NORTHWEST WINDS TO 40 KM/H.
LOW NEAR MINUS 16.
FRIDAY . . . FLURRIES AND SQUALLS TAPERING TO
SCATTERED FLURRIES. HIGH NEAR MINUS 7.
PROBABILITY OF PRECIPITATION IN PERCENT 90
TODAY. 90 TONIGHT. 70 FRIDAY.

METEO's machine output, without any human revision, reads as
follows:

LE GRAND TORONTO.
AUJOURD HUI . . . GENERALEMENT NUAGEUX ET
FROID AVEC QUELQUES AVERSES DE NEIGE. VENTS
VIFS D'OUEST A 50 KM/H. MAXIMUM D ENVIRON
MOINS 7.
CETTE NUIT . . . CIEL VARIABLE. AVERSES DE NEIGE
EPARSES. AFFAIBLISSEMENT DES VENTS. MINIMUM
D ENVIRON MOINS 15.
VENDREDI . . . CIEL VARIABLE. MAXIMUM D
ENVIRON MOINS 6.
PROBABILITE DE PRECIPITATIONS EN
POURCENTAGE 60 AUJOURD HUI. 30 CETTE NUIT. 20
VENDREDI.
WATERLOO-WELLINGTON-DUFFERIN
BARRIE-HURONIE
GREY-BRUCE
HURON-PERTH
. . . AVERTISSEMENT DE BOURRASQUES DE NEIGE
EN VIGUEUR . . .
AUJOURD HUI . . . NEIGE ET BOURRASQUES DE
NEIGE PAR ENDROITS. VENTS VIFS D OUEST A 50
KM/H OCCASIONNANT UNE VISIBILITE REDUITE
DANS LA POUDRERIE HAUTE ET BASSE.

ACCUMULATIONS DE 15 A 25 CENTIMETRES MAIS
JUSQU A 35 CENTIMETRES PAR ENDROITS SOUS LES
BOURRASQUES PLUS FORTES. MAXIMUM D
ENVIRON MOINS 9.
CETTE NUIT . . . AVERSES DE NEIGE ET
BOURRASQUES DE NEIGE PAR ENDROITS. VENTS DU
NORD-OUEST A 40 KM/H. MINIMUM D ENVIRON
MOINS 16.
VENDREDI . . . AVERSES DE NEIGE ET BOURRASQUES
SE CHANGEANT PROGRESSIVEMENT EN AVERSES DE
NEIGE EPARSES. MAXIMUM D ENVIRON MOINS 7.
PROBABILITE DE PRECIPITATIONS EN
POURCENTAGE 90 AUJOURD HUI. 90 CETTE NUIT. 70
VENDREDI.

GRAMR'S OTHER CHILDREN

Has anything else been developed with GramR?

There are, at present, three other GramR MT systems, two in operation and one still in development.

General TAO – the insurance industry

The first cannot really be called a machine-translation system as it performs no analysis of the incoming text and basically does a special kind of pattern matching.

Confederation Life Insurance Company's Montreal office is the location of the company's linguistic services department. On deciding to automate his department, Jean-Pierre Bernier carefully analyzed the needs and working habits of his translators. This resulted in his equipping his people with powerful Macintosh workstations, a made-to-measure project-management program, Microsoft Word as a text processor, a desk-top publishing program, a terminology bank and a local area network under TOPS software. A single MS-DOS machine was acquired to provide compatibility with other company departments and reliance placed on Apple file exchange to convert files.

Even with this environment to facilitate their work, however, the translators were spending considerable time putting together standard documents from an existing bank of pre-translated paragraphs. Discussions between Jean-Pierre Bernier and John Chandioux Consultants Inc. brought about the development of the Système Général de Traduction Assistée par Ordinateur (General TAO).

The principal objective of General TAO was to reduce or eliminate the routine cut-and-paste work required to translate these standard documents while respecting the very rigid formatting requirements of the lengthy texts (group insurance policies, descriptive employee booklets, benefit administration agreements, etc.). To complicate matters, the English texts are written on PCs using WordPerfect 5.0/5.1.

The challenge in this development was twofold: finding a system that would 'speak' to both PCs and Macintoshes, as well as a means of dealing with the enormous volume of text involved.

The solution was to use the PC compatible as a server for the system. Since the department's computers were already linked into a local-area network, it seemed much more efficient to practically dedicate the little-used PC to the General and use TOPS to publish the results on the network.

To deal with the volume and ensure that the required presentation is respected, the input is first stripped of most of its formatting information and an almost pure ASCII text is submitted to the GramR kernel which paginates through both the text and the 'overlays' containing the matched patterns. These pseudo-code files have reached a remarkable size: close to a megabyte for one single type of document. The pattern matching can best be described as 'fuzzy' with a series of variables to deal with dates, periods, amounts, etc. The overlays also contain mnemonic formatting codes which are converted to Microsoft's Rich Text Format on output, thus making the results easily interpretable by the Macintosh version of Microsoft Word.

The resulting document is perfectly formatted and, beause the French portions have all been standardized, thus requiring absolutely no revision, the translators need only ensure that any non-standard clauses which remain in English and which are flagged with a special character are correctly translated.

The following is an extract from a standard Confederation Life insurance policy and its translation by the General TAO system:

DEFINITIONS

Earnings: gross monthly earnings, excluding bonus, commissions and overtime. Earnings shall be determined where necessary on the basis of 40 hours per week, 4.33 weeks per month and 12 months per year.

Renewal date: January 1st.

GENERAL PROVISIONS

If an employee suffers a specified loss as a direct result of a covered accident, within 365 days after the date of such accident, the benefit will be paid provided CONFED receives proof of claim.

The amount payable is based upon the amount specified in the BENEFIT PLAN SUMMARY which is in effect at the time of loss and calculated using the percentage for the loss set out in the following table:

Loss of life	100%
Loss of both hands	100%
Loss of both feet	100%
Loss of sight of both eyes	100%
Loss of one arm	75%
Loss of one hand	66 2/3%

ADMINISTRATIVE PROVISIONS
POLICY RENEWAL

At the end of each policy year, CONFED will renew this policy for a further term of one policy year provided:

A the participation requirement of 100% of those employees eligible for coverage is met;

B the minimum premium requirement of $100 for each month of the policy year is met;

C the policyholder accepts any policy changes which CONFED considers necessary for renewal purposes; and

D CONFED receives the first premium due for the new policy year.

DÉFINITIONS

Salaire: rémunération mensuelle brute, à l'exclusion des gratifications, commissions et heures supplémentaires. Le salaire est calculé à raison de 40 heures par semaine, 4,33 semaines par mois et de 12 mois par année.

*Renouvellement: le 1er janvier, à minuit une minute.

CONDITIONS GÉNÉRALES

En cas de sinistre directement attribuable à un accident garanti, survenu dans les 365 jours qui suivent l'accident, CONFED verse la prestation après avoir reçu les pièces justificatives.

La prestation correspond à un pourcentage du capital stipulé *aux CONDITIONS PARTICULIÈRES au moment du sinistre, conformément au tableau ci-dessous:

Décès 100%
Perte des deux mains 100%
Perte des deux pieds 100%
Perte de la vision des deux yeux 100%
Perte d'un bras 75%
Perte d'une main 66 2/3%

GESTION ADMINISTRATIVE
RENOUVELLEMENT DU CONTRAT

A la fin de chaque année d'assurance, CONFED renouvelle le contrat sous réserve des conditions suivantes:

A participation de tous les salariés admissibles;
B paiement d'une prime minimale de 100$ par mois;
C acceptation par le titulaire de toute modification jugée nécessaire;
D paiement de la première prime de l'année suivante.

Here again the success of the development was assured by the assistance of the department's assistant manager, Paul Dupont, and the translators who were directly involved in testing from the beginning and in completing the grammars since October 1990. In December 1990, the translator who is now in charge of the system, David Harris, confirmed that he was able to produce a finished document from a General TAO output in 30 minutes as compared to several hours before the system was operational. Additional documents are being analyzed for possible inclusion in the system and a French–English counterpart using the same user interface is being considered.

DIGITRAD – the computer industry

In the case of Digital Equipment of Canada Limited, the translation problem entailed dealing with an inventory control system which contained some 165,000 entries, in abbreviated English to respect a 30-character field-length, and providing an equally short French version for each of the hardware and software items contained therein.

Francine Létourneau, translation manager in Montreal, approached John Chandioux for a first-phase solution which would deal with the software descriptions which represent some 70 percent of the volume.

The challenge in this case was to respect the 30-character limit and to decipher the English abbreviations which were produced by inventory control officers located in the United States. There were 80,000 entries requiring translation at the start of the project with constant updates coming in from the USA.

DIGITRAD runs in either batch or test mode. In the latter, the translator enters the English text on a PC compatible displaying a user-friendly interface quite similar to the General TAO system. The description is translated into clear French to ensure accuracy and, by successive calls to an abbreviation module via the return key, is reduced to the required length. In batch mode, the process is identical but without the translator's intervention.

DIGITRAD is a true machine translation system. It analyzes an input text written in a very specific sublanguage with its own vocabulary and grammar. The different elements of the descriptions can require translation, permutation and abbreviation.

Before DIGITRAD, the translator would access the database and, using the update function, call up one description after another and re-enter the full entry, translating where required. Three or four translators could work on the database without access to their colleagues' files, thereby duplicating some terminology work and creating different standards for the same types of descriptions. One translator could translate some 2,000 words a day. In early January 1991, Jean-Claude Bergeron, who edits the machine output, confirmed he had been able to translate 55,000 words in three days.

The following are sample entries from Digital's database:

QA–0JQAA–WZ UWS USER/ADMIN V4.1 UPD DOC K
QA–GEJAA–H5 20/20 RISC MED & DOC
QL–B16A9–JT WPS–PLUS VMS ED CW:6000
QL–GHVA9–JN DECmsgQ VMS RTO CW:2400
QT–0JXAG–9M WIN/TCP DPMC 16MT9
QT–YNCAM–8M DPRT PRT SVCS BSMC 16MT9

Translated:
QA–0JQAA–WZ UWS USER/ADMIN V4.1 M/J
ENSEMBLE DOC
QA–GEJAA–H5 20/20 RISC SUPP ENREG DOC
QL–B16A9–JT WPS–PLUS VMS LIC E ENS CW:6000
QL–GHVA9–JN DECmsgQ VMS OPTION EXEC CW:2400
QT–0JXAG–9M WIN/TCP F/M DECSUPPORT 16MT9
QT–YNCAM–8M DPRT PRT SVCS F/M SER BASE 16MT9

Abbreviated:
QA–0JQAA–WZ UWS USER/ADMIN V4.1 M/J ENS DOC
QA–GEJAA–H5 20/20 RISC SUPP DOC
QL–B16A9–JT WPS–PLUS VMS LIC E ENS CW:6000
QL–GHVA9–JN DECmsgQ VMS OPT EXEC CW:2400
QT–0JXAG–9M WIN/TCP F/M DECSUPP 16MT9
QT–YNCAM–8M DPRT PRT SVCS F/M SER BASE 16MT9

Canadian National Railways

Canadian National's system, which is still in development and has not yet been baptized, resembles Digital Equipment's in that it deals with an inventory control system. The items, however, are not as abbreviated and can contain up to six lines of text to describe the parts and supplies required to run the railroad.

In this case, the challenge is in dealing with some 70,000 descriptions, approximately half of which have already been translated. John Chandioux is in the process of writing a GramR program to match the English and French automatically and generate the translation rules by computer. The system should be in operation by mid-1992.

A FEW FINAL WORDS

Will an MT system solve most translation problems? No. But it can solve those problems which meet the following conditions: specificity, volume and repetitiveness.

Will a special development be required? Probably, as no one at present knows the exact proportions of all the possible language problems and a made-to-measure solution has a greater chance of consistently ensuring productivity gains in the 700 per cent to 800 per cent range.

In our view, a general translation system cannot work in the present state of the art. We are too far from fully understanding the nature of human language and its myriad linguistic representations. A workable general translation system will eventually grow from numerous specific translation projects, such as the ones we have developed at John Chandioux Consultants. Through our research and development activities we can slowly identify and solve linguistic ambiguities and ensure a quality output that substantially helps the translator to do what he or she is paid to do: translate realities from one reference system to another.

Like any good tool, GramR has been found useful in related fields for which it was not originally designed. Even though GramR was originally developed to deal with English–French translation problems, it is not specific to this language duo and can be used for most European languages. It can even be used for other linguistic applications.

John Chandioux Consultants Inc. has developed and launched several general-use software products, all of which deal with the French language: a spelling and grammar checker, a verb conjugator and, most recently, a program that converts standard French spelling to the 'reformed' spelling proposed by the Conseil Supérieur de la Langue Française in Paris on 6 December 1990. These are known as the GramR family of products: ORTOGRAF+, the name used in Canada for the spelling and grammar checker, CONJUGUONS! and L'ORTHOGRAPHE MODERNE.

The development of a similar class of products for the English language is under way and should prove interesting to people 'bilingually' involved.

NOTE

GramR, METEO and ORTOGRAF+ are registered trade marks and are the property of John Chandioux.

Chapter 4

The Perkins experience

John Newton

BACKGROUND

One of the most successful machine translation applications known to me is at Perkins Engines, Peterborough, England. It is an example of what can be achieved when a system is introduced in a thoroughly planned and methodical way into a restricted domain environment to process controlled-language source texts.

Perkins has been a leading manufacturer of diesel engines since 1932 and is well established in worldwide export markets. Frequent additions to the product range and modifications to existing products have created a need for rapid production of high-quality user documentation in five languages – English, French, German, Spanish and Italian.

Until 1985, all translation had been done manually: some overseas and some in the UK. The Technical Publications Manager, Peter Pym, was keen to ensure that the four translated versions did not differ too greatly in style or content from the English source texts or from each other; close scrutiny of existing translations had revealed minor semantic and stylistic divergences, as well as omissions and introduced elements (i.e. elements not derived from the source text). As these traits were particularly evident in translations produced or edited overseas, greater control from Peterborough was clearly desirable but the translations produced had to be acceptable to the overseas subsidiaries, given that they and their customers were the consumers.

When Peter Pym decided to explore the possibility of using MT, he already had a firm foundation on which to build: his department was using a form of controlled English known as Perkins Approved Clear English (PACE). PACE was initially based on the International Language for Service and Maintenance

(ILSAM), which in turn was based on Caterpillar Fundamental English (CFE). CFE comprised around 800 words of basic English, plus whatever technical terms were required to describe products. In 1990, the number of words in PACE stood at approximately 2,500, of which around 10 per cent were verbs. PACE is based on sound, commonsense principles: short sentences, avoidance of gratuitous synonymy (e.g. *right* is the opposite of *left*; its use in the sense of *correct* is therefore proscribed), avoidance of ellipsis, and great emphasis on clarity of expression. Founded on the principle 'one word, one meaning', the PACE dictionary lists and defines or exemplifies every word that is approved for use in technical publications, including articles, conjunctions, pronouns and prepositions. In the case of homographs, it specifies the parts of speech that can be used, e.g. *seal* is listed as both verb and noun, while *stroke* is listed only as a noun. The technical authors also apply a set of rules governing syntax and sentence patterns. This approach to writing grew out of a desire to convey technical information and instructions in as precise, clear and unambiguous a form as possible in the interests of safety and efficiency.

The following examples provide an illustration of these rules in practice:

Pre-PACE
The heavy duty oil bath cleaners are usually fitted with a centrifugal pre-cleaner mounted on top of the main cleaner.

Using PACE
Heavy-duty air cleaners of the oil bath type are usually fitted with a central pre-cleaner, which is mounted on top of the main cleaner.

Pre-PACE
There are a few engines fitted with spur gears instead of helical gears shown in this section.

Using PACE
Certain engines are fitted with spur gears, instead of helical gears which are shown in this section.

(Pym 1990: 86–7)

The texts produced in the technical publications department are models of stylistic homogeneity and terminological consistency. As was stated in the introduction to this volume, non-standard syntax and other deviations from linguistic norms are among the most serious obstacles inhibiting the widespread use of MT. Perkins' strict adherence to the rules and principles of PACE produces texts that are neutral in style and devoid of authors' quirks.

Peter Pym was aware that his department's controlled approach to technical writing could facilitate the introduction of MT, and in March 1984 he and his colleagues established their criteria for an 'ideal' system. After examining the (very few) systems that were available, they concluded that Weidner's MicroCat system matched their requirements most closely and a decision was taken to organize an operational trial using English–French. MicroCat is a PC-based system which processes translations in batch mode, using the transfer method, as described in Chapter 6.

DICTIONARY BUILDING AND UPDATING

The decision to conduct a test necessitated the creation of an English/French version of the PACE dictionary within the MicroCat system. Every word in PACE, including articles and prepositions, had to be entered into the new dictionary as the total control of the lexis that Peter Pym was seeking precluded the use of any other dictionary. Moreover, limiting the parts of speech in homographic entries (see below) to those that were allowed by PACE optimized the system's performance by reducing the number of available variants. Entries for non-technical words were, in most cases, copied from the system's core dictionary and modified as necessary. The core dictionary itself cannot be modified by the user but up to twenty-nine additional dictionaries can be created and sequenced as required for any particular task.

The existence of monolingual and bilingual dictionaries containing all the words used in Perkins' technical texts, along with definitions, usage examples and part-of-speech designations, greatly simplified the task of dictionary building. In an environment where vocabulary and terminology were not controlled and finite it would be necessary to use the system's vocabulary search function to identify lexical items that would need to be entered into the system's dictionaries.

Raw translation quality would be severely impaired in two ways if a text submitted for translation contained a substantial number of words that did not figure in the dictionaries specified for that task; first, the fact that no translation equivalents would be available for the 'unfound' elements would result in their being marked and left untranslated; second, and more important, the absence of 'flagged' information concerning the word type and other attributes of these elements would so limit the system's ability to perform its sentence-level syntactic analysis that it would invariably lead to a seriously confused rendering of any sentence thus affected.

During dictionary entry, the system elicits inflection rules and a considerable amount of semantic and syntactic information from the user. Correct entry of the inflection rules produces automatic generation of inflected forms of target-language verbs, nouns and adjectives, and recognition of English verbal adjectives ending in -ed and -ing and adverbs ending in -ly. The system also generates the appropriate forms of articles, forming contractions as necessary.

Entering inflected forms could interfere with the translation of identical forms functioning as other parts of speech; all source language words are therefore entered into the dictionary in their uninflected base form: English verbs in the infinitive and nouns in the singular. In the same way, target words that can inflect in the idiom must also be entered in their base form: verbs in the infinitive, nouns, adjectives and articles in their masculine singular form. For example, *lubricating oil* would need to be entered as *lubricate oil* to avoid interferance with the various -ing forms deriving from the entry for *lubricate*; accurate flagging of both entries would ensure that *lubricating oil* was correctly recognized and translated.

As dictionary updating plays such a key role in determining the quality of MicroCat's raw output, I felt that some readers would appreciate a rather more detailed description of the procedures involved; anyone less interested in this aspect of the subject should skip the remainder of this section and go directly to 'Adapting the working methods to the system' (page 53).

Multiple-word entry

The next step was to use the PACE English/French MicroCat dictionary to produce raw translations of texts that had been translated previously and then compare the machine's output with the human versions. This helped to identify recurrent structures requiring multiple-word-entry solutions in the MicroCat dictionary; for example, *big end bearing, always ensure that.*

In addition to catering for single-word source entries (maximum eighty characters) and homographs, MicroCat's dictionary structure permits the user to enter compound nouns and other multiple-word forms which are referred to as 'idioms'. In this context, 'idiom' is used to describe any dictionary source item which comprises more than one word; *drive belt* would therefore be regarded as an idiom. Source idioms can contain up to eight words (maximum 256 characters), and target idioms up to fourteen. In addition, 'idiom holes' allow idioms to contain variable elements which are translated independently of the idiom as a whole. Idiom holes are of two kinds: 'must match holes' mark positions in idioms that must be occupied by a word in order for the idiom to be 'found'; 'conditional match holes' mark positions that can either be occupied or left empty. This device allows a single entry to handle an infinite number of permutations; for instance, *be % % away*, given the translation *être à % %* (French), or *estar a % %* (Spanish), can handle any combination which follows this pattern, such as *the church is 2 miles away from the school, the keyboards were 10 centimetres away from the screens, the ladders will be several feet away from the wall*. This idiom has two 'must match holes', each represented by %. The first hole is flagged as a quantifier and the second as a noun; this means that any number or other quantifier will be accepted in the first hole, and any noun (singular or plural) in the second. The system would only apply the idiom entry if a combination of words matched this profile exactly; a combination such as *he is very far away* would therefore not result in the idiom being used. The 'idiom holes' feature allows the user to specify a single word type, or a number of word types, for each hole. If a single word type is chosen, various attributes can be selected to pinpoint qualifying words still further, e.g. gender, number, person, tense, mood, etc. The same entry procedure applies to 'conditional match holes', represented by $.

In the case of the text used for the Perkins English/French trial (a user's handbook), a large number of multiple-word entries were made after scrutiny of the machine output and the text was then retranslated using the updated dictionary. A trial and error process was thus begun in which consecutive dictionary updates and retranslations finally resulted in greatly improved raw output. 'Idiom hole' entries were used to provide solutions for frequently occurring constructions which were consistent with regard to pattern (i.e. the parts of speech of their component words and their relationships to each other) but variable as far as individual words in the 'hole' positions were concerned. It is easier and quicker to tackle less frequent occurrences at the post-editing stage, and it is in any case unwise to clutter the dictionary with a larger than necessary number of complex entries as this can increase processing time and confuse the system.

Homographic entries

For the purposes of the MicroCat system, a homograph is defined as a word that can function as more than one part of speech, in its base form, in an inflected form or in some combination of both. Because English verbs invariably have inflected forms that function as non-verbal parts of speech, e.g. adjectives ending in -*ing* and -*ed*, all verbs are treated as homographs. Provision is made for various homographic combinations, including: noun/adjective, noun/adjective/adverb, adjective/adverb, verb/adverb, verb/noun/ adverb, verb/noun/adjective and verb/noun/adjective/adverb, as well as verb homographs which allow for the existence of a gerund or other -*ing* noun, e.g. *swim (swimming)*, *build (building)*. Although the system provides for up to nine parts of speech for each homographic entry, it is unusual for more than five to be entered. The French translations entered for the source homograph *light* in a general context would probably be: *lumière* (noun), *éclairage* (-*ing* noun), *allumer* (verb), *léger* (adjective), and *qui allumer* (the so-called -*ing adjective*); the latter form is entered to cover cases where the -*ing* form is used adjectivally, e.g. *the boy lighting the candles, the man walking his dog*; however, *walking stick* would need a separate entry to avoid its being translated as *la canne qui marche*.

The system's ability to differentiate between the various parts of a homograph, as exemplified by its rendering of the nonsense sentence *the light lady lighting the lighting is lighting light lights* as *la dame légère qui allume l'éclairage allume des lumières légères*, is impressive.

Using idioms to preserve target language distinctions

The impressive capacity for resolving homographs described above does not overcome the problem of a source word or term which requires different translations in different sub-contexts within a given domain for a single part of speech; for example, the Perkins PACE English/French dictionary had no fewer than nine noun translations for *gear*. Multiple translation equivalents deriving from target language usage distinctions demand special attention, as a source language lexical item can be given only one translation per part of speech. Scrutiny of similar texts translated previously will usually reveal which equivalent occurs most frequently and this should be used for the main entry. Occurrences of the same word requiring different translations can often be accommodated through entering compound noun idioms. For example, the main entry for *gear* could be given the translation *engrenage*, while *crankshaft gear* could be entered as *pignon de vilebrequin*, and *worm gear* as *vis sans fin*. Any cases not resolved in this way would be addressed at the post-editing stage using extended Alt Mode commands to effect the appropriate substitutions.

Dictionary sequencing

In a situation where the prescribed vocabulary and terminology were not contained within a single fully customized dictionary, a hierarchical dictionary look-up sequence would be specified to guide the system in its choice of translation equivalents. Up to nine dictionaries can be sequenced by the user for any vocabulary search or translation task, and up to twenty-six different sequences can be resident at any time. In this mode, the system searches for source-text words and idioms in each dictionary in the specified sequence until it finds or finally fails to find the item in question. In an automotive context, a look-up sequence might contain a product-specific dictionary at the highest level, followed by a general in-house dictionary, a general automotive dictionary and the system's core dictionary. In this sequence, terms coined to describe features specific to the product would be found in the first dictionary specified, terms relating to the company's products in general would be located in the second, general automotive terms such as *steering wheel* and *small end bush* would be found in the third and the fourth would provide general words such as *number* and *blue*. Jumbling the sequence can produce amusing but predictable results; e.g. sequencing the core dictionary before the general automotive dictionary would result in *small end bush* being rendered as *le petit buisson de fin* but this would be attributable to human error (or mischief). The MicroCat PACE dictionary's total, yet exclusive, coverage of the requisite vocabulary and terminology made sequencing unnecessary at Perkins.

ADAPTING THE WORKING METHODS TO THE SYSTEM

When it was considered that little further improvement could be achieved through manipulation of the dictionary entries, it was decided to look at the English source text to see whether any general changes could be made which would improve the quality of raw translation. The starting point for this exercise was a marked-up copy of the raw output obtained using the repeatedly updated English/French MicroCat PACE dictionary. Sentences which had caused problems in translation were rewritten in ways which produced better renderings from the system but there was no compromise with regard to naturalness; there would clearly have been no point in distorting the content or 'feel' of the source text in order to accommodate the system's limitations. This activity, regarded as an extension of the PACE principle, did not in any way result in a sterile or 'unfriendly' style but it did produce a more than threefold increase in the number of verbs in the PACE dictionary: the total of eighty verbs listed at the beginning of the exercise rose to around 250. The technique used here was fundamentally different from pre-editing as discussed elsewhere in this volume because the text submitted for translation was the published source language version. Moreover, the stylistic practices that evolved were deemed to be generally applicable in the Perkins Technical Publications context. Where pre-editing is practised, it is aimed at generally improving a system's rendering of an individual source text, but the original, unedited version remains the 'official' source language document.

The amended source text was submitted for machine processing, and this time the output was of an extremely high standard, requiring very little post-editing; however, it must be said that some problems were intractable and could only be solved through post-editing. Although Perkins' policy of writing in controlled language optimizes the system's performance, MicroCat's analysis is limited to the sentence and this means that links and agreements (anaphora) cannot be carried beyond the sentence level; nevertheless, the quality overall was such that Peter Pym placed an order for software to translate the four language pairs that his department regularly handles.

Implementation

Because the groundwork had been done with English/French, this language pair was implemented first. However, as the text used for the trial was unlikely to have contained every approved word and idiom, a more thorough test of the customized dictionary was needed. Several previously translated service publications were therefore submitted to MicroCat for translation in order to expose the system to a broader range of typical text and to highlight dictionary entries still requiring attention. A series of retranslations and dictionary updates then followed until the dictionary was considered to be fully 'tuned' to the Perkins environment. When a multiple-word entry was needed to overcome a particular problem, model target-language idioms were gleaned from the existing translations. It should be emphasized that this exercise was confined to structures, as the vocabulary and terminology were already in the PACE dictionary.

When the first text written under the modified PACE rules was submitted for translation by MicroCat in 1986, the result was, if anything, even better than expected. A copy of the raw translation, processed overnight in batch mode, was sent to Perkins France for editing and the changes recommended were then implemented in Peterborough. After final proofreading by Perkins France, the text was approved for publication. Painstaking preparation had created conditions in which very short turnaround times were achievable with minimal post-editing.

Since this first pioneering effort, every new service publication produced by Perkins has been translated using MicroCat and, whenever possible, source texts have been created in the system's own word processor. Other language pairs have been brought on stream and UK-based post-editors have been commissioned to 'polish' the raw translations and so reduce turnaround time still further. Additional time savings are being achieved in production through source texts being fully coded for typesetting; this coding is automatically reproduced in the raw translations and the post-edited versions are then supplied to the printer on diskette.

The documentation's usefulness to end-users and to those responsible for marketing and servicing the products is optimized through the Perkins company in each of the main target markets remaining the authority for final approval and for all queries relating to terminology and usage.

Not surprisingly, it transpired that writing to accommodate the system's limitations resulted in even clearer communication and reinforced the advantages of PACE to non-native speakers who are obliged to use the English version if their mother tongue is not one of the five in which the documents are published (it is undoubtedly clearer for native speakers too).

Writing in controlled language produces texts which are more easily translatable, whatever method is used; it also results in greater homogeneity between different translated versions (i.e. versions in different target languages and versions produced by different translators into a single target language). As one might expect, different translations of a source text written in controlled and simplified language normally resemble each other more closely than versions derived from texts having a less regulated structure; comparing source texts written under varying degrees of constraint with back-translations usually illustrates this point.

MicroCat's vocabulary search function proved to be a useful tool for monitoring adherence to PACE rules in newly written texts. As I have stated above, if the PACE rules are strictly adhered to, a vocabulary search should reveal no 'unfound' words; however, any non-PACE words identified are examined in context to see if a new PACE entry is needed, and any selected for inclusion (possibly arising from the introduction of a new product or process) are first defined and then given part-of-speech designations. The next task is to identify and approve target-language equivalents in consultation with the overseas subsidiaries and, when these procedures are complete, entries are made in the PACE and MicroCat PACE dictionaries. Hard copies are then distributed to authors and post-editors. In addition, post-editors are encouraged to point out recurrent structural problems in the hope that they might be solved via the dictionary. This methodical, but open-minded, approach ensures that everyone concerned works within the same guidelines and that any new or deviant vocabulary or terminology is identified for approval, modification or rejection.

CONCLUSIONS

Not least of the benefits of Perkins' bold decision to automate the translation process was the opportunity it afforded for looking even more closely at what was being written and how it was being written. Introducing MT afforded Peter Pym a level of control that was previously unattainable and resulted in greater uniformity of content between source texts and their various translated versions:

> Using MicroCat, Perkins has been able to ensure consistent terminology and to reduce translation time as well as translation costs. Using the computerized databases, Perkins can control the source and target text at all stages of publishing. Producing translation using an MT system also ensures rigorous testing and control of the source text.
>
> (Pym 1990: 92)

The pre-existing systematic approach to writing, based on continous reappraisal, created ideal conditions for this project, as did the enthusiastic co-operation of the technical authors and the personnel in the overseas subsidiaries. The department's relations with the latter had already been strengthened through cooperation in compiling the bilingual versions of the PACE dictionary. Likewise, throughout the period of the MicroCat test (around six months), Peter Pym had kept his colleagues in France fully briefed on developments and had sought and acted upon their advice whenever any queries had arisen concerning terminology or usage.

In addition, I had demonstrated the system at Perkins' French subsidiary before the trial began and personnel from Perkins Engines France had attended meetings in Peterborough to help decide how it should be conducted and what form their co-operation would take; consulting all the parties involved in the project from the outset ensured their support. Translators from Perkins' parent company, Massey-Ferguson, were also involved throughout, as was Tony Hartley, a linguist from Bradford University, who advised Perkins regarding modifications to PACE and who devised a set of ten rules for simplified writing specifically designed to produce optimum results from MicroCat in the Perkins context.

At first sight, it may appear rash to have installed MT in a department which does not have any translators on its staff, but it must be borne in mind that linguists and post-editors were, and still are, consulted as external resources and Peter Pym has found this arrangement to be efficient, flexible and cost-effective.

Perkins' disciplined approach to the MicroCat trial, which had demanded and received all the preparation normally associated with full implementation, ensured that the actual implementation of English to French went very smoothly, as the system was delivered with the dictionary substantially tailored to the Perkins environment. Another factor which maximized the efficiency of the Perkins installation overall was the decision to introduce new language pairs only when those already in use were fully operational; this enabled the subsequent implementations to benefit from the lessons learned from those which had preceded.

More than anything else, however, the success of the Perkins application was made possible by the controlled and extremely consistent nature of the source texts and by a willingness on the part of all concerned to adapt the system to the working methods and the working methods to the system.

REFERENCE

Pym, P.J. (1990) 'Pre-editing and the use of simplified writing for MT: an engineer's experience of operating an MT system', in P. Mayorcas (ed.) *Translating and the Computer 10: The Translation Environment 10 Years On*, London: Aslib, 80–96.

Chapter 5

Machine translation in a high-volume translation environment

Muriel Vasconcellos and Dale A. Bostad

The real test of machine translation is whether or not it is effective in large-scale operations. These may be specialized applications, as in the case of Canada's METEO (see Chapter 3), or they may involve the translation of a broad variety of text types. In the latter case, the purpose of the translation will dictate the characteristics of the installation, particularly the human post-editing component. The purpose can run the gamut from publication for dissemination to 'information only'. For the product that has a public and undergoes scrutiny, a translator post-editor must be enlisted to eliminate all problems from the output, interpret connotations appropriately and make certain that the reader will understand precisely what the author intended to say. On the other hand, MT, by automatically generating a product where nothing existed before, has created a new mode of work in which a less than ideal translation can be provided for the consumer who merely needs to assimilate information and is not concerned with disseminating it.

The first type of application is exemplified by the Spanish to American (English) MT system (SPANAM) and English to Spanish MT system (ENGSPAN) at the Pan American Health Organization (PAHO) in Washington, DC, and the second by the SYSTRAN operation at the US Air Force's Foreign Technology Division in Dayton, Ohio.

TRANSLATION FOR CLOSE SCRUTINY: PAHO

MT has been enlisted in the service of general-purpose practical translation at PAHO[1] since January 1980. The first language combination to be implemented was Spanish–English, using SPANAM, the Organization's batch MT system developed in-house

(Vasconcellos and León 1988). ENGSPAN, a second, more sophisticated in-house product with a strong English parser,[2] followed suit
with English–Spanish in 1985 (León and Schwartz 1986).[3] Later,
SPANAM was entirely rebuilt using the conceptual design of
ENGSPAN. MT is now the principal mode of translation for these
two language combinations and is an integral part of the
Organization's translation and terminology service.[4]

PAHO undertook to develop MT with two broad purposes in
mind: to meet its internal translation needs more efficiently, and to
disseminate health information in the Latin American and
Caribbean countries. Very few of the translations done at PAHO
are for information only. There are occasional applications of this
kind but the majority must be of a quality that will stand close
scrutiny. Some are for publication although few serve as the basis
for important decisions, covering diverse subjects ranging from the
commitment of resources to primary care for sick children.

SPANAM and ENGSPAN, each with a robust parser and large
deeply coded dictionaries (63,000 and 55,000 terms respectively),
are capable of handling a broad range of subjects and dealing with
free syntax in a variety of genres. Among the most important
subject areas are medicine, public health, sanitary engineering,
agriculture, computer science, management and law, and there are
a number of others as well. Cross-cutting this spectrum is an even
broader range of styles and discourse genres: journal articles and
abstracts, textbooks, manuals (both for human health and for
software), proposals for funding, reports of missions, contracts and
agreements, minutes of meetings, business letters, diplomatic
exchanges, certificates, product specifications, supply lists, captions
for displays and even promotional materials and film scripts. This
type of variety actually presents more of a challenge than
differences in subject matter but SPANAM and ENGSPAN tackle
them all. For most applications the texts are post-edited by
professional translators working on-screen. The input texts are
never pre-edited or customized in any way. The only preprocessing
is a quick review by the clerical staff to ensure that the word-
processing document conforms to one of the standard formats used
in the Organization. Thus, from any perspective, it is safe to say
that MT at PAHO has been both designed and implemented as a
general-purpose product. Examples of SPANAM and ENGSPAN
output are shown in Figures 5.1 and 5.2.

Spanish		English
ILRAD	OK	ILRAD
LABORATORIO INTERNACIONAL DE INVESTIGACIONES SOBRE ENFERMEDADES ANIMALES	OK	INTERNATIONAL LABORATORY FOR RESEARCH ON ANIMAL DISEASES
El Laboratorio Internacional de Investigaciones sobre Enfermedades Animales (ILRAD) se fundó en 1974 con el objeto de ayudar al desarrollo de controles eficaces de dos importantes enfermedades que afectan a la ganadería: la	OK TU	The International Laboratory for Research on Animal Diseases (ILRAD) was founded in 1974 with the purpose of helping the development of effective controls of two important diseases that affect livestock raising:
tripanosomiasis y la teileriosis. En conjunto, estas dos enfermedades afectan a la producción ganadera de extensas zonas en unos 50 países en desarrollo de África, América Central y del Sur, el Oriente Medio, el subcontinente indio	OK	trypanosomiasis and theileriosis. Together, these two diseases affect the livestock production of extensive areas in some 50 developing countries of Africa, Central and South America, the Middle East, the Indian subcontinent and
y Asia. Las pérdidas totales que causan, de recursos humanos y económicos, son incalculables, no sólo en materia de leche y carne, sino también de cuero, lana,	OK	Asia. The total losses that cause, of human and economic resources, are untold, not only in terms of milk and meat, but also of hide, wool, fertilizers, animal power and other
fertilizantes, tracción animal y otros subproductos animales, y en posibles recursos de capital. Cientos de	PP 39 TU	animal by-products, and in possible capital resources. Hundreds of millons of persons, among them some of the
millones de personas, entre ellos algunos de los más pobres del mundo, resultan gravemente afectados. El ganado	NO 05	poorest in the world, result critically affected. Ruminant
rumiante transforma estos elementos a partir de vegetación que el hombre no puede comer, a menudo en terrenos que no	PP 15 TU GT	livestock transforms these elements from vegetation that man cannot eat, often in lands that it cannot utilize for
puede utilizar para cultivos. En otras zonas, es conveniente la producción integrada de ganado y cereales.	PP 12	*crops. In other areas, it is desirable the integrated production of earned and grains.
LA ESTRATEGIA DEL ILRAD	OK	THE STRATEGY OF ILRAD
Las dos enfermedades mencionadas son causadas por parásitos que son transmitidos por insectos.	OK	The two diseases mentioned are caused by parasites that are transmitted by insects.

Figure 5.1 Spanish–English unedited machine translation at PAHO.

La mosca tsetsé transmite los tripanosomas y la teileriosis OK
es transmitida por las garrapatas. En ambos casos las OK
relaciones entre parásitos, huéspedes y vectores son
complejas y sutiles, y por tanto la intervención es
difícil. Además, en ambos casos, otros animales salvajes y PP 20
domésticos sirven también como huéspedes de los parásitos,
creando así reservas de infección prácticamente
inaccesibles a las medidas de control.

Aun en el caso de que el control de los vectores fuer- PP 35
técnicamente posible, ello requeriría la aplicación de
medidas sistemáticas, oportunas y muy costosas, que están
evidentemente más allá de las capacidades del pequeño
agricultor del mundo en desarrollo. Por consiguiente, las OK
investigaciones del laboratorio hacen hincapié en la
identificación y elaboración de medios de control de
enfermedades basados en las reacciones inmunológicas de os
animales huéspedes.

Además de mantener un programa completo e innovador de PP 35 TU
investigaciones originales, el ILRAD sirve también como
centro de intercambio para integrar los diversos esfuerzos
de otras instituciones nacionales e internacionales que
laboran en los mismos problemas desde diferentes
perspectivas.

The tsetse fly transmits the trypanosomes and theileriosis
is transmitted by the ticks. In both cases the relations
between parasites, hosts and vectors are complex and
subtle, and accordingly the intervention is difficult. In
addition, in both cases, other wild animals and domestic
serve as well as hosts of the parasites, creating thus
reservoirs of infection practically inaccessible to the
measures of control.

Even if the control of the vectors were technically
possible, this would require the application of systematic,
timely and very expensive measures, that are evidently
beyond the capacities of the small farmer of the developing
world. Consequently, the research of the laboratory
emphasizes the identification and preparation of means of
disease control based on the +immunological+ reactions of
the host animals.

In addition to maintaining a complete and innovative
program of original research, ILRAD serves as well as
clearinghouse in order to integrate the various efforts of
other national and international institutions that work in
the same problems from different perspectives.

NT OK

S0015
EPIDEMIOLOGIC STUDIES OF CERVICAL CANCER IN LATIN AMERICA

OK TU TU

During the last five years, two large epidemiologic studies were conducted in Latin America to determine risk factors for cervical cancer in this high-risk population and to compare the prevalence and effects of different risk factors in this region and in Spain, where the incidence of invasive cervical cancer is very low.

SD PP 32

The Latin American Cervical Cancer Study was conducted in Bogotá, Colombia, Mexico City, Mexico, Costa Rica and Panama, by the National Cancer Institute of the United States (NCI) in collaboration with the "Gorgas Memorial Laboratory and research institutes in the participating countries, between January 1986 and July 1987. The study examined cases of invasive cervical cancer in patients

PP 24 TU

younger than 70 years of age at the major cancer referral hospitals in the areas of the study.

OK

For each case, two controls were selected: in Bogotá and Mexico City, two hospital controls were selected, matched according to age

OK TU TU

(in 5-year groups), excluding patients with diagnoses related to the exposures of interest.

S0015
ESTUDIOS EPIDEMIOLOGICOS DEL CANCER DEL CUELLO UTERINO EN AMERICA LATINA

Durante los últimos cinco años, dos grandes estudios epidemiológicos se realizaron en América Latina para determinar los factores de riesgo de cáncer del cuello uterino en esta población de alto riesgo y para comparar la prevalencia y los efectos de diferentes factores de riesgo en esta región y en España, donde la incidencia del cáncer invasivo del cuello uterino es muy baja.

El Estudio de Cáncer del Cuello Uterino Latinoamericano se realizó en Bogotá, Colombia, la Ciudad de México, México, Costa Rica y Panamá, por el Instituto Nacional del Cáncer de los Estados Unidos (INC) en colaboración con los Gorgas Memorial Laboratory y los institutos de investigaciones en los países participantes, entre enero de 1986 y julio de 1987. El estudio examinó los casos de cáncer invasivo del cuello uterino en las pacientes más jóvenes que 70 años de edad en los hospitales de referencia de cánceres principales en las áreas del estudio. Para cada caso, se seleccionaron dos controles: en Bogotá y la Ciudad de México, se seleccionaron dos controles del hospital, armonizado según la edad (en grupos de 5 años), excluyendo a las pacientes con diagnósticos relacionados con las exposiciones del interés.

Figure 5.2 English–Spanish unedited machine translation at PAHO.

In Costa Rica and Panama, one hospital and one community control were selected from census listings of the same areas of residence of the cases.

Overall, 99% of 766 eligible cases and 96% of 1532 controls agreed to participate and were interviewed on demographic, sexual, reproductive, medical, dietary and contraceptive history. A cervical swab was utilized to obtain cells from the cervical lesions of the cases and the cervical os of the controls to determine the presence of human papilloma virus (HPV). In addition, a blood sample was drawn for determination of micronutrients and antibodies against specific sexually transmitted agents. A physical examination was performed on participating males (78% of eligible case husbands and 71% of eligible control husbands) and a swab of the coronal sulcus and urethral canal were obtained to test for HPV.

En Costa Rica y Panamá, un hospital y un control de las comunidades se seleccionaron de los listados del censo de las mismas áreas de la residencia de los casos.

En total, 99% de 766 casos aptos y un 96% de 1532 controles acordaron participar y se entrevistaron en la historia demográfica, sexual, reproductiva, médica, alimenticia y anticonceptiva. Un hisopo cervical se utilizó para obtener células de las lesiones cervicales de los casos y el os cervical de los controles para determinar la presencia de +virus de papiloma humano+ (VPH). Además, una muestra sanguínea se extrajo para la determinación de los micronutrientes y los anticuerpos contra agentes de transmisión sexual específicos. Un examen físico se realizó en los varones participantes (78% de esposos del caso apto y 7% de esposos de control apto) y un hisopo del surco coronal y el canal uretral se obtuvieron para examinar para detectar el VPH.

The PAHO environment is distinguished by the fact that production and system development are carried on side by side as part of the same operation. As those who are working on a particular translation are in the best position to suggest appropriate target glosses, post-editors are encouraged to mark their copies of machine output with suggestions for the dictionaries (new technical terms being subject to review by the terminologist) and for system improvement in general. The computational linguists, for their part, conduct their research on production text and are constantly monitoring the output to ensure that the two systems are performing up to standard. Problems that are easy to solve are dealt with from one day to the next. In this way, the post-editors have the satisfaction of seeing their feedback incorporated. (More difficult problems take their place on a 'wish list,' in order of their priority). Some of the post-editors have learned how to update the dictionaries themselves, and whether they do or not they still get to see that they can have a personal hand in improving the quality of the output.

Over 8 million words delivered

Getting under way

As of 1990, SPANAM and ENGSPAN had generated some 34,800 pages (8.7 million words) in the service of production translation, with current machine output averaging around 6,000 pages (1.5 million words) a year. In 1989, MT was officially recognized as the Organization's primary mode of translation, as by that time it was supporting at least 60 per cent of all regular production in the two language directions. But the road to success had been bumpy at times. The use of MT at PAHO went through several phases, and it is of interest to take a look at this experience as it unfolded.

When SPANAM made its début, MT was operated as a separate unit in PAHO, offering direct competition to the existing human translation (HT) service. In view of the broad range of texts to be translated, its managers realized from the beginning that efficient and effective post-editing would be crucial to successful acceptance of MT. With this in mind, a certified translator was hired on a full-time basis to review and correct the output. This person also updated the dictionaries based on problems that came up in the course of day-to-day production. The first major application was the Organization's biennial program budget, for which it was possible to demonstrate savings of 61 per cent compared with human translation, as well as a reduction in staff days of 45 per cent (Vasconcellos 1984).

For the first five years, post-editing was done at no cost to the requesting office. The choice of whether to use MT was left to the end consumer. Many of the receiving units were pleased with the service, and the good word spread. Cost was undoubtedly a factor in the early popularity of MT, since the service was being offered for free, whereas HT sometimes had to be farmed out and the resulting cost charged to the client. Also, turnaround was faster. In addition, MT was welcomed with enthusiasm because the delivered product was machine readable, which was not true of HT at the time. Also, MT with light post-editing was occasionally used for information purposes only, and this service addressed a previously unmet need – yet another factor that added to its successful reputation. Since no one was forced to use MT, and since the service was free, there were virtually no complaints.

By 1984, MT production from Spanish into English was reaching 100,000 words (400 pages) a month, and ENGSPAN was being tried on an experimental application from English into Spanish. At the end of that year, in the wake of a series of personnel changes (including departure of the MT post-editor), the Organization's upper management decided to merge the MT and HT services and delay the recruitment of new translators until a study could be done on the overall allocation of human resources for translation. In the interim, MT continued to be an option but post-editing had to be done by contractors with the cost charged back to the requesting offices. The contractors, most of them freelance professional translators, were paid by the job at slightly more than half the then prevailing rate for HT, and they came to the PAHO offices to use the Organization's word-processing equipment. As a result of these changes, there was in fact a slight drop in MT production levels but the monthly average never fell below 67,000 words (268 pages).

In the fall of 1987, still without any conclusive data in hand and with several translator vacancies to be filled, PAHO's management decided to conduct an experiment that would yield concrete data for decisions about the appropriate mix of the four possible resources – namely, in-house MT, in-house HT, contract MT and contract HT.

The experiment

A formal eleven-month experiment was undertaken from October 1987 through August 1988 to establish whether machine translation in the PAHO environment was cost-effective, fast in turnaround and capable of supporting a higher level of year-round average production than human translation. The experiment also attempted to establish whether MT output post-edited by a professional translator was as serviceable as human translation.

Two temporary translators, one for each target language, were recruited to serve as post-editors for the duration of the experiment. MT ceased to be optional. All incoming work was screened to determine whether or not it could be submitted to the computer. A directive was issued instructing the requesting offices to submit their texts for translation on diskette. In this way new MT applications could be captured and use of the technology was maximized.

Interim statistics for the first eight and a half months of the experiment showed that MT, in-house and contract combined, was used to process 79 percent of the jobs into English (839,635 words or 3,359 pages, corresponding to 262 jobs) and 60 percent of those into Spanish (427,310 words or 1,709 pages, from 120 jobs).[5] MT was used less for Spanish because a large proportion of the input texts were from published sources outside the Organization and therefore not machine-readable. Optical character recognition (OCR) was used whenever possible to scan hard copy but it often turned out that cleaning up the scanner's mistakes was too time-consuming to be worth the effort.[6] In total, 74 percent of the jobs into English were machine readable and, of the rest, 5 percent could be scanned using the OCR but 21 percent could not. Into Spanish, on the other hand, only 54 percent were machine readable and, of the rest, 7 percent were scannable and 39 percent were not.

Data for the full twelve months showed a significantly greater volume translated by MT during the experiment than in previous years. The texts represented a broad range of subject areas and discourse types, as evidenced by the fact that more than 40 different 'clients' had been served.

The requesting offices, which usually did not know which mode was used, were asked to provide feedback on the serviceability of the product delivered to them. Responses were received for 30 percent of the jobs processed. Both modes drew praise and criticism but there was a slight preference for MT: 85.1 percent indicated satisfaction with jobs processed using MT, compared with 78.1 percent for HT. Interestingly, the lowest percentage of satisfaction (60 percent of total response) was for Spanish HT. Sometimes the client incorrectly assumed that the job had been done using MT when in fact it was HT. For example, the following comments were made about *human* translations: 'machine translation is not good enough. I practically had to rewrite it,' and 'the quality of the translation was more "rigid" than at other times; it seemed more like a machine translation without having a "human hand" go over it.'

The English in-house post-editor and some of the contractors were able to achieve daily outputs of 7,000 words and higher in the short term. In the long term, average daily in-house productivity for English, calculated according to standard methods used in the international organizations (i.e. net of leave, weekends and holidays) and *including periods without incoming translations* during which the translators worked on the dictionaries, was 2,546 words. This result exceeded the United Nations target of 2,000 words a day by 27 percent and far surpassed the real average of 1,200 words a day informally reported by many in-house services in the international organizations. As MT does not involve transcription and certain other types of general services support that were used for HT during the period, it was considered that the goal of 30 per cent savings over in-house HT had not only been achieved but in fact surpassed. For contract translation, the cost differential between HT and MT was self-evident, as MT post-editors were being paid 55 percent of the HT rate.

As a result of the experiment, a new policy was announced in February 1989 under which MT became the primary mode of translation in PAHO. The policy entailed a restructuring of the translation service so that as much incoming work as possible could be channeled in the direction of MT.

Current situation

The use of MT has not been stabilized in PAHO. The new technology continues to do the lion's share of the work. The decision to use MT, which rests entirely with the terminology and translation service, is based on the following characteristics of the input text:

1 machine readability (or optical 'scan-ability');
2 complexity of format; and
3 linguistic characteristics (e.g. grammar, discourse genre, need for between-the-lines interpretation, etc.).

These factors intersect with time-frame considerations, the availability of post-editors and the special strengths of the individual translators.

In-house translator positions have been established with post-editing built into the primary duty in the job description. At the same time, contractors are still employed for much of the work which, as always, comes in spurts. Compensation for contractors has been brought in line with the three-tiered scale of the US Department of State (general, semi-technical and technical). The pay for MT post-editors is the same as for State Department reviewers. A recent development is that most of the MT post-editing is now being done off-site by contractors working on their home computers.

The translator and the MT output

The experience of the last three years, since the mechanism for client feedback was formalized, has brought home increased awareness that it is the translator's skill, not the mode of work, that determines the quality of the final translation product.

At the same time, not all the PAHO translators have chosen to adapt to post-editing; some of the ones that we rely on have preferred not to try it, and of those who have tried it, not all have been equally successful. In total, about 30 post-editors have worked with SPANAM or ENGSPAN and, of these, six into Spanish and eight into English are now on the roster of contractors regularly used. An effort is made to give these 'regulars' an HT assignment every third or fourth time. There is a core group of translators, all of them veterans, who consistently prefer the MT mode.

Post-editing seems to be a special skill, somewhat related to traditional editing. It involves learning how to preserve as much of the machine's output as possible and 'zapping' the text at strategic points rather than redoing it from scratch. The post-editor quickly develops a set of context-dependent techniques for dealing with the patterns produced by the machine (Vasconcellos 1986, 1987a, 1987b; McElhaney and Vasconcellos 1988; Santangelo 1988).

There is a fine line to walk between allowing the output to stand and meeting the high standard of quality that needs to be applied to most of the translation jobs done at PAHO. In order to come up to this standard, the post-editor must be certain of all technical terminology, capture every nuance, provide accurate interpretations for coherence (Vasconcellos 1989a), ensure idiomatic equivalence, maintain a uniformly appropriate register, build in cohesiveness where it is lacking, provide adequate 'staging' (Grimes 1975: 323), and preserve the information structure (Halliday 1967; Vasconcellos 1986).

Sometimes, in addition to using approved terminology, the translation will call for special phraseology, as, for example, with resolutions of the organization's governing bodies. Here MT can present a problem: the post-editor cannot settle for an equally clear but unofficial version produced with the aid of the machine. In such cases it can be seen that in-house translators and 'regulars' are in a better position to make decisions about the MT output. To help the contractors in particular, the documentalist, who is very familiar with the workings of the Organization, reviews each incoming job and locates all the background materials the translator should have at hand.

When it is known that a translation will have only limited use – a first draft, for example, or an internal trip report – MT offers the possibility of delivering a less-than-ideal translation at a lower level of effort – i.e. by doing less post-editing. PAHO is currently attempting to implement an intermediate level of quality which would be acceptable in such situations. The text is syntactically and propositionally correct, but nuances may be sacrificed. So far, it has been difficult for the translators to 'lower their standards', but occasionally the press of time has been sufficient motivation for them to cut the right corners. In-house translators are more appropriate for such an approach, first because compensation is not at issue, but mainly because they are in a better position to sense the minimum level that will be acceptable. It is planned to experiment further with translations of intermediate quality.

Unfortunately, it does not necessarily follow that when a translation is of minor importance a raw or semi-polished MT product can be used. It often happens that when the input text has been prepared in a rush, maybe dictated but not read, or transcribed from an oral presentation, it contains incomplete fragments and grammatical lapses which throw the machine – and the post-editor – into a tailspin. Not only must the output be carefully post-edited, but the work of the post-editor is greatly slowed down, to the point where sometimes the effort has to be compensated at the full HT rate.

By far the most difficult challenge for the translators has been to know when to leave PAHO-specific terminology untouched. Terms that may look 'funny' to the uninitiated – such as *fertility regulation*, where *birth control* is the more common expression, or *harvesting* and its Spanish counterpart *cosecha* in reference to the culling of monkey populations – are apt to get changed by post-editors. Hypercorrections of this kind are the main source of complaints from clients. Again, the advantage of in-house translators or 'regulars' who know the technical terminology is obvious. To help deal with the problem, the entries in the SPANAM and ENGSPAN dictionaries can be coded so that a word or phrase will be flagged in the output, telling future post-editors that the term has been researched and is reliable. This resource has been implemented to a certain extent, but at the same time care needs to be taken not to clutter up the output with so many flags that the text becomes unreadable. And, of course, there is never a guarantee that a flagged term will not require a different translation in another context. Some of the other ways in which the post-editor can have some control over the output are described in the next section.

The translator and the dictionary

PAHO post-editors can gain a certain amount of power over the MT output by learning to manipulate the SPANAM and ENGSPAN dictionaries, which offer a wide variety of approaches for triggering expressions that are appropriate to the given context. As a first step, they are expected to mark up their hard side-by-side copy as they move along with each translation. The following kinds of information can be recorded: glosses for words that were not in the dictionary at all (which have averaged less then 0.5 percent since 1984), different or additional glosses for words that are in the dictionary, special translations for multiword phrases, reliability flags, and notes about syntactic errors the machine has made.

Perhaps the most immediately useful resource for the translator is the phrase-building capability. Whether or not the translator learns to enter these units in the dictionary personally, it is still rewarding to see them come up in future translations. If a particular term happens to have required research, the translator's efforts are captured once and for all, avoiding the duplication that is so common in translation services.

SPANAM and ENGSPAN can provide special translations in a wide variety of situations. Some examples are: different subject areas (English *core* for Spanish *núcleo* in an atomic energy text vs *nucleus* in an ordinary text); singular and plural forms of the same source word (*toxicity* for *toxicidad* and *toxic effects* for *toxicidades*); fixed phrases of two to five words in length (*in general* for *por lo general*) or *Pan American Health Organization*; long names of institutions and titles of publications; multiword phrases that can be parsed in more than one way if necessary; discontinuous phrasal verbs; glosses based on the syntactic or semantic features of associated words (the English source word *raise* with an inanimate object gives Spanish *levantar*; with an animate object, *criar*; with a human object, *educar*; and collocated with the word *flag*, *izar*). The post-editor can request these translations or learn to actually enter them in the dictionary.

The post-editor also brings recurring structural problems to the attention of the computational linguists.

Future applications

Thanks to ongoing dictionary work and system improvement, ENGSPAN now produces raw output of sufficiently reliable quality that consideration is being given to the translation of data bases and other applications in which users can access MT directly. Of particular interest are data bases that are available on compact disk read only memory (CD-ROM). Several proposals have been made and some of these may materialize into active projects.

The Consultative Group on International Agricultural Research (CGIAR) has been collaborating with the PAHO MT project since 1986 and provided support for the installation of ENGSPAN at the International Rice Research Institute in the Philippines and the International Center for Tropical Agriculture (CIAT) in Colombia. CGIAR is helping to form a donor consortium that will provide PAHO with funds to adapt ENGSPAN to a microcomputer and develop parallel systems from English into French and Portuguese, as well as establish an MT center within the CGIAR network that will support users and build specialized MT dictionaries in agriculture.

The availability of PAHO's MT systems on microcomputer will enable the organization to outplace this technology in its member countries, and this should contribute to the exchange and dissemination of types of needed health information which have not been translated in the past because of the cost and the limited availability of translators.

TRANSLATION FOR INFORMATION: FOREIGN TECHNOLOGY DIVISION, US AIR FORCE

Machine translation has undergone a long evolutionary develop-ment at the Air Force's Foreign Technology Division (FTD), extending over more than twenty years. While for many years the SYSTRAN Russian–English system was the sole MT operation, with time additional language pairs were acquired: French–English, German–English, Japanese–English and, recently, Spanish–English. A large-scale machine translation environment has been created, with some fifteen people inputting data, six or seven people editing the data, and, since 1975, a group of four to seven people constantly working on improving the dictionaries and the parsing algorithms. At all times, development of the various systems has gone hand in hand with use of the systems to translate texts on a daily basis.

The SYSTRAN machine translation systems are used to translate large amounts of information – roughly 50,000 to 60,000 pages of source text per year. The translations are used by scientific and technical analysts who need to keep abreast of foreign developments in a wide range of technical fields and to prevent technological surprise that could threaten the United States.

FTD got involved early with machine translation and has consistently been a supporter of MT because it was enamored with the prospects of what MT could do in the early years, and because it was believed that machine translation was the only way to translate massive amounts of material and get the translations back to the requesters while the information was still useful. The early intuition that machine translation could provide this service has proven correct, and FTD has not veered from its solid commitment to MT for over twenty years.

However, the way of producing machine-translation products

has evolved over time at FTD, and it is of interest to briefly discuss how FTD got started in the MT business and where it is now.

In the 1960s and the first years of the 1970s the Russian–English system was used to produce a very rough hard-copy translation. Post-editors edited the translation extensively – almost rewriting it – and then the edited version was sent to a 'recomposition' pool where it was retyped. Alternatively, some translators used the rough machine translation as a 'pony' when they dictated the translation on tape. The translator picked and selected those parts of the machine translation that were valuable – certain technical terms and phrases – and worked directly from the Russian text. The dictated translation was then transcribed. Machine translation was really only used as an aid to the translator. The end translation was a quite accurate finished product.

Because this method was slow and productivity was low, in 1974 it was discarded and a very lightly edited hard-copy translation was instituted. It was decided that this was the only way to cope with an immense backlog that had built up. The degree of post-editing was at the discretion of the editor, but speed was the name of the game. Changes were written in ink on large fanfold computer printout. There were no stylistic changes. The end product could only be called fairly crude and the format primitive – a low-quality utilitarian product whose one saving grace was that it got the information quickly to the requester and allowed an immense backlog to be eliminated. This was FTD's first effort at producing what we call 'partially edited machine translation.'

In 1976 a dedicated input/editing minicomputer system using a DEC PDP 11/05 and sixteen workstations was designed and installed. This allowed the first on-line computer revision of machine translation, and in 1977 the first version of EDITSYS was written. EDITSYS is a software module called at the end of the Russian–English analysis that identifies certain potential problem areas in the output and brings these conditions to the attention of the post-editor. When a given condition is met, the program generates a full-page-width string of characters (a 'flag') immediately in front of the condition. The post-editor must react to the 'highlighted' condition and verify the machine translation version or make a revision. The flag is removed during a later step in the post-processing. Such conditions as 'not-found' words, rearrangement, acronyms, problem words, mistyped words that produce spurious match-ups, etc., are highlighted. Post-editing is thus determined by a software program that tells the editors the minimum number of conditions that have to be reviewed, although the editors can – and some of them do – post-edit beyond the flagged conditions. But sentences and blocks of text basically go through unscrutinized by an editor. This type of partially edited text has been our mainstay for the last fifteen years. The translation is then printed on high-quality paper on a laser printer and has a much better appearance than the previous product. This product has been well received by FTD analysts.

As stated above, some editors do edit to a certain extent beyond the flags. There are also other exceptions to the procedure just described. Some short translations for dissemination require careful sentence-by-sentence editing. Moreover, medical and biology texts, at present, are closely edited for technical accuracy. Approximately 5 per cent of MT translations receive this type of post-editing. Finally, some fifty to 100 translations per year, ranging from one paragraph to two pages, are removed from the 'first-in-first-out' queue, translated by MT, and then edited on hard copy by translators who do not normally do post-editing. The idea is to get the jobs done quickly and out the door; otherwise they tend to stagnate behind larger jobs. Requesters expect fast turnaround on very short translations; they understand that a 300-page book, for example, takes longer.

In 1987, FTD developed a new MT application which we call 'interactive machine translation.' This system gives all users individual access to MT at their own terminals. It is now available to users via hookup with approximately 1,600 PCs within FTD. This is raw machine translation without the mediation of translators. The system is designed so that a user can rapidly determine the significance of the material he wants translated and weed out extraneous information. It is best used for rapid translation of titles of books, tables of contents, captions of tables and graphs, and individual sentences and paragraphs. However, it can also be used effectively to translate complete short articles and to get back a rapid translation instead of going through the sometimes time-consuming operation of routing translations through the formal bureaucracy. One very effective use of the system is for 'gisting' a large book – that is, determining the significant parts of the book and then routing this material through the normal translation procedures. For example, if a user has a 350-page book, the system might be used to determine that only Chapters 3, 7 and

12–15 are really pertinent to the research in question. Obviously, the use of such a tool makes for tremendous cost savings by eliminating the translation of irrelevant material.

FTD has conducted three extensive surveys of machine translation over the last ten years to analyze the effectiveness and use of MT and gain insights into how to improve the product. The two most important insights coming out of the surveys are:

1 speed of translation is the most important consideration for FTD analysis; and
2 the existing product, partially edited MT, is deemed satisfactory in meeting most users' translation requirements.

There has been some feedback spelling out deficiencies in certain technical disciplines, and there was a small percentage of users who found MT unsatisfactory as a translation product but overall the acceptance rate has been very high.

The most recent survey, taken in December 1990, covered users of both partially edited MT and interactive MT. Sixty surveys were sent out; thirty-three were returned, for a return rate of 55 percent. In addition, within this number, six users were personally interviewed. According to the survey, 73 per cent of the respondents felt that the current post-edited MT product was meeting or exceeding their requirements for technical accuracy. An even higher proportion – 82 percent – stated that the post-edited product was meeting or exceeding their requirements for readability! There was high praise for the interactive system. However, because the analysts themselves have to input the data, it was not deemed effective for longer documents. More analysts would be willing to use raw MT if the data could be input for them. They would foresake the current post-editing if the translation directorate would input the documents and send the raw MT product electronically to them directly after translation. Very recently the utility of raw MT was emphasized by the fact that 600 pages of French had to be translated in two weeks and, due to the time constraint and the lack of post-editors from French, the only translation that could be produced was raw MT. The requester accepted the raw MT in order to get quick access to the data and meet his deadline.

Recently an assessment of Russian partially edited MT was made by an independent group of scientists conducting Air Force research in a subfield of physics. For one particular portion of a

book they had access to both a human translation (done for
another government agency) and a machine translation. Their final
report contained the following unsolicited comments on the quality
of the two English translations:

> While the [human] translation read somewhat more smoothly, it
> seemed to use inappropriate or erroneous terminology more
> often than the [machine] translation did. Consequently, we
> relied primarily on the [machine] translation, using the
> [human] translation mainly for reference.

FTD is now embarked on an ongoing project to improve the
efficiency of its MT operation. The areas being addressed include:
incorporation of software for individual users to modify dictionaries; OCRs to scan Russian, French and German; expansion
into other language pairs; and continued refinement of specialist
dictionaries.

NOTES

1   Regional Office of the World Health Organization for the Americas.
    WHO is a specialized agency in the United Nations system.
2   Developed with partial assistance from the US Agency for Interna-
    tional Development (AID) under Grant DEP–5443–G–SS–3048–00.
    ENGSPAN is installed at AID and runs there on an IBM 3081 (OS/
    VMS).
3   SPANAM and ENGSPAN are written in PL/1 and run on PAHO's
    IBM mainframe computer, currently an IBM 4381 (DOS/VSE/SP),
    which is used for many other purposes.
4   The Organization's working languages are Spanish and English. The
    English–Spanish and Spanish–English combinations account for 90 per
    cent of the translation workload. Portuguese and French, which
    together make up the other 10 per cent, are also official languages of
    the Organization but are handled by a separate service.
5   For a detailed review of the data from the experiment, see Vasconcellos
    1989b.
6   The equipment on hand was already old at the time of the experiment.
    Current OCR technology would undoubtedly do much better.

BIBLIOGRAPHY

Grimes, J.E. (1975) *The Thread of Discourse*, The Hague: Mouton.
Halliday, M.A.K. (1967) 'Notes on transitivity and theme in English', part
    2, *Journal of Linguistics* 3: 199–244.

Hartmann, R.R.K. and Stork, F.C. (1976) *Dictionary of Language and Linguistics*, New York: Wiley.

Hutchins, W.J. (1988) 'Future perspectives in translation technologies', in M. Vasconcellos (ed.) *Technology as Translation Strategy* (American Translators Association Scholarly Monograph Series, vol. II), Binghamton, New York: State University of New York.

León, M. and Schwartz, L.A. (1986) 'Integrated development of English–Spanish machine translation: from pilot to full operational capability: technical report of Grant DPE–5543–G–SS–3048–00 from the US Agency for International Development', coordinated by M. Vasconcellos, Washington, DC: Pan American Health Organization.

McElhaney, T. and Vasconcellos, M. (1988) 'The translator and the postediting experience', in M. Vasconcellos (ed.) *Technology as Translation Strategy* (American Translators Association Scholarly Monograph Series, vol. II), Binghamton, New York: State University of New York.

Santangelo, S. (1988) 'Making an MT system work: perspective of a translator', in M. Vasconcellos (ed.) *Technology as Translation Strategy* (American Translators Association Scholarly Monograph Series, vol. II), Binghamton, New York: State University of New York.

Vasconcellos, M. (1984) 'Machine translation at the Pan American Health Organization: a review of highlights and insights', *Newsletter*, British Computer Society Natural Language Translation Specialist Group.

—— (1985) 'Theme and focus: cross-language comparison vis translations from extended discourse', unpublished PhD dissertation, Georgetown University, Washington, DC.

—— (1986) 'Functional considerations in the postediting of MT output: dealing with V(S)O versus SVO', *Computers and Translation* 1, 1: 21–38.

—— (1987a) 'Postediting on-screen: machine translation from Spanish into English', in C. Picken (ed.) *A Profession on the Move: Proceedings of Translating and the Computer 8*, London: Aslib.

—— (1987b) 'A comparison of MT postediting and traditional revision', in K. Kummer (ed.) *Proceedings of the 28th Annual Conference of the American Translators Association*, Medford, New Jersey: Learned Information.

—— (1989a) 'Cohesion and coherence in the presentation of machine translation products', in *Georgetown University Round Table on Languages and Linguistics 1989*, Washington, DC: Georgetown University Press.

—— (1989b) 'Long-term data for an MT policy', *Literary and Linguistic Computing* 4, 3: 203–13.

Vasconcellos, M. and León, M. (1988) 'SPANAM and ENGSPAN: machine translation at the Pan American Health Organization', in J. Slocum (ed.) *Machine Translation Systems*, Cambridge: Cambridge University Press.

Chapter 6

Esperanto as an intermediate language for machine translation

Klaus Schubert

PRESTIGE

According to an unconfirmed rumour, on the occasion of a prestigious machine translation conference held in Japan in 1989, a senior representative of a major Japanese computer manufacturer reported that his company had sold X number of machine translation systems and he proudly added that *10 per cent are actually used*. This cannot make sense unless 90 per cent of the customers buy machine-translation systems like Van Gogh paintings: for prestige.

True or untrue, the story may well confirm that a trade as uncertain as machine translation, with its extremely long payback periods, is indeed sensitive to prestige considerations. It could therefore seem risky to include in a machine translation project a language like Esperanto which has the unmerited but undeniable quality that the mere mentioning of its name calls forth the most emotional rejections from both laymen and linguists (Forster 1987; Piron 1987).

Despite all this, the idea of using Esperanto in machine translation is almost as old as the attempts to make computers translate. In recent years, the idea has become a reality, and I shall here address the question, 'what is so special about Esperanto that a prestige-sensitive software company chose to adopt it?'.

The first section gives a short history of how Esperanto became involved in machine translation. The second section prepares the discussion about Esperanto as an intermediate language, explaining why an intermediate language is needed at all. The third section points out that the choice of an intermediate language is conditioned by the basic design of the machine translation system. The fourth section discusses the virtues and drawbacks of alternative intermediate representations, and the fifth section shows under which circumstances the best choice is Esperanto. The final section describes in greater detail those properties of Esperanto that make it particularly suitable for functioning within a machine translation system.

ESPERANTO'S ROAD INTO MACHINE TRANSLATION

Esperanto became associated with computational linguistics (which in the early decades was almost exclusively machine translation) in three stages (Schubert 1989a: 26–9). These may be labelled:

1 'the idea';
2 'Esperanto on equal terms'; and
3 'Esperanto for its specificity'.

The first stage, 'the idea', had its origin in the very early years of machine translation in the late 1940s and early 1950s. After the first wishful attempts, it was soon understood that natural language is more intricate than the decoding tasks the first computers had performed well for military and intelligence applications. When natural languages turned out to be too difficult, it was suggested that something more consistent be tried, such as, for instance, Esperanto. Yehoshua Bar-Hillel put forward this suggestion in his famous state-of-the-art report of 1951 (Bar-Hillel 1951; Hutchins 1986: 33–4).

This first stage of ideas about Esperanto in computational language processing was preceded by a period when various scholars used Esperanto as a kind of universal syntactic representation. Most interesting in this respect are Lucien Tesnière's dependency syntax (Tesnière 1959/1982: 64) and Petr Smirnov-Trojanskij's method of machine translation developed prior to the computer age (Denisov 1965: 80ff.). Both systems were developed in the 1930s.

The second stage, 'Esperanto on equal terms', begins when Esperanto is actually used in computational linguistics. First, a series of studies appear which merely investigate the feasibility of the idea (Sjögren 1970; Kelly 1978; Dietze 1986), then smaller programs are written of which only a minority may have been published (Ben-Avi 1977), and, finally, larger implementations are realized. Such implementations are carried out, for example, within the SUSY machine-translation project in Saarbrücken (Maas 1982, 1985, 1987: 40), at Chubu University in Aichi, Japan (Katumori and Hukuda 1984; Makino *et al.* 1986) and at the Chinese Academy of Social Sciences in Peking (Li Wei 1986) and in other places. In the age of the personal computer, much work was done by individuals (Kat 1985; Mohai 1986; Briem 1990). Esperanto was also addressed in speech processing (Sherwood 1978, 1982, 1985; Gordos 1985; Koutny *et al.* 1988), in computer-aided instruction (Sherwood and Sherwood 1982; Janot-Giorgetti 1985) and even in combined systems including both machine-translation and speech-processing functions (Sato and Kasuya 1987; Sato 1989: 165–76). I call this stage 'Esperanto on equal terms', as in these projects and systems Esperanto is treated basically as any other, ethnic, language. There is only a difference of degree in that Esperanto turns out to be easier to handle than ethnic languages, because of its great formal consistency.

The third stage, which I term 'Esperanto for its specificity', begins with the DLT machine-translation project. Distributed language translation (DLT) is the name of a long-term research and development effort by the Dutch software company Buro voor Systeemontwikkeling (BSO), in Utrecht. Based on an invention by Toon Witkam of BSO in 1979, DLT took shape in 1984–7, when a first prototype version was implemented (feasibility study: Witkam 1983; prototype architecture: Schubert 1986; syntax: Schubert 1987; prototype semantics: Papegaaij *et al.* 1986; latest news: Sadler forthcoming), followed by an improved one in 1988.

In the DLT system, Esperanto functions as the intermediate language. The original idea was to include in international datacommunications networks a facility that would allow each subscriber to read and to contribute messages in their own language. Potential applications are not confined to public or corporate electronic mail; they include document management, information retrieval and other functions where variable volumes of text are stored, accessed and updated in several languages. The transmission form in such a network would then be the DLT system's intermediate language, i.e. Esperanto. Translation from the source language into Esperanto takes place in the sender's office, before the text enters the network, and translation from Esperanto into the target language is carried out in the computer where the receiver reads the message. (Hence the term *distributed* in the system's name.)

It is not the aim of this chapter to give a full account of the linguistic and computational developments that were required to realize this idea to the extent to which it has been accomplished at the time of writing. Here, I shall only address the question, 'which properties of Esperanto make it suitable for this application?'.

WHEN IS AN INTERMEDIATE LANGUAGE NEEDED?

Before answering the question, 'under what circumstances should the intermediate language of a machine translation system be Esperanto?', it may be useful to explain why an intermediate language is needed at all.

Translating is an intricate intellectual process, and attempting to have it done by a computer does not by any means make the task easier. Machine translation necesarily involves a series of steps which use linked but distinct modules. Representations are therefore needed for partially processed versions of the text. As soon as the design of the system includes more than two languages, combinatorial problems arise. The so-called transfer systems link each pair of a source and a target language directly via a series of intermediate steps specific to that language pair. It is well known that systems with this architecture need for n languages $n(n - 1)^2$ transfer modules with as many language-pair-specific representations. A transfer system for the nine official languages of the European Community, for instance, would thus need no fewer than seventy-two translation modules. The transfer representations are usually made up of elements from the two languages involved, plus some formal symbols. The more languages such a system contains, the more expensive it becomes to add yet another language: $2\,n$ interfaces to and from the n languages already included (eighteen new modules for adding a tenth language).

A remedy for this combinatorial explosion is a true intermediate representation. The $n(n - 1)^2$ formula is based on the assumption that every source language is linked directly with every target language. If these direct links can be given up in favour of a single, central representation, the combinatorial problem is removed. Then a text from whatever source language is first translated into the intermediate representation and from there into the target language(s) chosen. This set-up requires only $2\,n$ modules, and the addition of a new language requires only two modules (thus eighteen instead of seventy-two modules for the EC example, two more for a tenth language).

Thus, if a system is designed to be *multilingual*, an intermediate representation is required to keep the *complexity* of the architecture to a minimum and, at the same time, to make the system easily *extensible*.

CONDITIONS FOR THE INTERMEDIATE LANGUAGE

In principle, most of what was said in the previous section is basic knowledge for anyone acquainted with machine translation. It is not always fully acknowledged, however, that the reasons which motivate the inclusion of an intermediate representation in the architecture of a system inherently imply a number of conditions for the *nature* of that representation.

First, an intermediate representation can only help to avoid combinatorial explosion if it is the sole link between any source and target language. The system's architecture can only shed the combinatorial problems (and their cost) if each language is connected to the intermediate representation only. No direct links to other languages can be permitted. To achieve this goal, it does not suffice merely to allow the data to flow technically through the one intermediate representation. It is essential that the source and target language modules be truly independent. Second, therefore, a text represented in the intermediate form must not contain any features that are specific to a given source or target language. The first requirement addresses, so to speak, the external combinatorial explosion. The second requirement seeks to avoid a similar explosion that would otherwise occur within the intermediate representation.

The second condition is less obvious. A transfer system without a central intermediate representation needs its $n(n - 1)^2$ transfer modules, as, for instance, translating from English requires one set of rules and dictionaries when the target language is German, and a different one when the target language is Italian, and translating into Portuguese requires one set of rules and dictionaries when the source language is Danish, and a different one when the source language is Greek. In a system with an intermediate representation, this combinatorial problem must necessarily be removed as well, otherwise the system cannot profit from its less explosive architecture. If this condition is not observed, there may be $2 n$ modules but there will nevertheless have to be $n(n - 1)^2$ transfer rule systems and dictionaries. This is what I call the internal explosion. In small 'toy' systems it can be circumvented, but in real production-scale machine translation systems the internal explosion is disastrous and should be avoided in the basic design of the system architecture.

As a consequence of all this, an essential requirement for the intermediate representation is that it should be fully independent of the source and target languages. At this stage of the reasoning, this does not necessarily mean that the words (or other symbols for semantic elements) in the intermediate representation could not be taken from a language which also functions as a source and target language in the system. The requirement only means that a text, represented in intermediate form, must not bear any particular traces of its original language that would be needed to translate it in any specific form into the target languages.

At this stage of the argument, one might well build an intermediate representation using English words. In the case of the DLT system, other considerations make this impossible and make Esperanto preferable.

ALTERNATIVE INTERMEDIATE REPRESENTATIONS

When an intermediate representation is designed, several basic decisions have to be made. The first decision is between a *language* and an *artificial symbol system*. If one opts for a language, the next decision is between an *ethnic language* and a *planned language*. And finally, in the group of ethnic languages there are several thousands to choose from, in the group of planned languages several hundreds (Duličenko 1989: 51).

As is often the case in language-related system design, the decisions are in reality not as clear-cut as they appear to be in theory. The most commonly adopted solution is a more or less strongly artificial symbol system with words, morphemes or other elements from an ethnic language among the symbols. Such a representation is on the artificial side of the scale, but it is not totally devoid of linguistic elements. The opposite solution is a text in a plain human language, ethnic or planned, normally with a few enrichments or precisions for which artificial, non-linguistic, symbols are applied. The DLT solution belongs to the latter kind.

The independence requirement, formulated above, does not at first sight appear to have much bearing on the question, 'what kind of elements should the intermediate representation be made up of?' Nonetheless, it has a corollary which is so obvious that its consequences are often overlooked. As the intermediate representation by virtue of the independence requirement must not contain any source or target language-specific features, it should itself be self-contained and fully capable of expressing the complete content of the text being translated.

From one of the classics of linguistic theory, Louis Hjelmslev, we learn an interesting consequence of this expressiveness requirement. Hjelmslev has investigated the relationship between artificial symbol systems and human language. Interestingly enough, he arrives at a criterion which establishes a direct link to the issue discussed here: *translatability*. Hjelmslev shows that meaning expressed in an artificial symbol system can always be translated into a human language, whereas a text in a human language cannot always be translated into a given artificial symbol system. In other words, according to Hjelmslev, artificial symbol systems are inherently less expressive than human languages (Hjelmslev 1963: 101; Schubert 1988: 137). More precisely, artificial symbol systems are so much less expressive than human languages that it is impossible to *translate* the full content of an ordinary text into an artificial system. Thus, the difference in expressiveness between an artificial symbol system and a human language is not merely one of degree but one of *quality*.

If Hjelmslev is right in this finding, the attempts to use artificial symbol systems as intermediate representations in machine translation are in obvious contradiction to the independence requirement and to its corollary, the expressiveness requirement.

As a consequence of Hjelmslev's diagnosis, artificial symbol systems cannot fulfil the function of an intermediate representation in machine translation. A single scholar's opinion may not be accepted as a proof, but, to say the least, the experience of the machine translation community with intermediate representations so far certainly does not suggest the contrary! A possible solution, then, is to adopt a human language for the intermediate function, that is, to opt for an intermediate *language* instead of an intermediate representation.

The experience in both literary and informative translation shows that translating through a bridge language is without any doubt possible but normally leads to a lower-quality result. A high-quality machine translation system therefore needs an 'upgraded' version of a human language. Such a solution has been tried out with considerable success in the DLT project. The discussion in the next sections shows that, contrary to what critics sometimes assume, the solution found for the DLT system is not being put forward as a universal and generally applicable remedy for all machine translation systems of whatever type, but that it is a carefully chosen, made-to-measure instrument for a specific, well-described purpose. It is in this context that the choice of Esperanto should be understood and appreciated.

ESPERANTO AS A CONSEQUENCE OF SYSTEM DESIGN

Belonging to a new generation which is not yet on the market, the DLT machine translation system was given a clearly more ambitious design than existing systems. From the very first plan drawn up by its inventor, Toon Witkam, DLT's design has been ambitious in a fundamental way: it is aimed at the monolingual layman user. This is noteworthy, as the DLT designers subscribe to the generally agreed finding of the 1950s that fully automatic high-quality translation is impossible. The basic parameters of the DLT architecture therefore include – in addition to the inter-mediate language, the primary functions of which are to avoid combinatorial explosion and to maintain the extensibility of the system – a system-initiated disambiguation dialogue. The dialogue takes place during the first half of the translation process, i.e., when the text is being translated from the source language into the intermediate language. In the dialogue, the user is asked to decide such cases of structural or semantic ambiguity in the source text that cannot with sufficient confidence be resolved by the system itself. The dialogue is carried out entirely in the source language and its wording is arranged in such a way that no knowledge of grammar, of linguistic terminology or of the target language(s) is needed, let alone of Esperanto.

Along with the requirement for expressiveness formulated above, the goal of high-quality output places a severe condition on the intermediate language. Because of the distributed architecture, a disambiguation dialogue can reasonably be included only in the source-to-intermediate part of the overall translation process, so that there is interaction once for each text, but not once for each text and each target language. A logical consequence is that the intermediate-to-target parts have to be fully automatic, and obviously they should deliver translation of a high quality. Existing machine translation systems require post-editing, an activity to be carried out by a skilled translator or reviser for each of the target languages involved. By contrast, the DLT design aims at ready-to-use high-quality output which does not need post-editing.

In the DLT setting, the intermediate language should thus allow for fully automatic high-quality translation, a thing which is known to be impossible between 'normal' human languages. As I have shown above, the combinatorial considerations suggest the use of some intermediate language, no matter which. The additional requirement of fully automatic translation *from* the intermediate language places a severe restriction on the designer's freedom of choice. Given this requirement, the intermediate language has to be much more precise than the source and target languages, as it has to render the results of the disambiguation process. It is through the additional information gathered in the disambiguation steps, plus the inherent clarity of the intermediate language itself, that fully automatic high-quality translation can be achieved in the second half of the process.

This is the essence of the reason for choosing Esperanto as the intermediate language: the expressiveness requirement makes it necessary that the language *into* which texts from all source languages are translated be a human language rather than an artificial symbol system. The requirement of fully automatic high-quality translation *from* the intermediate language into any one of a number of target languages makes it necessary for the intermediate language to be fundamentally clearer and more precise than ordinary languages. In the DLT setting, Esperanto has been found to offer an excellent way out of this seemingly contradictory situation.

WHAT MAKES ESPERANTO SO WELL-SUITED FOR MACHINE TRANSLATION?

In the previous sections I have discussed the external aspects of the situation in which Esperanto functions as an intermediate language in the DLT system. The essence of the argument so far is the insight that Esperanto combines the expressiveness of an ethnic language with the extreme clarity of an artificial symbol system. I have not yet offered much proof of this. In this section, therefore, I shall go more deeply into the grammatical (and even sociolinguistic) properties that make Esperanto especially suitable for this purpose.

In order to make this discussion interesting for those readers who are not especially interested in the particulars of the DLT machine translation system, I have chosen as a starting point a rather fundamental view of machine translation, or, in fact, of natural-language processing in general.

The essential problem of natural-language processing

Natural-language processing, and in particular its oldest endeavour, machine translation, sometimes seems to be a never-ending struggle towards a goal that ultimately cannot be reached. In my view, the essence of the problem lies in the fact that language is infinite. Language is an open-ended system. There is always more than what can be covered by explicit rules or enumerated in dictionaries or in lists of exceptions to the rules. There are no sharp borderlines, especially between grammatical and ungrammatical utterances, between existing and non-existing words and expressions, between allowed and forbidden combinations of words or meanings, etc. All this makes language vague, but this vagueness is an extremely fruitful prerequisite for language to cope with the infinite multitude and diversity of situations that people need to communicate about. A symbol system which is not infinite in this vast and multi-layered sense is insufficient. Hjelmslev understood this.

As a consequence of this infiniteness of language it is often impossible to cover every phenomenon encountered in a text to be translated in pre-formulated rules that range over finite or enumerable sets of elements. A significant stream of research interest in general and computational linguistics has, therefore, for quite some time been focusing on *corpora* as the basic source of knowledge about language. In current work on natural-language processing at the BSO software company, this approach has been rigidly adhered to. Based on the experience gained with the DLT prototypes. Victor Sadler has developed a method of using corpora not only to inspire grammarians and lexicographers (who would then write explicit rules and entries), but directly as a knowledge source in machine translation (Sadler 1989: Part II; Schubert 1990: 219). It may be noteworthy that a corpus in this sense is a set of examples. A technique with direct use of corpora thus implies that the knowledge needed for the automated translation process is derived from examples, and translating on the basis of examples means that the basic principle used is *analogy*. If properly applied, this principle caters very smoothly for the infiniteness of language: instead of trying to describe the precise *limits* of linguistic phenomena, the analogy-based technique uses *typical* examples of constructions, translation equivalents, etc., that are known to be correct and *extrapolates* from those to new texts previously unknown to the system.

The details of this approach are far beyond the scope of this chapter. For the discussion here it is interesting that, as a consequence of a technique which takes into account the infiniteness of language, the capacity to accommodate extrapolation processes in a comfortable and expedient way becomes a touchstone for an intermediate language in machine translation.

Removing syntactic ambiguity

The DLT feasibility study devoted extensive attention to modifications in the grammar of Esperanto that were felt necessary for its function in DLT (Witkam 1983: IV–1–IV–111). During the development of the prototypes, however, it was found that most of these modifications could be abandoned, so that DLT's intermediate language became more and more similar to common Esperanto as it is spoken and written by humans. (This obviously facilitated the transition to corpus-based techniques later on, for which it is advantageous for texts in undoctored language to be incorporated in a straightforward manner.) At the end of the prototype phase, the difference between common Esperanto and DLT's version can be summarized under a single condition; DLT's Esperanto is *syntactically* unambiguous. The term *syntax* is meant in a broad sense which covers all grammatical properties on the formal side of the linguistic sign (Schubert 1987: 14–16). Essentially, this is achieved by the insertion of two kinds of delimiter. As Witkam (1983: IV–93) had suggested, extra spaces between words are used as markers for the end of a syntagma (a phrase). This resolves most of the notorious attachment problems that are extensively discussed in syntax and parsing theory. (*Ni aĉet'as libr'o'n de Goethe* 'We buy a-book by Goethe': normal single space before *de*, thus *de Goethe* belongs to *libr'o'n* and translates as 'by'; *Ni aĉet'as libr'o'n #de Goethe* 'We buy a-book from Goethe'; extra space [shown as #] before *de*, indicating a syntagma boundary so that *de Goethe* cannot belong to the [closed] syntagma *libr'o'n* and accordingly belongs to *aĉet'as* and translates as *buy from*.) As Esperanto is totally agglutinative, DLT also introduced overt markers of morpheme boundaries as shown above. In this way, ambiguity in the analysis of words is excluded. (Common Esperanto *sendata* becomes either *sen'dat'a* 'without' + 'date' + adjective marker = 'undated' or *send'at'a* 'send' + passive progressive participle + adjective marker = 'being sent'.)

It may be surprising that these two minor artificial elements should suffice to make a human language unambiguous, albeit only at the word- and sentence-syntactic level. Obviously, this is possible in Esperanto only because the language has a highly unambiguous structure anyway. A well-known feature is the word class system: all content words bear an identifying morpheme (e.g. *a* for adjectives, see above), and the function words are a finite list. With the exception of a handful of function words, no word class ambiguity exists. This may not seem much but in view of the enormous problems such a simple thing as word class recognition brings about in parsing and corpus analysis efforts for English, this clear structure of Esperanto is a major asset.

Productive word-formation

One of the central and most efficient aspects of the infiniteness of language is the possibility of combining existing linguistic signs to express new meanings. In all languages, the formation of syntagmata and sentences offers an opportunity for the expression of new meanings, but many languages also have a very productive combinatorial capacity within words. Productive word formation is a major instrument of infinite expressiveness. In English, this possibility is marginal, in Esperanto, as in all agglutinative languages, it is an essential feature.

Esperantology has brought about a highly elaborated theory of word formation (Schubert 1989b). On the basis of a grammatical foundation which was designed as an *open*, extensible system and under the influence of the pragmatic factors to be discussed below, Esperanto has, in its hundred-year history, developed a highly compositional system of word-formation. As a consequence, the language provides a powerful mechanism for forming new words from existing roots, while at the same time, the derivation of the meaning of these words can be automated to a high degree. (This derivation mechanism cannot be fully exhaustive for theoretical reasons. A language in which this were possible would have lost its infiniteness in a crucial field.)

The ability to isolate the component elements of complex words using automated processes is extremely important for a good and effective functioning of word-based knowledge banks such as those used in DLT, where the basic knowledge source is made up of structured corpora. A speciality of Esperanto is, in this respect, its unusually high degree of compositionality. This means that the meaning of an extremely high percentage of complex words can be inferred in a straightforward manner from the individual meanings of their component elements. This is the case with Esperanto, as its design objective was ease of learning and inferability is an obvious advantage in language learning. As it turns out, the same characteristic pays off in machine translation as well. The fact that Esperanto not only started with a perspicuous word-formation system but maintained this system intact throughout a hundred years of uncontrolled use can be attributed to the pragmatic factors addressed below.

Why semantic ambiguity cannot be removed

It is not sufficient to remove ambiguity at the syntactic level. More intricate and more challenging to machine translation is ambiguity at the semantic level. What about Esperanto in this regard?

The sceptics rail against Esperanto with an endless store of arguments and prejudice. The optimists, on the other hand, sometimes smile complacently and say, 'Oh, I understand, with this Esperanto of yours, you have found a totally unambiguous language for the computer!' The sceptics have been proved wrong by the experience gained in DLT practice, and elsewhere. But the optimists are mistaken, too. At the semantic level, Esperanto is not unambiguous, because there is no such thing as semantic unambiguity. Slogans like 'one word – one meaning' are nonsensical, as they presuppose that there is an objective, cross-linguistically valid, dissection of meaning in discrete portions. There is, however, plenty of evidence that no such portions exist. This is amply borne out by the unsuccessful attempts at defining basic sets of such portions of meaning, normally called semantic atoms or semantic primitives. The art, then, is not the dissection of meaning with a view to achieving basic, universally valid elements that cannot be subdivided further and constructing therefrom an intermediate representation; it is the handling of meaning in whatever shape it takes in different, fully expressive languages.

In addition, it should be borne in mind that the main problem in machine translation is not the 'semantic ambiguity' that some scholars attempt to resolve at the monolingual level. The main problem is the ambiguity at the *translation* level, that is, the semantic ambiguity in lexical or structural transfer. In other words, the main hurdle is the ambiguity *between* languages, rather than the ambiguity within languages. To put it simply: if your English–Chinese dictionary offers you ten translations for *machine*, which one do you choose, what are your criteria for choosing it and how do you automate this choice?

The DLT approach addresses this problem by aligning parallel corpora of translated texts and taking them as the basic knowledge source. DLT's 'bilingual knowledge banks' are built from these corpora, one side of which is in Esperanto. The bilingual knowledge banks are based on the principle of extrapolation. For extrapolation, obviously, a regular language structure is a major advantage.

A word about pragmatics

Compositionality in the semantic part of a language's grammar is expedient for machine translation. Many readers will agree with that. In Esperanto, as in other languages, compositionality is not total. So, what is so special about Esperanto?

The answer is twofold: first, Esperanto has developed from a deliberately constructed grammatical system, initiated only a century ago, and has thus been able to preserve its compositionality to a very considerable extent. This gives it a quantitative advantage compared to ethnic languages. Second, however, being a language spoken in an *international* language community, Esperanto has a qualitative advantage over other languages. As Esperanto's main and almost exclusive function is *international* communication, it has always maintained its special suitability for communication between people with radically different linguistic backgrounds and preconceptions. This condition has favoured a development on the basis of the intrinsic regularities of the language itself, rather than through imitating other languages and adopting loan patterns. Because of this pragmatic factor, Esperanto has always developed with a natural tendency towards consistency. This is an important asset for its function in machine translation.

Two prejudices

Finally, a few words about two frequently heard prejudices concerning Esperanto that are closely related to the subject of this discussion. First a practical, then a theoretical one.

Prejudice 1

'I understand that some simple corespondence among pen pals and stamp collectors is possible in Esperanto. But, of course, you can't say everything in that language, can you?' Of course you can. Like any other language, Esperanto can express everything which has already been expressed in it. This sounds contradictory but it holds for all languages, English as well as Yoruba: if you have to prove that something can be said in a language, you will only succeed if this has been done (and recorded) before. So the problem resides not only in existing language use but in the language's capacity to develop. 'Western' languages like English, German or Russian have very rich vocabularies, but terminologists still work hard to extend them, as unfortunately, they experience that you cannot really say everything in English, German or Russian. The same holds true for Esperanto. The language has the capacity to develop, and it has developed whenever it was necessary for it to do so. Unlike ethnic languages, however, Esperanto develops in the sociolinguistically unique setting of international communication.

Prejudice 2

'You argue that artificial symbol systems are insufficient. But Esperanto is an artificial language par excellence, isn't it?' It is not. What is often overlooked in this sort of discussion is the fact that Esperanto has already entered its second century. When the first textbook of Esperanto was published in 1887, Esperanto *was* artificial, and it was not yet a language. But since then, Esperanto has, in a slow and unnoticed development, become a language spoken by people. According to Detlev Blanke (Blanke 1985: 105ff and *Tabelle* 2), Esperanto is the only project of a planned language which has totally accomplished the transition from an artificial system to a real language. So, the argument should now be based on a serious study of Esperanto as it exists today, not on remarks quoted by journalists from outdated encyclopaedias.

CONCLUSION

The experience of the DLT machine translation project so far has shown that Esperanto fulfils a specific requirement in language technology: it can be used to good advantage as an intermediate language in machine translation, when fully automatic high-quality translation from the intermediate language into the target language(s) is aimed at.

BIBLIOGRAPHY

Bar-Hillel, Y. (1951) 'The state of machine translation in 1951', *American Documentation* 2: 229–37.

Ben-Avi, S. (1977) 'An investigation into the use of Esperanto as an intermediate language in a machine translation project', PhD Thesis, Manchester.

Blanke, D. (1985) *Internationale Plansprachen*, Berlin: Akademic-Verlag.

Briem, S. (1990) 'Maskinoversaettelse fra esperanto til islandsk', in J. Pind and F. Rögnvaldsson (eds) *Papers from the Seventh Scandinavian Conference of Computational Linguistics (Reykjavík 1989)*, Reykjavik: Institute of Lexicography/Institute of Linguistics, 138–45.

Denisov, P.N. (1965) *Principy modelirovanija jazyka (na materiale vspomogatel'nych jazykov dlja avtomatičeskogo poiska i perevoda)*, Moscow: Moskovskij Universitet.

Dietze, J. (1986) 'Projekt der rechnergestützten Erarbeitung eines Wörterbuchs von Esperantowurzeln', *Wissenschaftliche Zeitschrift der Universität Halle*, 35 [G, 5]: 90–1.

Duličenko, A.D. (1989) 'Ethnic language and planned language, and its place in language science', in K. Schubert (ed.) *Interlinguistics. Aspects of the science of planned languages*, Berlin/New York: Mouton de Gruyter, 47–61.

Forster, P.G. (1987) 'Some social sources of resistance to Esperanto', in José-Luis Melena Jiménez *et al.* (eds) *Serta gratvlatoria in honorem Juan Régulo*, vol. 2: *Esperantismo*, La Laguna: Universidad, 203–11.

Gordos, G. (1985) 'Parol-sintezo kun limigita vortaro', in I. Koutny (ed.) *Perkomputila tekstoprilaboro*, Budapest: Scienca Eldona Centro, 11–29.

Hjelmslev, L. (1963) *Sproget*, 2nd edn, Copenhagen: Berlingske forlag.

Hutchins, W.J. (1986) *Machine Translation: Past, Present, Future*, Chichester: Ellis Horwood.

Janot-Giorgetti, M.T. (1985) 'Parol-rekono kun limigita vortaro, ĝia apliko en la lernado de parolataj lingvoj', in I. Koutny (ed.) *Perkomputila tekstoprilaboro*, Budapest: Scienca Eldona Centro, 57–68.

Kat, J.O. de (1985) 'Traduko el la internacia lingvo al naciaj', in I. Koutny (ed.) *Perkomputila tekstoprilaboro*, Budapest: Scienca Eldona Centro, 259–66.

Katumori, H. and Hukuda, M. (1984) 'Esuperanto o tyûkai-gengo to suru kikai-hon´yaku no kokoromi', *WGNL meeting 1984–7–26*.

Kelly, I.D.K. (1978) 'How Esperanto can aid machine translation', *Computer Weekly* 19 January 1978.

Koutny, I., Olaszy, G. and Kisfaludy, K. (1988) 'Esperanto speech synthesis and its application in language learning', in T. Szende (ed.) *From Phonology to Applied Phonetics*, Magyar Fonetikai Füzutek//Human Papers in Phonetics, 19, Budapest: Linguistics Institute of the Hungarian Academy of Sciences, 47–54.

Li Wei (1986) 'Aŭtomata tradukado el la internacia en la ĉinan kaj anglan lingvojn (Esperanta–angla/ĉina maŝintraduka sistemo)', *Grundlagenstudien aus Kybernetik und Geisteswissenschaft/Humankybernetik* 27: 147–52.

Maas, H.D. (1982) 'Aŭtomata tradukado en kaj el Esperanto', in H.F. Yashovardhan and B. Frank-Böhringer (eds) *Lingvokibernetiko kaj aliaj internacilingvaj aktoj de la IX-a Internacia Kongreso de Kibernetiko//Sprachkybernetik und andere internationalsprachige Akten vom IX. Internationalen Kybernetikerkongreß*, Tübingen: Narr, 75–81.

—— (1985) 'Pri kelkaj strategioj por fraz-analizo', in I. Koutny (ed.) *Perkomputila tekstoprilaboro*, Budapest: Scienca Eldona Centro, 175–205.

—— (1987) 'The MT system SUSY', in M. King (ed.) *Machine Translation Today: the State of the Art*, Edinburgh: Edinburgh University Press, 209–46, 392–435.

Makino, S., Hirata, M. and Katumori, H. (1986) 'Esuperanto o tyûkai-gengo to suru kikai hon´yaku', *WGNL meeting 1986–3–28*.

Mohai, L. (1986) 'Komputila tradukprogramo el Esperanto hungaren', in P. Broczkó, I. Koutny and A. Lukács (eds) *Language Cybernetics, Educational Cybernetics//Lingvokibernetiko, pedagogia kibernetiko//Cybernétique de la langue, cybernétique de l'éducation*, Budapest: Neumann Society, 47–51.

Papegaaij, B.C., Sadler, V. and Witkam, A.P.M. (eds) (1986) *Word Expert Semantics: an Interlingual Knowledge-based Approach* (Distributed Language Translation 1), Dordrecht/Riverton: Foris.

Piron, C. (1987) 'Esperanto: l'immagine e la realità', in A. Chiti-Batelli (ed.) *La comunicazione internazionale tra politica e glottodidattica*, Milan: Marzorati, 68–116.

Sadler, V. (1989) *Working with Analogical Semantics. Disambiguation Techniques in DLT*, Dordrecht/Providence: Foris.

—— (forthcoming) 'Machine translation project reaches watershed', *Language Problems and Language Planning* 15.

Sato, S. (1989) 'Phonetic form generation in a semantics-to-speech system of Japanese', Sendai: Dissertation, Tohoku University.

Sato, S. and Kasuya, H. (1987) 'Automatic translation/speech synthesis of Japanese from written Esperanto incorporating a linguistic knowledge base editor', in J. Laver and M.A. Jack (eds) *European Conference on Speech Technology (Edinburgh 1987)*, vol. 2, Edinburgh: CEP, 414–17.

Schubert, K. (1986) 'Linguistic and extra-linguistic knowledge', *Computers and Translation* 1: 125–52.

—— (1987) *Metataxis. Contrastive Dependency Syntax for Machine Translation*, Dordrecht/Providence: Foris.

—— (1988) 'Ausdruckskraft und Regelmäßigkeit. Was Esperanto für automatische Übersetzung geeignet macht', *Language Problems and Language Planning* 12: 130–47.

—— (1989a) 'Interlinguistics – its aims, its achievements, and its place in language science', in K. Schubert (ed.) *Interlinguistics. Aspects of the Science of Planned Languages*, Berlin/New York: Mouton de Gruyter, 7–44.

—— (1989b) 'An unplanned development in planned languages. A study of word grammar', in K. Schubert (ed.) *Interlinguistics. Aspects of the Science of Planned Languages*, Berlin/New York: Mouton de Gruyter, 249–74.

—— (1990) 'Kunskap om världen eller kunskap om texten? En metod för korpusstödd maskinöversättning', in J. Pind and E. Rögnvaldsson (eds) *Papers from the Seventh Scandinavian Conference of Computational Linguistics (Reykjavík 1989)*, Reykjavik: Institute of Lexicography/Institute of Linguistics, 218–28.

Sherwood, B.A. (1978) 'Fast text-to-speech algorithms for Esperanto, Spanish, Italian, Russian and English', *International Journal of Man–Machine Studies* 10: 669–92.

—— (1982) 'Raporto pri sintezo de Esperanta parolado', in I. Koutny (ed.) *Homa lingvo kaj komputilo*, Budapest: NJSzT//Societo Neumann, 64–75.

—— (1985) 'Komputila tradukado de esperanta teksto', in I. Koutny (ed.) *Perkomputila teksloprilaboro*, Budapest: Scienca Eldona Centro, 153–60.

Sherwood, J.N. and Sherwood, B.A. (1982) 'Computer voices and ears furnish novel teaching options', *Speech Technology* [1982]: 46–51.

Sjögren, S. (1970) *En syntax för datamaskinell analys av esperanto*, FOA P rapport C 8264–11(64), Stockholm: Försvarets forskningsanstalt.

Tesnière, L. (1959) *Eléments de syntaxe structurale*, 2nd edn, 4th print. 1982, Paris: Klincksieck.

Witkam, A.P.M. (1983) *Distributed Language Translation. Feasibility Study of a Multilingual Facility for Videotex Information Networks*, Utrecht: BSO.

Chapter 7

Limitations of computers as translation tools

Alex Gross*

As should be more than evident from other contributions to this volume, the field of computer translation is alive and well – if anything, it is now entering what may prove to be its truly golden era. But there would be no need to point this out if certain problems from an earlier time had not raised lingering doubts about the overall feasibility of the field. Just as other authors have stressed the positive side of various systems and approaches, this chapter will attempt to deal with some of these doubts and questions, both as they may apply here and now to those planning to work with computer translation systems and also in a larger sense as they may be connected to some faulty notions about language held by the general public and perhaps some system developers as well. Explaining such doubts and limitations forthrightly can only help all concerned by making clear what is likely – and what is less likely – to work for each individual user. It can also clarify what the underlying principles and problems in this field have been and to some extent still are.

To begin with, the notion of computer translation is not new. Shortly after the Second World War, at a time when no one dreamt that word processors, spreadsheets, or drawing programs would be widely available, some of the computer's prime movers, Turing, Weaver and Booth among them, were already beginning to think about translation.[1] They saw this application mainly as a natural outgrowth of their wartime code-breaking work, which had helped to defeat the enemy, and it never occurred to them to doubt that computer translation was a useful and realizable goal.

The growing need to translate large bodies of technical information, heightened by an apparent shortage of translators, was one factor in their quest. But perhaps just as influential was a coupling of linguistic and cultural idealism, the belief that removing 'language barriers' was a good thing, something that would promote international understanding and ensure world peace. Two related notions were surely that deep down all human beings must be basically similar and that piercing the superstratum of language divisions could only be beneficial by helping people to break through their superficial differences.[2] Underlying this idealism was a further assumption that languages were essentially some kind of code that could be cracked, that words in one tongue could readily be replaced by words saying the same thing in another. Just as the key to breaking the Axis code had been found, so some sort of linguistic key capable of unlocking the mysteries of language would soon be discovered. All these assumptions would be sorely tested in the decades ahead.

SOME BASIC TERMS

Some of the most frequently used terms in this field, although also defined elsewhere in this book, will help the reader in dealing with the subject. It will quickly become evident that, merely by providing these definitions, I will also have touched upon some of the field's major problems and limitations, which can then be explained in greater detail. For example, a distinction is frequently made between machine translation (usually systems that produce rough text for a human translator to revise) and computer-assisted translation devices (usually but not invariably software designed to help translators do their work in an enhanced manner). These are often abbreviated as MT and CAT respectively. So far, both approaches require the assistance or active collaboration to one extent or another of a live, human translator. Under machine translation one finds a further distinction between batch, interactive and interlingual approaches. A batch method has rules and definitions which help it 'decide' on the best translation for each word as it goes along. It prints or displays the entire text thus created with no help from the translator (who need not even be present but who nonetheless may often end up revising it). An interactive system pauses to consult with the translator on various words or asks for further clarification. This distinction is blurred by the fact that some systems can operate in either batch or interactive mode. The so-called interlingual approach operates on the theory that one can devise an intermediate 'language' – in at least one case a form of Esperanto – that can encode sufficient linguistic information to serve as a universal intermediate stage – or pivot point – enabling translation back and forth between numerous pairs of languages, despite linguistic or cultural differences. Some skepticism has been voiced about this approach, and to date no viable interlingual system has been unveiled.

Batch and interactive systems are sometimes also referred to as transfer methods to differentiate them from interlingual theories, because they concentrate on a trade or transfer of meaning based on an analysis of one language pair alone. I have tried to make these distinctions as clear as possible, and they do apply to a fair extent to the emerging PC-based scene. At the higher end on mini- and mainframe computers, there is, however, a certain degree of overlap between these categories, frequently making it difficult to say where CAT ends and MT begins.

Another distinction is between pre-editing (limiting the extent of vocabulary beforehand so as to help the computer) and post-editing (cleaning up its errors afterwards). Usually only one is necessary, although this will depend on how perfect a translation is sought by a specific client. 'Pre-editing' is also used to mean simply checking the text to be translated beforehand so as to add new words and expressions to the system's dictionary. The work devoted to this type of pre-editing can save time in post-editing later. A more extreme form of pre-editing is known as controlled language, the severely limited vocabulary of which is used by a few companies to make MT as foolproof as possible.

Advocates of MT often point out that many texts do not require perfect translations, which leads us to our next distinction, between output intended for information-only skimming by experts able to visualize the context and discount errors, and 'full-dress' translations, for those unable to do either. One term that keeps cropping up is FAHQT for fully automatic high-quality translation, which most in the field now concede is not possible (although the idea keeps creeping in again through the back door in claims made for some MT products and even some research projects).[3] Closer to current reality would be such descriptions as FALQT (fully automatic low-quality translation) and PAMQT (partly automatic medium-quality translation). Together, these terms cover much of the spectrum offered by these systems.

Also often encountered in the literature are percentage claims purportedly grading the efficiency of computer translation systems. Thus, one language pair may be described as '90 percent accurate' or '95 percent accurate' or occasionally only '80 percent accurate.' The highest claim I have seen so far is '98 percent accurate.' Such ratings may have more to do with what one author has termed spreading 'innumeracy' than with any meaningful standards of measurement.[4] On a shallow level of criticism, even if we accepted a claim of 98 percent accuracy at face value (and even if it could be substantiated), this would still mean that every standard double-spaced typed page would contain five errors – potentially deep substantive errors, as computers, barring a glitch, never make simple mistakes in spelling or punctuation.

It is for the reader to decide whether such an error level is tolerable in texts that may shape the cars we drive, the medicines and chemicals we take and use, and the peace treaties that bind our nations. As for 95 percent accuracy, this would mean one error on every other line of a typical page, while with 90 percent accuracy we are down to one error in *every line*. Translators who have had to post-edit such texts tend to agree that with percentage claims of 90 percent or below it is easier to have a human translator start all over again from the original text.

On a deeper level, claims of 98 percent accuracy may be even more misleading – does such a claim, in fact, mean that the computer has mastered 98 percent of perfectly written English or rather 90 percent of minimally acceptable English? Is it possible that 98 percent of the latter could turn out to be 49 percent of the former? There is a great difference between the two, and so far these questions have not been addressed. Thus, we can see how our brief summary of terms has already given us a bird's-eye view of our subject.

PRACTICAL LIMITATIONS

There are six important variables in any decision to use a computer for translation: speed, subject matter, desired level of accuracy, consistency of translation, volume and expense. These six determinants can in some cases be merged harmoniously together in a single task but they will at least as frequently tend to clash. Let us take a brief look at each:

Speed

This is an area where the computer simply excels – one mainframe system boasts 700 pages of raw output per night (while translators are sleeping), and other systems are equally prodigious. How raw the output actually is – and how much post-editing will be required, another factor of speed – will depend on how well the computer has been primed to deal with the technical vocabulary of the text being translated. Which brings us to our second category:

Subject matter

Here, too, the computer has an enormous advantage, provided a great deal of work has already gone into codifying the vocabulary of the technical field and entering it into the computer's dictionary. Thus, translations of aeronautical material from Russian to English can be not only speedy but can perhaps even graze the '98 percent accurate' target, because intensive work over several decades has gone into building up this vocabulary. If you are translating from a field the computer vocabulary of which has not yet been developed, you may have to devote some time to bringing its dictionaries up to a more advanced level. Closely related to this factor is the third category:

Desired level of accuracy

I have already mentioned the former in referring to the difference between full-dress translations and work needed on an information-only basis. If the latter is sufficient, only minimal post-editing – or none at all – may be required, and considerable cash savings can be the result. If a full-dress translation is required, however, then much post-editing may be in order and there may turn out to be – depending once again on the quality of the dictionaries – no appreciable savings.

Consistency of vocabulary

Here the computer rules supreme, always assuming that correct prerequisite dictionary building has been done. Before computer translation was readily available, large commercial jobs with a deadline would inevitably be farmed out in pieces to numerous translators with perhaps something resembling a technical glossary distributed among them. Sometimes the task of 'standardizing' the final version could be placed in the hands of a single person of dubious technical attainments. Even without the added problem of a highly technical vocabulary, it should be obvious that no two translators can be absolutely depended upon to translate the same text in precisely the same way. The computer can fully exorcize this demon and ensure that a specific technical term has only one translation, provided that the correct translation has been placed in its dictionary (and provided, of course, that only one term with only one translation is used for this process or entity).

Volume

From the foregoing, it should be obvious that some translation tasks are best left to human beings. Any work of high or even medium literary value is likely to fall into this category. But volume, along with subject matter and accuracy, can also play a role. Many years ago a friend of mine considered moving to Australia, where he heard that sheep farming was quite profitable on either a very small or a very large scale. Then he learned that a very small scale meant from 10,000 to 20,000 head of sheep, a very large one meant over 100,000. Anything else was a poor prospect, and so he ended up staying at home. The numbers are different for translation, of course, and vary from task to task and system to system but the principle is related. In general, there will be – all other factors being almost equal – a point at which the physical size of a translation will play a role in reaching a decision. Would-be users should carefully consider how all the factors I have touched upon may affect their own needs and intentions. Thus, the size and scope of a job can also determine whether or not you may be better off using a computer alone, some computer–human combination or having human translators handle it for you from the start. One author proposes 8,000 pages per year in a single technical specialty with a fairly standardized vocabulary as minimum requirements for translating text on a mainframe system.[5]

Expense

Given the computer's enormous speed and its virtually foolproof vocabulary safeguards, one would expect it to be a clear winner in this area. But for all the reasons I have already mentioned, this is by no means true in all cases. The last word is far from having been written here, and one of the oldest French companies in this field has just recently got round to ordering exhaustive tests comparing the expenses of computer and human translation, taking all factors into account.[6]

As we can see quite plainly, a number of complications and limitations are already evident. Speed, wordage, expense, subject matter and accuracy/consistency of vocabulary may quickly become mutually clashing vectors affecting your plans. If you can make allowances for all of them, then computer translation can be of great use to you. If the decision-making process involved seems prolonged and tortuous, it perhaps merely reflects the true state of the art not only of computer translation but of our overall knowledge of how language really works. At least some of the apparent confusion about this field may be caused by a gap between what many people believe a computer should be able to do in this area and what it actually can do at present. What many still believe (and have, as we shall see, continued to believe over several decades, despite ample evidence to the contrary) is that a computer should function as a simple black box: you enter a text in language A on one side, and it slides out written perfectly in language B on the other. Or, better still, you read it aloud, and it prints or even speaks it aloud in any other language you might desire.

This has not happened and, barring extremely unlikely developments, will not happen in the near future, assuming our goal is an unerringly correct and fluent translation. If we are willing to compromise on that goal and accept less-than-perfect translations, or wish to translate texts within a very limited subject area or otherwise restrict the vocabulary we use, then extremely useful results are possible. Figure 7.1 provides a rough indication of the suitability or otherwise of various text types for MT. Some hidden expenses may also be encountered; these can involve retraining translators to cooperate with mainframe and minicomputers and setting up electronic dictionaries to contain the precise vocabulary used by a company or institution. Less expensive systems running on a PC with built-in glossaries also require a considerable degree of customizing to work most efficiently, as such smaller systems are far more limited in both vocabulary and semantic resolving power than their mainframe counterparts.

Furthermore, not all translators are, at present, prepared to make the adjustments in their work habits needed for such systems to work at their maximum efficiency. And even those able to handle

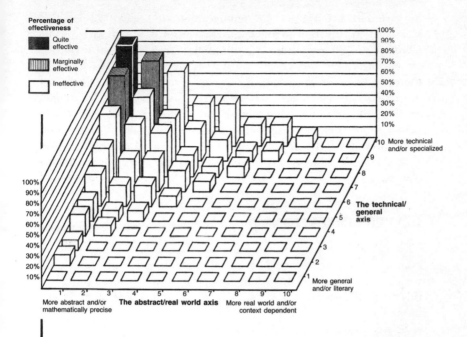

Percentage of effectiveness

- Quite effective
- Marginally effective
- Ineffective

100%
90%
80%
70%
60%
50%
40%
30%
20%
10%

10 More technical and/or specialized
9
8
7
6 The technical/ general axis
5
4
3
2
1 More general and/or literary

100%
90%
80%
70%
60%
50%
40%
30%
20%
10%

1'   2'   3'   4'   5'   6'   7'   8'   9'   10'
More abstract and/or   **The abstract/real world axis**   More real world and/or
mathematically precise   context dependent

If machine translation techniques were 100% effective in all cases, the above graph would be a solid block of black. The extent of white space shown reflects the current situation. The areas where these techniques can be quite effective or marginally effective are probably limited to the three bars on the upper left, though even here some post-editing by a translator may be needed for the computer output to be read by non-specialists. It is important to stress, however, that much technical and industrial translation does fall into this area of the graph where computer techniques can be of use. It should be clear from the graph that wherever language is more general or literary or is more dependent on context or real-world understanding, computer techniques are less effective. One author recommends their use where the annual volume of restricted vocabulary technical text for a single language direction (e.g. French to English) is 5,000 pages or more (Newman 1988). Statistics for this chart are based on a face-value acceptance of accuracy claims published by MT vendors, these figures should therefore be treated with some caution.

Figure 7.1 The effectiveness of computer translation.
Prepared by Alex and Ilene Gross

the transition may not be temperamentally suited to making such systems function at their most powerful level. All attempts to introduce computer translation systems into the work routine depend on some degree of adjustment by all concerned, and in many cases such adjustment is not easy. Savings in time or money are usually only achieved at the end of such periods. Sometimes everyone in a company, from executives down to stock clerks, will be obliged to change their accustomed vocabularies to some extent to accommodate the new system.[5] Such a process can on occasion actually lead, however, to enhanced communication within a company.

DEEPER LIMITATIONS

This section explains how changing standards in the study of linguistics may be related to the limitations in machine translation we see today and perhaps prefigure certain lines of development in this field. Those interested only in the practical side should turn immediately to p. 115.

Some practical limitations of MT and even of CAT should already be clear enough. Less evident are the limitations in some of the linguistic theories which have sired much of the work in this field. On the whole, Westerners are not accustomed to believing that problems may be insoluble and, after four decades of labor, readers might suppose that more progress had been made in this field than appears to be the case. To provide several examples at once, I can remember standing for some time by the display booth of a prominent European computer translation firm during a science conference at MIT and listening to the comments of passers-by. I found it dismaying to overhear the same attitudes voiced over and over again by quite sane and reasonable representatives from government, business and education. Most of what I heard could be summed up as:

1 language can't really be that complex as we all speak it;
2 language, like nature, is an alien environment which must be conquered and tamed;
3 there has to be some simple way to cut through all the nonsense about linguistics, syntax and semantics, and achieve instant high-quality translation;
4 why wasn't it all done yesterday?

To understand the reasons behind these comments and why they were phrased in this particular way – and also to understand the deeper reasons behind the limitations of computer translation – it may be helpful to go back to the year 1944, when the first stirrings of current activity were little evident and another school of linguistics ruled all but supreme. In that year Leonard Bloomfield – one of the three deans of US linguistics along with Edward Sapir and Benjamin Lee Whorf[7] – was struggling to explain a problem that greatly perturbed him.

Bloomfield was concerned with what he called 'secondary responses to language.' By these he meant the things people say and seem to believe about language, often in an uninformed way. He called such opinions about language 'secondary' to differentiate them from the use of language in communication, which he saw as 'primary.' People delivering such statements, he observed, are often remarkably alert and enthusiastic: their eyes grow bright, they tend to repeat these opinions over and over again to anyone who will hear and they simply will not listen – even those who, like the ones I met at MIT, are highly trained and familiar with scientific procedures – to informed points of view differing from their own. They are overcome by how obvious or interesting their own ideas seem to be.[8]

I would add here that what Bloomfield seems to be describing is a set of symptoms clinically similar to some forms of hysteria. As he put it:

> It is only in recent years that I have learned to observe these secondary . . . responses in anything like a systematic manner, and I confess that I cannot explain them – that is, correlate them with anything else. The explanation will doubtless be a matter of psychology and sociology.
>
> (Hockett 1970: 420)

If it is indeed hysteria, as Bloomfield seems to suggest, I wonder if it might not be triggered because some people, when their ideas about language are questioned or merely held up for discussion, feel themselves under attack at the very frontier of their knowledge about reality. For many people, language is so close to what they believe that they are no longer able to tell the difference between reality and the language they use to describe it. It is an unsettling experience for them, one they cannot totally handle, somewhat like tottering on the edge of their recognized universe. The relationship between one's language habits and one's grasp of reality has not been adequately explored, perhaps because society does not yet train a sufficient number of bilingual, multilingual or linguistically oriented people qualified to undertake such investigations.[9]

Bloomfield went even further, to define 'tertiary responses to language' as innately hostile, angry or contemptuous comments from those whose secondary responses are questioned in any serious way. They would be simply rote answers or rote repetitions of people's 'secondary' statements whenever they were challenged on them, as though they were not capable of reasoning any further about them. Here he seemed to be going even further in identifying these responses with irrational or quasi-hysterical behavior.

What was it that Bloomfield found so worrisome about such opinions on language? Essentially he – along with Whorf and Sapir – had spent all his life building what most people regarded as the 'science of linguistics.' It was a study which required extended fieldwork and painstaking analysis of both exotic and familiar languages before one was permitted to make any large generalizations even about a single language, much less about languages in general. Closely allied to the anthropology of Boas and Malinowski, it insisted on careful and thoughtful observations and a non-judgmental view of different cultures and their languages. It was based on extremely high standards of training and scholarship and could not immediately be embraced by society at large. In some ways he and his colleagues had gone off on their own paths, and not everyone was able to follow them. Whorf and Sapir had, in fact, both died only a few years earlier, and Bloomfield himself would be gone five years later. Here are a few of the 'secondary' statements that deeply pained Bloomfield and his generation of linguists:

Language A is more _____ than language B ('logical', 'profound', 'poetic', 'efficient', etc., *fill in the blank yourself*).

The structure of language C proves that it is a universal language, and everyone should learn it as a basis for studying other languages.

Language D and language E are so closely related that all their speakers can always easily understand each other.

Language F is extremely primitive and can only have a few hundred words in it.

Language G is demonstrably 'better' than languages H, J and L.

The word for '_____' (*choose almost any word*) in language M proves scientifically that it is a worse – better, more 'primitive' or 'evolved,' etc. – language than language N.

Any language is easy to master, once you learn the basic structure all languages are built on.

(Bloomfield 1944: 413–21)

All of these statements are almost always demonstrably false upon closer knowledge of language and linguistics, yet such opinions are still quite commonly heard. In this same piece Bloomfield also voiced his sadness over continual claims that 'pure Elizabethan English' was spoken in this or that region of the American South (a social and historical impossibility – at best such dialects contain a few archaic phrases) or boasts that the Sequoyan Indian language was so perfect and easy to learn that all citizens of the State of Oklahoma should study it in school (Hockett 1970: 414–16). What he found particularly disturbing was that this sort of linguistic folklore never seemed to die out, never yielded to scientific knowledge, simply went on and on seemingly repropagating itself with a life of its own. Traces of it could even be found in the work of other scholars writing about language and linguistics.

Bloomfield's views were very much a reflection of his time. They stressed a relativistic view of language and culture and the notion that languages spoken by small indigenous groups of people had a significance comparable to that of languages spoken by much larger populations. They willingly embraced the notion that language, like reality itself, is a complex matrix of factors and tended to reject simplistic generalizations of any sort about either language or culture. Moreover, Bloomfield certainly saw his approach as being a crucial minimum stage for building any kind of true linguistic science.

Less than ten years after his death these ideas were replaced, also in the name of science, by a set of different notions, which Bloomfield would almost certainly have dismissed as 'secondary responses to language.' These new observations, which shared a certain philosophical groundwork with computational linguistics, constitute the credo of the Chomskian approach, now accepted as the dominant scientific view. They include the following notions:

1 All languages are related by a 'universal grammar'.

2 It is possible to delineate the meaning of any sentence in any language through knowledge of its deep structure and thereby replicate it in another language.

3 A diagram of any sentence will reveal this deep structure.

4 Any surface-level sentence in any language can easily be related to its deep structure, and this in turn can be related to universal grammar in a relatively straightforward manner through a set of rules.

5 These and related statements are sufficient to describe not only the structure of language but the entire linguistic process of development and acculturation of infants and young children everywhere and can thus serve as a guide to all aspects of human language, including speech, foreign-language training and translation.

6 The similarity of these deep- and surface-level diagrams to the structure of computer languages, along with the purported similarity of the human mind to a computer, may be profoundly significant.[10]

These ideas are clearly not ones Bloomfield could have approved of. They are not relativistic or cautious but universalist and all-embracing; they do not emphasize the study of individual languages and cultures but leap ahead into stunning generalizations. As such, he would have considered them examples of 'secondary responses' to language. In many ways they reflect the USA of the late 1950s, a nation proud of its own new-found dominance and convinced that its values must be more substantial than those of 'lesser' peoples. Such ideas also coincide nicely with a seemingly perennial need academia feels for theories offering a seemingly scientific approach, suggestive diagrams, learned jargon and a grandiose vision.

We all know that science progresses by odd fits and starts and that the supreme doctrines of one period may become the abandoned follies of a later one. But the turnabout we have described is surely among the most extreme on record. It should also be stressed that the outlook of Bloomfield, Whorf and Sapir has never truly been disproved or rejected and still has followers today.[11] Moreover, there is little proof that these newer ideas, while they may have been useful in describing the way children learn to speak, have ever helped a single teacher to teach languages better or a single translator to translate more effectively. Nor has anyone ever succeeded in truly defining 'deep structure' or 'universal grammar.'

No one can, of course, place the whole responsibility for machine translation today on Noam Chomsky's theories about language – certainly his disciples and followers[12] have also played a role, as has the overall welcome this entire complex of ideas has received. Furthermore, their advent has certainly also coincided with the re-emergence of many other 'secondary responses', including most of the comments I mentioned overhearing at MIT. Much of the literature on machine translation has owed – and continues to owe – a fair amount to this general approach to linguistic theory. Overall understanding of language has certainly not flourished in recent times, and the old wives' tale of a single magical language providing the key to the understanding of all other tongues now flourishes again as a tribute both to Esperanto and the Indian Aymara language of Peru.[13] Disappointment with computer-translation projects has also been widespread throughout this time, and at one point even Chomsky seemingly washed his hands of the matter, stating that, 'as for machine translation and related enterprises, they seemed to me pointless as well as probably quite hopeless' (Chomsky 1975: 40).

Even such lofty notions as those favored by Turing and Weaver, that removing 'language barriers' would necessarily be a good thing, or that different languages prevent people from realizing that they are 'really all the same deep down,' could turn out to be 'secondary responses'. It may also be that language barriers and differences have their uses and virtues, and that enhanced linguistic skills may better promote world peace than a campaign to destroy such differences. But popular reseeding of such notions is, as Bloomfield foresaw, quite insidious, and most of these ideas are still very much with us, right along with the proof that they may be unattainable. This is scarcely to claim that the end is near for computers as translation tools, though it may mean that further progress along certain lines of enquiry is unlikely.

There are probably two compelling sets of reasons why computers can never claim the upper hand over language in all its complexity, one rooted in the cultural side of language, the other in considerations related to mathematics. Even if the computer were suddenly able to communicate meaning flawlessly, it would still fall short of what humans do with language in a number of ways. This (as linguists have long been aware) is because communication of meaning is only one among many functions of language. Others are:

1 demonstrating one's class status to the person one is speaking or writing to;
2 simply venting one's emotions, with no real communication intended;
3 establishing non-hostile intent with strangers, or simply passing time with them;
4 telling jokes;
5 engaging in non-communication by intentional or accidental ambiguity, sometimes also called 'telling lies';
6 two or more of the above (including communication) at once.

Under these circumstances it becomes very difficult to explain how a computer can be programmed merely to recognize and distinguish these functions in language A, much less make all the adjustments necessary to translate them into language B. As we have seen, computers have problems simply with the communications side, not to mention all these other undeniable aspects of language. This would be hard enough with written texts but with spoken or 'live' language, the problems become all but insurmountable.

Closely related here is a growing awareness among writers and editors that it is virtually impossible to separate the formulation of even the simplest sentence in any language from the audience to whom it is addressed. Said another way, when the audience changes, the sentence changes. Phrased even more extremely, there is no such thing as a 'neutral' or 'typical' or 'standard' sentence – even the most seemingly innocuous examples will be seen on closer examination to be directed towards one audience or another, whether by age, education, class, profession, size of vocabulary, etc. While those within the target audience for any given sentence will assume its meaning is obvious to all, those on its fringes must often make a conscious effort to absorb it, and those outside its bounds may understand nothing at all. This is such an everyday occurrence that it is easy to forget how common it really is. And this, too, adds a further set of perplexities for translators to unravel, as they must duplicate not only the 'meaning' but also the specialized 'angling' to an analogous audience in the new language. Perhaps the most ironic proof of this phenomenon lies in the nature of the 'model' sentences chosen by transformational and computational linguists to prove their points. Such sentences rarely reflect general usage – they are often simply the kinds of sentences used by such specialists to impress other specialists in the same field.

Further proof is provided here by those forms of translation often described as 'impossible', even when performed by humans – stage plays, song lyrics, advertising, newspaper headlines, titles of books or other original works and poetry. Here it is generally conceded that some degree of adaptation may be merged with translation. Theatre dialogue, in particular, demands a special level of 'fidelity.' Sentences must be pronounceable by actors as well as literally correct, and the emotional impact of the play must be recreated as fully as possible. A joke in language A must also become a joke in language B, even if it isn't. A constantly maintained dramatic build-up must seek its relief or 'punch lines' at the right moments. This may seem far from the concerns of a publications manager anxious to translate product documentation quickly and correctly. But in a real sense all use of words is dependent on building towards specific points and delivering 'punch lines' about how a product or process works. The difference is one of degree, not of quality. It is difficult to imagine how computers can begin to cope with this aspect of translation.

Cross-cultural concerns add further levels of complexity, and no miraculous 'universal structure'[14] exists for handling them. Languages are simply not orderly restructurings of each other's ideas and processes, and a story I have told elsewhere[15] may perhaps best illustrate this. It relates to a real episode in my life when my wife and I were living in Italy. At that time she did most of the shopping to help her learn Italian, and she repeatedly came home complaining that she couldn't find certain cuts of meat at the butcher's. I told her that if she concentrated on speaking better Italian, she would certainly find them. But she still couldn't locate the cuts of meat she wanted. Finally, I was forced to abandon my male presumption of *bella figura* and go with her to the market, where I patiently explained in Italian what it was we were looking for to one butcher after another. But even together we were still not successful. What we wanted actually turned out not to exist.

The Italians cut their meat differently from the way Americans do. There are not only different names for the cuts but actually *different cuts* as well. Their whole system is built around it – they feed and breed their cattle differently so as to produce these cuts. So one might argue that the Italian steer itself is different; technically and anatomically, it might just qualify as a different subspecies.

This notion of 'cutting the animal differently' or of 'slicing reality differently' can turn out to be a factor in many translation problems. It is altogether possible for whole sets of distinctions, indeed whole ranges of psychological or even tangible realities, to vanish when going from one language to another. Those which do not vanish may still be mangled beyond recognition. It is this factor which poses one of the greatest challenges even for experienced translators. It may also place an insurmountable stumbling block in the path of computer-translation projects, which are based on the assumption that simple conversions of obvious meanings between languages are readily possible.

Another cross-cultural example concerns a well-known wager AI pioneer Marvin Minsky has made with his MIT students. Minsky has challenged them to create a progam or device that can unfailingly tell the difference, as humans supposedly can, between a cat and a dog. Minsky has made many intriguing remarks on the relation between language and reality[16] but he shows in this instance that he has unwittingly been manipulated by language-imposed categories. The difference between a cat and a dog is by no means obvious, and even 'scientific' Linnaean taxonomy may not provide the last word. The Tzeltal Indians of Mexico's Chiapas State in fact classify some of our 'cats' in the 'dog' category, rabbits and squirrels as 'monkey,' and a more doglike tapir as a 'cat,' thus proving in this case that whole systems of animals can be sliced differently. Qualified linguistic anthropologists have concluded that the Tzeltal system of naming animals – making allowance for the fact that they know only the creatures of their region – is ultimately just as useful and informative as Linnaean latinisms and even includes information that the latter may omit.[17] Comparable examples from the other cultures are on record.[18]

An especially dramatic cross-cultural example suggests that at least part of the raging battle as to whether acupuncture and the several other branches of Chinese medicine can qualify as 'scientific' springs from the linguistic shortcomings of Western observers. The relationships concerning illness the Chinese observe and measure are not the ones we observe, their measurements and distinctions are not the same as ours, their interpretation of such distinctions is quite different from ours, the diagnosis suggested by these procedures is not the same and the treatment and interpretation of a patient's progress can also diverge radically from our own. Yet the whole process is perfectly logical and consistent in its own terms and is grounded in an empirical procedure.[15] The vocabulary is fiendishly difficult to explain to non-specialists in this highly developed branch of the Chinese language. No one knows how many other such instances of large and small discontinuities between languages and their meanings may exist, even among more closely related tongues like French and English, and no one can judge how great an effect such discontinuities may have on larger relationships betwen the two societies or even on ordinary conversations between their all-too-human representatives.

Just as the idea that the earth might be round went against the grain for the contemporaries of Columbus, so the notion that whole ranges of knowledge and experience may be inexpressible as one moves from one language to another seems equally outrageous to many today. Such a notion, that language A cannot easily and perfectly replicate what is said in language B, simply goes against what most people regard as 'common sense.' But is such insistence truly commensensical or merely another instance of Bloomfield's 'secondary responses'? Something like this question lies at the root of the long-continuing and never fully resolved debate among linguists concerning the so-called Whorf–Sapir hypothesis.[7]

Mathematical evidence suggesting that computers can never fully overtake language is quite persuasive. It is also, in part, fairly simple and lies in a not terribly intricate consideration of the theory of sets. No subset can be larger than the set of which it is a part. Yet all mathematics – and, in fact, all science and technology, as members of a linguistics school known as Glossematics[19] have argued – can be satisfactorily identified as a subcategory, and possibly a subset, of language. According to this reasoning, no set of its components can ever be great enough to serve as a representation of the superset they belong to, namely language. Allowing for the difficulties involved in determining the members of such sets, this argument, by analogy alone, would tend to place language and translation outside the limits of solvable problems and consign them to the realm of the intractable and un-decidable.[20]

The theory of sets has further light to shed. Let us imagine all the words of language A as comprising a single set, within which each word is assigned a number. Now let us imagine all the words of language B as comprising a single set, with numbers once again assigned to each word. We'll call them set A and set B. If each numbered word within set A meant exactly the same thing as each word with the same number in set B, translation would be no problem at all, and no professional translators would be needed. Absolutely anyone able to read would be able to translate any text between these two languages by looking up the numbers for the words in the first language and then substituting the words with the same numbers in the second language. It would not even be necessary to know either language. And computer translation in such a case would be incredibly easy, a mere exercise in 'search and replace,' immediately putting all the people searching through books of words and numbers out of business.

But the sad reality of the matter – and the real truth behind machine translation efforts – is that word # 152 in language A does not mean exactly what word # 152 in language B means. In fact, you may have to choose between words 152, 157, 478 and 1,027 to obtain a valid translation. It may further turn out that word 152 in language B can be translated back into language A not only as 152 but also 149, 462 and 876. In fact, word # 152 in language B may turn out to have no relation to word # 152 in language A at all. This is because forty-seven words with lower numbers in language B had meanings that spilled over into further numbered listings. It could still be argued that all these difficulties could be sorted out by complex trees of search and 'goto' commands. But such altogether typical examples are only the beginning of the problems faced by computational linguists, as words are rarely used singly or in a vacuum but are strung together in thick, clammy strings of beads according to different rules for different languages. Each bead one uses influences the number, shape and size of subsequent beads, so that each new word in a language A sentence compounds the problems of translation into language B by an extremely non-trivial factor, with a possible final total exceeding by several orders of magnitude the problems confronted by those who program computers for the game of chess.

There are, of course, some real technical experts, the linguistic equivalents of chess grandmasters, who can easily determine most of the time what the words mean in language A and how to render them most correctly in language B. These experts are called *translators*, though thus far no one has attributed to them the power or standing of chess masters. Another large irony: so far, the only people who have proved capable of manipulating the extremely complex systems originally aimed at replacing translators have, in fact, been translators.

TRANSLATORS AND MT DEVELOPERS: MUTUAL CRITICISMS

None of the preceding necessarily makes the outlook for machine translation or computer-aided translation all that gloomy or unpromising. This is because most developers in this field long ago accepted the limitations of having to produce systems that can perform specific tasks under specific conditions. What prospective users must determine, as I have sought to explain, is whether those conditions are also their conditions. Although there have been a few complaints of misrepresentation, this is a situation most MT and CAT developers are prepared to live with. What they are not ready to deal with (and here let's consider their viewpoint) is the persistence of certain old wives' tales about the flaws of computer translation.

The most famous of these, they will point out with some ire, are the ones about the expressions 'the spirit is willing but the flesh is weak' or 'out of sight, out of mind' being run through the computer and coming out as 'the vodka is good but the meat is rotten' and 'invisible idiot' respectively. There is no evidence for either anecdote, they will protest, and they may well be right. Similar stories circulate about 'hydraulic rams' becoming 'water goats' or the headline 'Company posts sizeable growth' turning into 'Guests mail large tumour'. Yet such resentment may be somewhat misplaced. The point is not whether such and such a specific mistranslation ever occurred but simply that the general public – the same public equally prepared to believe that 'all languages share a universal structure' – is also ready to believe that such mistranslations are likely to occur. In any case, these are at worst only slightly edited versions of fairly typical MT errors – for instance, I recently watched a highly regarded PC-based system render a 'dead key' on a keyboard (*touche morte*) as 'dead touch.' I should stress that there are perfectly valid logical and human reasons why such errors occur, and that they are at least as often connected to human as to computer error. There are also perfectly reasonable human ways of dealing with the computer to avoid many of these errors.

The point is that the public is really quite ambivalent – even fickle – not just about computer translation but about computers in general, indeed about much of technology. Lacking Roman gladiators to cheer, they will gladly applaud at the announcement that computers have now vanquished all translation problems but just as readily turn thumbs down on hearing tales of blatant mistranslations. This whole ambivalence is perhaps best demonstrated by a recent popular film where an early model of a fully robotized policeman is brought into a posh boardroom to be approved by captains of industry. The board chairman instructs an impeccably clad flunky to test the robot by pointing a pistol at it. Immediately the robot intones, 'if you do not drop your weapon within twenty seconds, I will take punitive measures.' Naturally the flunky drops his gun, only to hear, 'if you do not drop your weapon within ten seconds, I will take punitive measures.' Some minutes later they manage to usher the robot out and clean up what is left of the flunky. Such attitudes towards all computerized products are widespread and coexist with the knowledge of how useful computers can be. Developers of computer translation systems should not feel that they are being singled out for criticism.

These same developers are also quite ready to voice their own criticisms of human translators, some of them justified. Humans who translate, they will claim, are too inconsistent, too slow or too idealistic and perfectionist in their goals. It is, of course, perfectly correct that translators are often inconsistent in the words they choose to translate a given expression. Sometimes this is inadvertent, sometimes it is a matter of conscious choice. In many Western languages we have been taught not to repeat the same word too often: thus, if we say the 'European problem' in one sentence, we are encouraged to say the 'European question' or 'issue' elsewhere. This troubles some MT people, although computers could be programmed easily enough to emulate this mannerism. We also have many fairly similar ways of saying quite close to the same thing, and this also impresses some MT people as a fault, mainly because it is difficult to program for.

This whole question could lead to a prolonged and somewhat technical discussion of 'disambiguation,' or how and when to determine which of several meanings a word or phrase may have – or, for that matter, of how a computer can determine when several different ways of saying something may add up to much the same thing. Although the computer can handle the latter more readily than the former, it is perhaps best to assume that authors of texts will avoid these two extreme shoals of 'polysemy' and 'polygraphy' (or perhaps 'polyepeia') and seek out the smoother sailing of more standardized usage.

Perhaps the most impressive experiments on how imperfect translation can become were carried out by the French several decades ago. A group of competent French and English translators and writers gathered together and translated various brief literary passages back and forth between the two languages a number of times. The final results of such a process bore almost no resemblance to the original, much like the game played by children sitting in a circle, each one whispering words just heard to the neighbour on the right (Vinay and Darbelnet 1977: 195–6). Here, too, the final result bears little resemblance to the original words.

The criticisms of slowness and perfectionism/idealism are related to some extent. While the giant computers used by the CIA and NSA can, of course, spew out raw translation at a prodigious rate, this is our old friend fully automatic low-quality output and must be edited to be clear to any but an expert in that specialty. There is, at present, no evidence suggesting that a computer can turn out high-quality text at a rate faster than a human – indeed, humans may in some cases be faster than a computer, if FAHQT is the goal. The claim is heard in some MT circles that human translators can only handle 200 to 500 words per hour, which is often true, but some fully trained translators can do far better. I know of many translators who can handle from 800 to 1,000 words per hour (something I can manage under certain circumstances with certain texts) and have personally witnessed one such translator use a dictating machine to produce between 3,000 and 4,000 words per hour (which, of course, then had to be fed to typists).

Human ignorance – not just about computers but about how languages really work – creeps in here again. Many translators report that their non-translating colleagues believe it should be perfectly possible for a translator simply to look at a document in language A and 'just type it out' in flawless language B as quickly as though it were the first language. If human beings could to this, then there might be some hope of computers doing it. Here again we have an example of Bloomfield's secondary responses to language: the absolute certainty that any text in one language is exactly the same in another, give or take some minimal word juggling. There will be no general clarity about computer translation until there is also a greatly enhanced general clarity about what languages are and how they work.

In all this the translator is rarely perceived as a real person with specific professional problems, as a writer who happens to specialize in foreign languages. When MT systems are introduced, the impetus is most often to retrain and/or totally reorganize the work habits of translators or replace them with younger staff whose work habits have not yet been formed, a practice likely to have mixed results in terms of staff morale and competence. Another problem, in common with word processing, is that no two MT systems are entirely alike, and a translator trained on one system cannot fully apply experience gained on it to another. Furthermore, very little effort is made to persuade translators to become a factor in their own self-improvement. Of any three translators trained on a given system, only one at best will work to use the system to its fullest extent and maximize what it has to offer. Doing so requires a high degree of self-motivation and a willingness to improvise glossary entries and macros that can speed up work. Employees clever enough to do such things are also likely to be upwardly mobile, which may mean soon starting the training process all over again, possibly with someone less able. Such training also forces translators to recognize that they are virtually wedded to creating a system that will improve and grow over time. This is a great deal to ask in either the USA's fast-food job market or Europe's increasingly mobile work environment. Some may feel it is a bit like singling out translators and asking them to willingly declare their life-long serfdom to a machine.

AND THE FUTURE?

Computer translation developers prefer to ignore many of the limitations I have suggested, and they may yet turn out to be right. What MT proponents never stop emphasizing is the threefold increase in computer capacity awaiting us in the not so distant future: increasing computer power, rapidly dwindling size and plummeting prices. Here they are undoubtedly correct, and they are also probably correct in pointing out the vast increase in computer power that advanced multi-processing and parallel processing can bring. Equally impressive are potential improvements in the field of artificial intelligence, allowing for the construction of far larger rule-based systems likely to be able to make complicated choices between words and expressions.[21] Neural nets,[22] along with their Hidden Markov Model cousins,[23] also loom on the horizon with their much publicized ability to improvise decisions in the face of incomplete or inaccurate data. Beyond that stretches the prospect of nanotechnology,[24] an approach that will so miniaturize computer pathways as to single out individual atoms to perform tasks now requiring an entire circuit. All but the last are already with us, either now in use or under study by computer companies or university research projects. We also keep hearing advanced warnings of the imminent Japanese wave, ready to take over at any moment and overwhelm us with all manner of 'voice writers', telephone translators and simultaneous computer interpreters.

How much of this is simply more of the same old computer hype, with a generous helping of Bloomfield's secondary responses thrown in? Perhaps the case of the 'voice writer' can help us to decide. This device, while not strictly a translation tool, has always been the audio version of the translator's black box: you say things into the computer, and it immediately and flawlessly transcribes your words into live on-screen sentences. In most people's minds, it would take just one small adjustment to turn this into a translating device as well.

In any case, the voice writer has never materialized (and perhaps never will) but the quest for it has now produced a new generation of what might best be described as speaker-assisted speech-processing systems. Though no voice writers, these systems are quite useful and miraculous enough in their own way. As you speak into them at a reasonable pace, they place on the screen their best guess for each word you say, along with a menu showing the next best guesses for that word. If the system makes a mistake, you can simply tell it to choose another number on the menu. If none of the words shown is yours, you still have the option of spelling it out or keying it in. This ingenious but relatively humble device, I predict, will soon take its place as a useful tool for some translators. This is because it is user controlled rather than user supplanting and can help those translators who already use dictation as their means of transcribing text. Those who lose jobs because of it will not be translators but typists and secretaries.

Whenever one discovers such a remarkable breakthrough as

these voice systems, one is forced to wonder if just such a breakthrough may be in store for translation itself, whether all one's reasons to the contrary may not be simply so much rationalization against the inevitable. After due consideration, however, it still seems to me that such a breakthrough is unlikely for two further reasons beyond those already given. First, the very nature of this voice device shows that translators cannot be replaced, simply because it is the speaker who must constantly be on hand to determine whether the computer has chosen the correct word, in this case in the speaker's native language. How much more necessary does it then become to have someone authoritative nearby, in this case a translator, to ensure that the computer chooses correctly amid all the additional choices imposed where two languages are concerned? And second, really a more generalized way of expressing my first point, whenever the suspicion arises that a translation of a word, paragraph or book may be substandard, there is only one arbiter who can decide whether this is or is not the case: another translator.

There are no databases, no foreign language matching programs, no knowledge-engineered expert systems sufficiently supple and grounded in real world knowledge to take on this job. Writers who have tried out any of the so-called 'style-checking' and 'grammar-checking' programs for their own languages have some idea of how much useless wheel-spinning such programs can generate for a single tongue and so can perhaps imagine what an equivalent program for 'translation checking' would be like. Perhaps such a program could work with a severely limited vocabulary but there would be little point to it, as it would only be measuring the accuracy of those texts computers could already translate. Based on current standards, such programs would at best produce verbose quantities of speculations which might exonerate a translation from error but could not be trusted to separate good from bad translators except in the most extreme cases. It could end up proclaiming as many false negatives as false positives and become enshrined as the linguistic equivalent of the lie detector. And, if a computer cannot reliably check the fidelity of an existing translation, how can it create a faithful translation in the first place?

Which brings me almost to my final point: no matter what gargantuan stores of raw computer power may lie before us, no matter how many memory chips or AI rules or neural nets or

Hidden Markov Models or self-programming atoms we may lay end to end in vast arrays or stack up in whatever conceivable architecture the human mind may devise, our ultimate problem remains:

1 to represent, adequately and accurately, the vast interconnections between the words of a single language on the one hand and reality on the other;
2 to perform the equivalent task with a second language; and
3 to map out completely and correctly, all the interconnections between them.

This is ultimately a linguistic problem and not an electronic one at all, and most people who take linguistics seriously have been racking their brains over it for years without coming anywhere near a solution.

Computers with limitless power will be able to do many things today's computers cannot do. They can provide terminologists with virtually complete lists of all possible terms to use, they can branch out into an encyclopedia of all related terms, they can provide spot logic checking of their own reasoning processes, they can even list the rules which guide them and cite the names of those who devised the rules and the full text of the rules themselves, along with extended scholarly citations proving why they are good rules. But they cannot reliably make the correct choice between competing terms in the great majority of cases. In programming terms, there is no shortage of ways to input various aspects of language nor of theories on how this should be done; what is lacking is a coherent notion of what must be output and to whom, of what should be the ideal 'front end' for a computer translation system. Phrased more impressionistically, all these looming new approaches to computing may promise endless universes of artificial spiders' webs in which to embed knowledge about language but will the real live spiders of language – words, meaning, trust, conflict, emotion – actually be willing to come and live in them?

And yet, Bloomfieldian responses are heard again: there must be some way around all these difficulties. Throughout the world, industry must go on producing and selling; no sooner is one model of a machine on the market than its successor is on the way, urgently requiring translations of owners' manuals, repair manuals and factory manuals into a growing number of languages. This is the driving engine behind computer translation that will not stop, the belief that there *must* be a way to bypass, accelerate or outwit the translation stage. If only enough studies were made, enough money spent, perhaps a full-scale program like those intended to conquer space, to conquer the electron, DNA, cancer, the oceans, volcanoes and earthquakes. Surely the conquest of something as seemingly puny as language cannot be beyond us. But at least one computational linguist has taken a radically opposite stance:

> A Manhattan project could produce an atomic bomb, and the heroic efforts of the Sixties could put a man on the moon, but even an all-out effort on the scale of these would probably not solve the translation problem.
>
> (Kay 1982: 74)

He goes on to argue that its solution will have to be reached incrementally if at all and specifies his own reasons for thinking this can perhaps one day happen in at least some sense:

> The only hope for a thoroughgoing solution seems to lie with technology. But this is not to say that there is only one solution, namely machine translation, in the classic sense of a fully automatic procedure that carries a text from one language to another with human intervention only in the final revision. There is in fact a continuum of ways in which technology could be brought to bear, with fully automatic translation at one extreme, and word-processing equipment and dicating machines at the other.
>
> (Kay 1982: 74)

The real truth may be far more sobering. As Bloomfield and his contemporaries foresaw, language may be no puny afterthought of culture, no mere envelope of experience but a major functioning part of knowledge, culture and reality, their processes so interpenetrating and mutually generating as to be inseparable. In a sense humans may live in not one but two jungles, the first being the tangible and allegedly real one with all its trials and travails. But the second jungle is language itself, perhaps just as difficult to deal with in its way as the first.

At this point I would like to make it abundantly clear that I am no enemy either of computers or of computer translation. I spend endless hours at the keyboard, am addicted to downloading all manner of strange software from bulletin boards and have even ventured into producing some software of my own. As I also love translation, it is natural that one of my main interests would lie at the intersection of these two fields. Perhaps I risk hyperbole but it seems to me that computer translation ought to rank as one of the noblest of human undertakings, as in its broadest aspects it attempts to understand, systematize and predict not just one aspect of life but all human understanding itself. Measured against such a goal, even its shortcomings have a great deal to tell us. Perhaps one day it will succeed in such a quest and lead us all out of the jungle of language and into some better place, although for all the reasons I have mentioned this appears somewhat unlikely.

Despite having expressed a certain pessimism, I foresee, in fact, a very optimistic future for those computer projects which respect some of the reservations I have mentioned and seek limited, reasonable goals in the service of translation. These will include computer-aided systems with genuinely user-friendly interfaces, batch systems which best deal with the problem of making corrections and – for those translators who dictate their work – the new voice-processing systems I have mentioned. There also seems to be considerable scope for using AI to resolve ambiguities in technical translation with a relatively limited vocabulary. Beyond this, I am naturally describing my reactions based on a specific moment in the development of computers and could, of course, turn out to be quite mistaken. In a field where so many developments move with such remarkable speed, no one can lay claim to any real omniscience, and so I will settle at present for guarded optimism over specific improvements, which will not be long in overtaking us.

NOTES

* I wish to express my gratitude to the following individuals, who read this piece in an earlier version and assisted me with their comments and criticisms: John Báez, Professor of Mathematics, Wellesley College; Alan Brody, computer consultant and journalist; Sandra Celt, translator and editor; André Chassigneux, translator and Maître de Conférences at the Sorbonne's École Supérieure d'Interprètes et de Traducteurs (L'ESIT); Harald Hille, English terminologist, United Nations; Joseph Murphy, Director, Bergen Language Institute; Lisa Raphals, computer consultant and linguist; Laurie Treuhaft, English Translation Department, United Nations; Vieri Tucci, computer consultant and translator; Peter Wheeler, Director, Antler Translation

Services; and Apollo Wu, reviser, Chinese Department, United Nations. ~~I would also like to extend my warmest thanks to John Newton, the~~ editor of this volume, for his many helpful comments.

1   In 1947 Alan Turing began work on his paper 'Intelligent machinery,' published the following year. Based on his wartime experience in decoding German naval and general staff messages, this work foresaw the use of 'television cameras, microphones, loudspeakers, wheels and "handling servo-mechanisms" as well as some sort of "electric brain."' It would be capable of:

(i)   various games . . .
(ii) the learning of languages
(iii) *translation of languages* [my emphasis]
(iv) cryptography
(v)   mathematics

(Hodges on Turing 1985)

Further details on Turing's role are found in Hodges (1985). The best overview of this entire period, as well as of the entire history of translating computers is, of course, provided by Hutchins (1986).

2   See especially Weaver (1955).

3   Typical among these have been advertisements for Netherlands-based Distributed Language Technology, which read in part:

DLT represents the safe route to truly automatic translation: without assistance from bilinguals, polyglots, or post-editors. But meeting the quality standards of professional translators – no less . . . . The aim is a translation machine that *understands*, that knows how to tell sense from nonsense . . . . In this way, DLT will surpass the limitations of formal grammar or man-made dictionaries.

At various times during its long development, this system has boasted the use of pre-editing, gigantic bilingual knowledge banks, an Esperanto interlingual architecture, artificial intelligence and the ability to handle 'a vast range of texts on general and special subjects.' (Source: advertisements in *Language Technology/Electric Word*, in most 1989 issues.) On the research side, Jaime G. Carbonell and Masaru Tomita announced in 1987 that Carnegie Mellon University 'has begun a project for the development of a new generation of MT systems whose capabilities range far beyond the current technology.' They further specified that, with these systems, '. . . unlike current MT systems, no human translator should be required to check and correct the translated text' (Carbonell and Tomita 1987). This treatment is found in Sergei Nirenburg's excellent although somewhat technical anthology (Nirenburg 1987).

4   According to an influential book in the United States, innumeracy is as great a threat to human understanding as illiteracy (Paulos 1989).

5   Newman as included in Vasconcellos 1988a. In addition to this excellent piece, those obtaining this volume will also want to read Jean Datta's candid advice on why computer translation techniques should be introduced into a business or institution slowly and carefully, Muriel

Vasconcellos' own practical thoughts on where the field is headed and Fred Klein's dose of healthy skepticism.

6   'In the testing phase, some 5,000 pages of documentation, in three types of text, will be processed, and the result compared with human translation of the same text in terms of quantity, time taken, deadlines met, and cost', (Kingscott 1990). This piece describes the B'VITAL/ ARIANE method now being used by the French documentation giant SITE. To my knowledge, this is the first reasonably thorough test proposed comparing human and machine translation. Yet, it is limited to one system in one country under conditions which, after the fact, will most probably be challenged by one party or another. Human translators will certainly demand to know whether full set-up costs, on-the-job training courses and software maintenance expenses have been fully amortized. For their part, machine translation advocates might conceivably ask how human translators were chosen for the test and/or what level of training was provided. These are all questions which merit further consideration if a fair discussion comparing computer and human translation is to take place.

7   Both Sapir and Whorf carried out extensive studies of American Indian languages and together evolved what has come to be called the Whorf–Sapir hypothesis. Briefly stated, this theory states that what humans see, do and know is *to a greater or lesser extent* based on the structure of their language and the categories of thought it encourages or excludes. The prolonged and spirited debate around this hypothesis has largely centered on the meaning of the phrase *to a greater or lesser extent*. Even the theory's most outright opponents concede it may have validity in some cases, although they see something resembling strict determinism in applying it too broadly and point out that translation between languages would not be possible if the Whorf–Sapir hypothesis were true. Defenders of the theory charge that its critics may not have learned any one language thoroughly enough to become fully aware of how it can hobble and limit human thinking and further reply that some translation tasks are far more difficult than others, sometimes bordering on the impossible.

8   Bloomfield, 'Secondary and tertiary responses to language' (Hockett 1970: 412–29). This piece originally appeared in *Language* 20: 45–55. The author's major work in the field of linguistics was *Language* (1933/ 1984).

9   As so many people in so many countries speak two or more languages, it might be imagined that there is a broad, widely-shared body of accurate knowledge about such people. In point of fact there is not, and the first reasonably accessible book-length account of this subject is by Grosjean. Some of this book's major points, still poorly appreciated by society at large:

> Relatively few bilingual people are able to translate between their two languages with ease. Some who try complain of headaches, many cannot do it at all, many others do it badly but are not aware of this. Thus, bilingualism and translation skills are two quite

different abilities, perhaps related to different neurological processes.

No bilinguals possess perfectly equal skills in both their languages. All favor the one or the other at least slightly, whether in reading, writing, or speaking. Thus, the notion of being brought up perfectly bilingual is a myth – much of bilingualism must be actively achieved *in both languages*.

One does not have to be born bilingual to qualify as such. Those who learn a second language later, even as adults, can be considered bilingual to some extent, provided they actively or passively use a second language in some area of their lives.

(Grosjean 1982)

10 Although presented here in summarized form, these ideas all form part of the well-known Chomskian process and can be found elaborated in various stages of complexity in many works by Chomsky and his followers (Chomsky 1957, 1965 and 1975).

11 The bloodied battlefields of past scholarly warfare waged over these issues are easily enough uncovered. In 1968 Charles Hockett, a noted follower of Bloomfield, launched a full-scale attack on Chomsky (Hockett 1968). Those who wish to follow this line of debate further can use his bibliography as a starting point. Hostilities even spilled over into a *New Yorker* piece and a book of the same name (Mehta 1971). Other starting points are the works of Chomsky's teacher (Harris 1951) or a unique point of view related to computer translation (Lehmann 1987). Throughout this debate, there have been those who questioned why these transformational linguists, who claim so much knowledge of language, should write such dense and unclear English. When questioned on this, Mehta relates Chomsky's reply as follows:

'I assume that the writing in linguistics is no worse than the writing in any other academic field', Chomsky says. 'The ability to use language well is very different from the ability to study it. Once the Slavic department at Harvard was thinking of offering Vladimir Nabokov an appointment. Roman Jakobson, the linguist, who was in the department then, said that he didn't have anything against elephants but he wouldn't appoint one a professor of zoology'. Chomsky laughs.

(Mehta 1971)

12 See, for example, Fodor (Fodor and Katz 1964) or Chisholm (Chisholm 1981).

13 See Note 3 for reference to Esperanto. The South American Indian language Aymara has been proposed and partially implemented as a basis for multilingual machine translation by the Bolivian mathematician Iván Guzmán de Rojas, who claims that its special syntactic and logical structures make it an ideal vehicle for such a purpose. On a surface analysis, such a notion sounds remarkably close to Bloomfieldian secondary responses about the ideal characteristics of the

Sequoyan language, long before computers entered the picture (Guzmán de Rojas 1985).

14 The principal work encouraging a search for 'universal' aspects of language is by Greenberg. Its findings are suggestive but inconclusive (Greenberg 1963).

15 This section first appeared in a different form as a discussion between Sandra Celt and the author (Celt and Gross 1987).

16 Most of Marvin Minsky's thoughts on language follow a strictly Chomskian framework – thus, we can perhaps refer to the overall outlook of his school as a Minskian–Chomskian one (Minsky 1986: Sections 19–26).

17 See Hunn for a considerably expanded treatment (Hunn 1977).

18 A rich literature expanding on this theme can be found in the bibliography of the book mentioned in the preceding note (Hunn 1977).

19 Glossematics is, in the USA, a relatively obscure school of linguistics, founded by two Danes, Louis Hjelmslev and Hans Jorgen Uldall, earlier this century. Its basic thesis has much in common with thinking about computers and their possible architectures. It starts from the premise that any theory about language must take into account all possible languages that have ever existed or can exist, that this is the absolute minimum requirement for creating a science of linguistics. To objections that this is unknowable and impossible, its proponents reply that mathematicians regularly deal with comparable unknowables and are still able to make meaningful generalizations about them. From this foundation emerges the interesting speculation that linguistics as a whole may be even larger than mathematics as a whole, and that 'linguistics' may not be that science which deals with language but that the various so-called sciences with their imperfect boundaries and distinctions may in fact be those branches of linguistics that deal for the time being with various domains of linguistics. Out of this emerges the corollary that taxonomy is the primary science, and that only by naming things correctly can one hope to understand them more fully. Concomitant with these notions also arises an idea that ought to have attracted computer translation researchers, that a glossematic approach could lay down the basis for creating culture-independent maps of words and realities through various languages, assigning precise addresses for each 'word' and 'meaning', although it would require a truly vast system for its completion and even then would probably only provide lists of possible translations rather than final translated versions. The major theoretical text of Glossematics, somewhat difficult to follow like many linguistic source books, is Hjelmslev (Hjelmslev 1961). One excellent brief summary in English is by Whitfield (Whitfield 1969); another, available only in Spanish or Swedish, is by Malmberg (Malmberg 1967).

20 Different strands of this argument may be pursued (Nagel and Newman 1989; Harel 1987; Godel 1931).

21 In correct academic terms, artificial intelligence is not some lesser topic related to machine translation, rather machine translation is a branch

of artificial intelligence. Some other branches are natural-language understanding, voice recognition, machine vision and robotics. The successes and failures of AI constitute a very different story and a well-publicized one at that – it can be followed in the bibliography provided by Minsky (Minsky 1986). On AI and translation, see Wilks (Wilks 1984).

22 Neural nets are once again being promoted as a means of capturing knowledge in electronic form, especially where language is concerned. The source book most often cited is *Parallel Distributed Processing* (Rumelhart and McClelland 1987).

23 Hidden Markov Models, considered by some as merely a different form of neural nets but by others as a new technology in their own right, are also being mentioned as having possibilities for machine translation. They have, as noted, proved quite effective in facilitating computer-assisted voice transcription techniques.

24 The theory of nanotechnology visualizes a further miniaturization in computers, similar to what took place during the movement from tubes to chips but in this case actually using internal parts of molecules and even atoms to store and process information. Regarded with skepticism by some, this theory also has its fervent advocates (Drexler 1986).

BIBLIOGRAPHY

Bloomfield, L. (1933) *Language*, New York: Holt, Rinehart & Winston (reprinted in great part in 1984, University of Chicago).

—— (1944) 'Secondary and tertiary responses to language', in *Language* 20: 45–55 and in C.F. Hockett (ed.) (1987) *A Leonard Bloomfield Anthology*, Chicago: University of Chicago Press.

Booth, A.D. (ed.) (1967) *Machine Translation*, Amsterdam: North Holland.

Brower, R.A. (ed.) (1959) *On Translation*, Cambridge, Mass.: Harvard University Press.

Carbonell, J.G. and Tomita, M. (1987) 'Knowledge-based machine translation, the CMU approach', in S. Nirenburg (ed.) *Machine Translation: Theoretical and Methodological Issues*, Cambridge: Cambridge University Press.

Celt, S. and Gross, A. (1987) 'The challenge of translating Chinese medicine', *Language Monthly* 43: 19–21.

Chisholm, W.S. Jr. (1981) *Elements of English Linguistics*, London: Longman.

Chomsky, N. (1957) *Syntactic Structures*, The Hague: Mouton.

—— (1965) *Aspects of the Theory of Syntax*, Cambridge, Mass.: MIT Press.

—— (1975) *The Logical Structure of Linguistic Theory*, Chicago: University of Chicago Press.

Coughlin, J. (1988) 'Artificial intelligence and machine translation: present developments and future prospects', *Babel* 34: 1, 1–9.

Datta, J. (1988) 'MT in large organizations: revolution in the workplace', in M. Vasconcellos (ed.) *Technology as Translation Strategy* (American Translators Association Scholarly Monograph Series, vol. II), Binghamton, New York: State University of New York Press.

Drexler, E.K. (1986) *Engines of Creation*, New York: Anchor Press.

Fodor, J.A. and Katz, J.J. (1964) *The Structure of Language*, New York: Prentice-Hall.

Godel, K. (1931) 'Über formal unentscheidbare Sätze der Principia Mathematica und verwandte Systeme I', *Monatshefte für Mathematik und Physik* 38: 173–98.

Greenberg, J. (1963) *Universals of Language*, Cambridge, Mass.: MIT Press.

Grosjean, F. (1982) *Life with Two Languages: an Introduction to Bilingualism*, Cambridge, Mass.: Harvard University Press.

Guzmán de Rojas, I. (1985) 'Logical and linguistic problems of social communication with the Aymara people', Ottawa: The International Development Research Center.

Harel, D. (1987) *Algorithmics: The Spirit of Computing*, Addison-Wesley.

Harris, Z. (1951) *Structural Linguistics*, Chicago: University of Chicago Press.

Hjelmslev, L. (1961) *Prolegomena to a Theory of Language*, Madison: University of Wisconsin Press.

Hockett, C.F. (1968) *The State of the Art*, The Hague: Mouton.

—— (ed.) (1987) *A Leonard Bloomfield Anthology*, Chicago: University of Chicago Press.

Hodges, A. (1983) *Alan Turing: The Enigma*, New York: Simon & Schuster.

Hunn, E.S. (1977) *Tzeltal Folk Zoology: The Classification of Discontinuities in Nature*, New York: Academic Press.

Hutchins, W.J. (1986) *Machine Translation: Past, Present, Future*, Chichester: Ellis Horwood.

Jakobson, R. (1959) 'On linguistic aspects of translation', in R.A. Brower (ed.) *On Translation*, Cambridge Mass.: Harvard University Press.

Kay, M. (1982) 'Machine translation', *American Journal of Computational Linguistics*, April–June, 74–8.

Kingscott, G. (1990) 'SITE buys B'Vital: relaunch of French national MT project', *Language International*, April.

Klein, F. (1988) 'Factors in the evaluation of MT: a pragmatic approach', in M. Vasconcellos (ed.) *Technology as Translation Strategy* (American Translators Association Scholarly Monograph Series, vol. II), Bingghamton, New York: State of New York University Press.

Lehmann, W.P. (1987) 'The context of machine translation', *Computers and Translation* 2.

Malmberg, B. (1967) 'Los nuevos caminos de la lingüística', *Siglo Veintiuno*, Mexico: 154–74.

Mehta, V. (1971) *John is Easy to Please*, New York: Ferrar, Straus & Giroux.

Minsky, M. (1986) *The Society of Mind*, New York: Simon & Schuster.

Nagel, E. and Newman, J.R. (1989) *Godel's Proof*, New York: New York University Press.

Newman, P.E. (1988) 'Information-only machine translation: a feasibility study', in M. Vasconcellos (ed.) *Technology as Translation Strategy* (American Translators Association Scholarly Monograph Series, vol. II), Binghamton, New York: State University of New York Press.

Nirenburg, S. (ed.) (1987) *Machine Translation: Theoretical and Methodological Issues*, Cambridge: Cambridge University Press.

Paulos, J.A. (1989) *Innumeracy, Mathematical Illiteracy and its Consequences*, New York: Hill & Wang.

Rumelhart, D.E. and McClelland, J.L. (1987) *Parallel Distributed Processing*, Cambridge, Mass.: MIT Press.

Sapir, E. (1921) *Language: An Introduction to the Study of Speech*, New York: Harcourt, Brace & World.

Saussure, F. de (1916) *Cours de linguistique générale*, Paris: Payot.

Slocum, J. (ed.) (1988) *Machine Translation Systems*, Cambridge: Cambridge University Press.

Vasconcellos, M. (ed.) (1988a) *Technology as Translation Strategy* (American Translators Association Scholarly Monograph Series, vol. II), Binghamton, New York: State University of New York.

—— (1988b) 'Factors in the evaluation of MT: formal vs functional approaches', in M. Vasconcellos (ed.) *Technology and Translation Strategy* (American Translators Association Scholarly Monograph Series, vol. II), Binghamton, New York: State University of New York.

Vinay, J.-P. and Darbelnet, J. (1977) *Stylistique comparée du français et de l'anglais*, Paris: Didier.

Weaver, W. (1955) 'Translation', in W.N. Locke and A.D. Booth (eds) *Machine Translation of Languages*, New York: Wiley, 15–23.

Whitfield, F. (1969) 'Glossematics', in A.A. Hill (ed.) *Linguistics*, Voice of America Forum Lectures.

Whorf, B.L. (1956) *Language, Thought and Reality* (collected papers), Cambridge, Mass.: MIT Press.

Wilks, Y. (1984) 'Machine translation and the artificial intelligence paradigm of language processes', *Computers in Language Research* 2.

Chapter 8

Computerized term banks and translation

Patricia Thomas

Advances in the coding of messages in the Second World War and the application of computers to areas other than mathematics led to the notion that translation could be done 'automatically'. Early computing research workers who were not linguists tended to think that translation could be effected by substituting a word in one language for its lexical equivalent in another and, while morphology was addressed, syntax and semantics were hardly considered; the frequently hilarious results have been well documented (Knowles 1979, *inter alia*). Two more or less parallel developments to produce computerized aids for translators began to take shape: the creation of machine translation systems in the late 1940s and the building of computerized dictionaries in the form of multilingual terminology data banks (term banks) in the early 1960s. Initially these developments took place independently but in recent years there has been a merging of the two forms, in which the terminographical information in a term bank may be incorporated into machine translation systems in the form of 'back-up' dictionaries. Latterly, the information has been used to provide the data for expert systems which may help, for example, with the semantic problems in machine translation.

TERM BANKS

Generally, little is known about term banks as, apart from one or two, they have not received the same press as machine translation (MT). Why is this? There seem to be three main reasons: first, it is only now becoming possible to buy a term bank 'off the shelf' as one might a personal computer (PC) version of an MT system. Second, many are 'in-house' developments which are only available to specific users. Third, there seems to be reluctance on the part of the general public, at least in the UK, to explore the possibilities available to them from, for example, British Telecom via a telephone and a modem.

What sort of help can term banks provide? The principal functions of term banks are the storage of terms in large numbers, ease of updating, rapid retrieval and, probably most important, their standardization or indication of preferred usage. They may provide domain classification, relationships with other terms, definitions, examples of terms in context, bibliographic references for further information and indication of copyright.

The first term banks evolved as computerized dictionaries and were mono- or multilingual. In 1976, a survey of scientific and technical databases was carried out jointly by the Association for Information Management (Aslib) in the UK and the European Association of Scientific Information Dissemination Centres (EUSIDIC). It emerged that 66 per cent of the databases had English as a 'carrier' language; that is, they were built using English as the base language and their query language is English, whereas only 7 per cent had some multilingual functions; that is, with links between the languages as opposed to plurilingual, where there is no link between the languages (Iljon 1977). There are currently some seventy-five term banks in operation, a number of which transcend national boundaries (Terminological Data Banks 1989). Early examples are the European Commission's EURO-DICAUTOM, the Federal Republic of Germany's LEXIS at the Bundessprachenamt and the Canadian government's TERMIUM, the development of which was accelerated by the adoption of the laws on bilingualism in Canada between 1969 and 1977. Many have been developed by large institutions such as the International Monetary Fund and the United Nations and by international commercial enterprises to satisfy in-house needs. In recent years, more term banks have been developed at national levels to cover not only the specialized and mainly commercial needs within a country, such as TERMDOK in Sweden and NoTe-Bergen in Norway (the latter being developed for the Norwegian North Sea oil industry), but also in response to the requirements of increased trade between countries, necessitating technical manuals and other documentation in the buyer's language.

Access to term banks, which are generally available on-line, may be gained by a subscriber paying an annual fee, plus 'connection' time for each search; however, on-line access to EURODICAUTOM and to TERMIUM is free. TERMIUM is also available via an off-line print service or by telephone query; since 1990 it has been available on Compact Disc Read-Only Memory (CD-ROM). From the UK, access to EURODICAUTOM is via the International Packet Switch Stream (IPSS) from British Telecom's PSS Dialplus.[1] The user requires a telephone, a modem and a terminal or microcomputer and needs to obtain a password (£60 plus £15 quarterly in 1990) from British Telecom who will provide an agreement which gives access to more than 130 networks world-wide, including the European Commission Host Organisation (ECHO) which offers on-line access to a range of EC-sponsored databases. There is a 'volume' charge which for Europe amounted to around 9p per full screen of information in 1990. A quicker method for users who already have access to a packet switch stream (PSS) system is a telephone call to the EURODICAUTOM help-line in Luxembourg.[2] Their personnel will provide a temporary password to enable the database to be searched until a permanent contract can be arranged. EURODICAUTOM's database is in French but queries are posed in English. Answers may correspond exactly to what has been requested, or contain several answers if the query is for a compound term; the search mechanism has an automatic truncation function. The content of EURO-DICAUTOM is described in the next section.

France is particularly well served via Minitel which is also available in the rest of Europe and the USA at US$10 per hour (1990 rate), giving access to NORMATERM, the database of the French standards organization, to FRANTEXT, the database of the National Institute of the French Language and to LEXICOM, the term bank of the Audiovisual and Computerised Data Centre for Social Communication, Analysis and Diffusion (DAICADIF). The system is, however, slow because it was designed as a service network and requires a separate action to be taken to work from word processor to Minitel.

Specific domains may be requested from a number of term banks in the form of glossaries on floppy disks. Some organizations have adopted software and, in certain cases, terminology, from another term bank (e.g. Ruhrgas from EURODICAUTOM; the Deutsches Institut für Normung, DIN (the German standards institute) from Siemens' TEAM), yet so far there has been little attempt at co-operation between the compilers of term banks to incorporate standardized or prescribed terminology in order to prevent ambiguities. Any attempt at prescription carries with it inherent problems of national pride and the changing nature of language, yet it is desirable in technical and scientific domains where safety is often an important factor.[3]

Some term banks record the standardized terminology of a country; these are, perhaps not surprisingly, countries with a long-standing tradition of preserving the quality of their language, such as France with NORMATERM at the Association Française de Normalisation (AFNOR), Germany with DIN and the former USSR with ASITO at the VNIIKI/GOSSTANDART (The All-Union Research Institute). Although the storage of terminology was a prime motive in the development of early term banks, it is clear that standardized terminology is necessary for translators and that term banks provide a valuable tool, giving them recourse to previously translated texts and access to up-to-date terminology. However, surveys of the ways translators work show that very few use term banks, although many expressed a wish to do so (Smith and Tyldesley 1986; Fulford et al. 1990), as they regard terminology work as a 'time waster'.

Term acquisition and representation: the record format

The point of departure in terminology work is the acquisition of terms. This involves consulting expert sources to define and delimit the chosen domain and to decide which word or words are used to express the concepts and thus constitute the terms of that domain. The next step is to provide a means of recording the terms and their associated data; this is done by devising a record format for each term. The two figures which follow give examples of record formats of varying degrees of complexity. Figure 8.1 shows the descriptive, linguistic and documentary information which accompanies each term and which comprises the record format of EURODICAUTOM, which contains some 500,000 records of which 90,000 are acronyms and abbreviations. It is strong in the domains of agriculture, medicine and law but, interestingly, there is comparatively little on defence.

Figure 8.2 shows an early example of the format used at the University of Surrey, based on that of the Danish term bank, DANTERM. Within a domain, this format will be the same for each term and will comprise a number of fields which may be

NI = serial number: a seven-character code indicating the term number
TY = type: a five-character alphanumeric code indicating the collection from which the term emanates
BE = originating office: a three-letter code (Brussels or Luxembourg)
PH = phrase: phraseological entry or illustrative context
DF = definition: may be more than one, with one or more contexts
VE = headword: may consist of one or more lexical units in each Community language
NT = note: any additional useful information
RF = reference: indicates the source(s) of the terminological information
CF = reliability code: rating from 0 (no quotable source) to 5 (information taken from standards or documents of equivalent status)
AU = author of term record
CM = subject code: a three-character alphanumeric code, based on the EC's system of classification devised by Dr. Lenoch

Figure 8.1 Information provided for each term in EURODICAUTOM.

grouped into different types of data such as administrative (e.g. date of entry, update, initials of terminologist), linguistic (e.g. grammar), conceptual (e.g. those which help to 'site' the term in a thesaurus-like structure, such as broader, narrower and related terms, as well as synonyms and antonyms) and those which enlarge the user's knowledge of the field (e.g. bibliographic references); it is possible for a database of these texts to be available for immediate access. These categories are not exhaustive and other data types, or fields, will be found in different term banks. TERMIUM, the Canadian government's term bank, contains data in English, French, German and Spanish, with a maximum of two languages being dealt with on a terminology record. It covers all domains, with scientific, technical, administrative and economics being the most actively used.

With term record formats being developed more or less simultaneously in different term banks for disparate needs, it is inevitable that the fields deemed necessary to provide information in any domain should sometimes be adequate, are usually comprehensive, but will invariably be widely divergent. However, with the need for exchanges of data between term banks both nationally and internationally, it is clear that a universal record

FIELD

NO.	CONTENT	COMPLETED RECORD
0	Key	000005
1	Record origin	SUR
2	Record pool	0001
3	Originator	PCT
4	Date of record	23.05.85
5	Update	16.07.90
6	Updater	PCT
7	Source of update and copyright	Directory and Dictionary of Animal, Bacterial and Plant Viruses (1989) ed. R. Hull, F. Brown and C. Payne. London: Macmillan Reference Books
8	Updated text	Causes an acute febrile illness in children. Associated with cough, coryza and conjunctivitis, spots on the buccal mucosa and rash on the head and neck, spreading to the remainder of the body. Encephalitis also occurs in some cases. Can cause death in undernourished children. Sub-acute sclerosing panencephalitis, a progressive degenerative disease of the central nervous system [. . .]
9	Subject	VIR
10	Language and country code	EN/UK
11	Entry	Measles virus
12	Source origin	Not applicable
13	Source type	DCT
14	Source no. and page	0001 (listed in separate file); 0133
15	Updated source no. and page	0006: 0128
16	Synonyms	Rubeola virus; rougeole virus; morbillivirus
17	Abbreviation/acronym	
18	Contextual synonyms	
19	Deprecated term	
20	Definition	Cough, coryza and conjunctivitis occur about ten days after infection.

21	Bibliographic reference	Prodromal stage 4–5 days, followed by mounting fever. Koplik's spots on the buccal mucosa and rash on head and neck spreading to trunk and limbs. Usually rapid recovery but can be fatal in undernourished children. [. . .] A Dictionary of Virology (1981). ed. K.E.K. Rowson, T.A.L. Rees and B.W.J. Mahy
22	Context/usage	
23	Conceptual position	Family (i.e. superordinate 1): Paramyxoviridae; genus (i.e. superordinate 2): Morbillivirus
24	Antonyms	
25	Related terms	Distemper virus (affects dogs), rinderpest virus (affects cattle, sheep, pigs, goats), peste des petits ruminants virus (affects sheep and goats)
26	Grammatical note	Noun
27	Classification	UDC: 578. Nordic: G 7430
28	Copyright	Blackwell Scientific Publications, Oxford; Macmillan Reference Books, London
29	Phonetic form	(to be added)
30	Language/Country code 2	FR/FR
31	Foreign language equivalent 2	la rougeole
32	Synonym 2	le morbillivirus
33	Deprecated term 2	
34	Scope note 2	
35	Bibliographic reference 2	Degree of equivalence etc.
40–3	Third language as for second, and so on	

Figure 8.2 Example of a completed record for the entry term 'measles virus' in the Surrey term bank with British English as the source language (SL). Not all record fields are necessarily completed. (The record format is under revision.)

format is required which contains a mandatory common core of
fields, to which others may be added as required.

Exchange of data between term banks

The magnetic tape exchange format (MATER) was instigated by
DIN and developed by the International Standards Organization
Technical Committee (ISO TC 37) in conjunction with terminologists working on term banks in many different countries
(ISO 6156, 1987). MATER is a standard terminological record
format comprising a common core of mandatory fields, and further
optional fields, which is used for exchanging, on tapes, term bank
data stored on mainframe computers by means of an input/output
facility which links the format of the individual bank to that of
MATER.

However, to answer the needs of microcomputers, MicroMATER
has been developed at Brigham Young University, Provo, in co-
operation with Infoterm, Vienna, and this format can be
adapted using various software tools (Melby forthcoming). Its files
comprise selected standard 7-bit ASCII characters to allow
transmission by electronic mail. It is designed to be flexible,
consisting of term records, each of which has an open-ended
number of fields of varying lengths. Each record begins with an
asterisk and each field name is enclosed in curly brackets. The
record is terminated by a commerical 'at' and an exclamation mark
(@!). Escape characters preceded by '@' are used to represent
diacritics and are linked to IBM extended (8-bit) ASCII
characters. MicroMATER, unlike MATER which is used only for the
exchange of data, can be manipulated to provide, for example,
reversal of a bilingual glossary[4] with its corresponding information;
this step, however, needs careful assessment of synonyms and
quasi-synonymous terms.

The future of term banks

It was soon realized that the potential of term banks was greater
than their use solely as a repository for terminology. By using a
relational database, links could be made between linguistic aspects
of terms such as synonyms and antonyms, and between ter-

minological aspects such as logical and generic relations (ISO 2788, 1974); in other words, hierarchical structures which lend themselves to representation in this type of database. Thus the scope for retrieval of the information contained within a relational database was greatly enhanced. Given that a number of terms may be embedded in the definition of a single term, it became evident that the knowledge contained within the text of the definition needed to be structured and deployed for the purpose of 'intelligent' retrieval, which allows the machine to make deductions from the information it contains and to propose options to the user. The birth of the next generation of term banks is being witnessed. These can provide for the data relating to a term, which have been structured hierarchically, to be channelled directly into an expert system which in turn will enable greater interaction between translators and the data available in the term bank. Skuce and Meyer discuss the evolution of term banks into multifactional knowledge bases. These authors also state that 'it is still extremely rare to find in terminology banks or publications any systematic attempts to represent the conceptual organization of a field, whether textually or graphically' (Skuce and Meyer 1990: 188–9), and stress the importance of good graphical representations for terminology as 'in our experience, the terminologists referred to the graph constantly'.

Hence the term 'record format', i.e. the 'fields' it contains and, in particular, the structure of the definition, assumes a vital role because of the growing need to supply terminology for 'treatment' by artificial intelligence. The current research in text analysis is facilitated if careful consideration has been given to the input stage of the term record.

Current developments

Since in the context of translation term banks are often linked into machine translation systems, the current situation of both types of help for translators will be reviewed, together with related aids. Renewed interest in MT and particularly machine-assisted translation (MAT) in recent years is due to a greater insistence on the use of the mother tongue because of export marketing, with a trend towards a lesser use of English. Industry's need to penetrate foreign markets has created an increasing and largely unsatisfied demand for multilingual documentation. In addition to the established term banks, and as an intermediate stage between these and large MT systems, there is a flourishing growth in interactive computerized dictionary 'tools' of varying sophistication available to the translator who likes to have dictionaries integrated with word processors (McNaught 1988) and to be able to compile personal glossaries. Most translators, in fact, limit their use of computers to word processing, while, as already mentioned, a small number have access to term banks. However, in addition to these tools, a wide range of facilities is available such as access to both general and specialized dictionaries, optical character readers (OCR) for reading texts into a computer, external communications (telex, fax, electronic mail), text editing (including spelling, grammar and style checkers in various languages, and hyphenation) and text analysis (concordancing and word frequency programs). This list is not exhaustive, nor are all the facilities found in all the systems; one system being developed under the aegis of the European Commission is the translator's workbench, ESPRIT II Project no: 2315 (Ahmad *et al.* 1990).

Among commercially available systems, Ericsson Vertriebs-Partner in Stuttgart has produced INTERDOC as an electronic language-independent support for translators, as the company considers fully automatic systems to be too limited and electronic support more rewarding to use. INTERDOC is language independent because Ericsson does not provide terminology but it provides font generation for the user to create non-Latin scripts and characters. In addition to word-processing and communication facilities, a terminologist allocates points on a scale from 0 to 9 for close to distant relationships between terms, forming a 'semantic net' to help the translator identify synonymous terms in the same text, even when these are unknown to the translator; it is, for example, quite common to find different names being allocated to the same chemical by different departments in the same company.

Among the most used of other commercial products are 'INK TextTools' (Netherlands) which also run on IBM PCs and compatibles, and have specialized dictionaries compiled by translators, as well as a general dictionary, together with a text analyser, 'TEXAN', and text editor, 'TED'; 'TERMEX', now known as 'MTX', from Linguatech (Provo, USA), which can draw data from the Siemens TEAM (Germany) terminology data bank and for which it is planned to do the same from EURODICAUTOM (EC) and from Collins On-Line Electronic Dictionaries (available on floppy disks for IBM PC XTs, ATs and true compatibles); 'Tron' from Transword (Netherlands), limited to bilingual dictionaries; and SITE (France) with PHENIX terminology management and AQUILA technical dictionaries. There are drawbacks, however: for example, some systems with text analysers only work out of English and in some cases their screen layout and manuals leave much to be desired.

One significant development is Harrap's CD-ROM Multilingual Dictionary database which gives very rapid access via English to eighteen general and specialized (scientific/technical and business) dictionaries in twelve languages, mostly bilingual, and includes Chinese and Japanese characters. This program is memory-resident, requiring 170 kilobytes (Kb) of random-access memory (RAM) in addition to the disk operating system (DOS) and word-processing software, and a Hitachi, Philips, Sanyo, Sony or Toshiba CD-ROM drive for interfacing to an IBM PC XT, AT, PS/2 or true compatible.

In addition, desk-top publishing (DTP) is an innovation which will speed translation work to a final product. One example is that available from Arrow Technical Translations, which can function in fourteen languages, post-translation, with a screen which operates on the WYSIWYG ('what you see is what you get') principle. In the UK, the University of Manchester Institute of Science and Technology (UMIST) is developing a system for a user who does not know the target language (TL) (Hutchins and Somers 1992) and, in France, C. Boitet's team in Grenoble aims to develop a similar, interactive product called LIDIA (large internationalization of documents by interacting with their authors) using HyperCard on an Apple Macintosh to prompt the writer to 'standardize' input text either on screen or using synthetic speech.[5]

MT research and development activity is intense in Japan, where it is allied to research in AI and is committed to producing massive 'knowledge bases'. The Fifth Generation project announced in 1982 has immense Japanese government and industrial support, as well as individual support in the USA and Europe, to enable Japan to keep abreast of Western developments and to export its goods effectively in a world market. Translations of documentation are almost entirely from Japanese into English and *vice versa*. About twenty groups, some large by European standards, have full-time researchers working on MT; the universities involved are Kyushu,

Kyoto, Osaka and Fukuoka, and interested commercial organizations, where most research is undertaken, include Fujitsu, Toshiba, NEC, Nippon Telegraph and Telephone, and a joint venture by Hitachi and Quick. All these systems have dictionaries of approximately 30,000 words, typed by students! The Toshiba system has a particularly good interface with a bilingual word processor. A linguistic machine editor can change sentences from the active to the passive voice and, where ambiguities occur, alternative translations are proffered. It can run interactively or off-line, in the latter case producing more than one default translation for ambiguous words, terms or structures. The Fujitsu system is less flexible but contains Japanese–German and Japanese–Korean, using English as the interlingua. A semantics-based MT system, ATLAS, aiming at translating 20,000 words an hour, is under development.

The major current development in Europe is the European Commission's sequel to SYSTRAN, the EUROTRA multilingual MT system for which design planning started in February 1978. EUROTRA is based on a monolingual analysis of the source text, with generation via multilingual transfer modules to a monolingual generation in the target language. It is planned to be the world's largest MT system and is destined to handle translation in the nine official Community languages, i.e. seventy-two language pairs. Results from the early stages have been evaluated and, while it is clear that an advanced MT system will not be realized by the end of phase III of the project, Danzin *et al.* recommend in their assessment report (Danzin *et al.* 1990) that the research in computational linguistics (CL) be continued and that the next phase in the language development of EUROTRA should concentrate primarily on monolingual applications. One of these could be the production of terminologies.

The future of MT and term banks

What is likely to be the structure of future systems? In MT, research is being continued in two disciplines, AI and CL. It seems likely that a surface syntactic analysis of a source language (SL) will be underpinned by a semantic analysis, which could be used for comparison against prototypes in the form of 'frames' or 'scripts' in an expert system. To provide material to complete the 'slots' for frames and scripts, scanners or OCRs may be used to 'read in' texts from which an event could be inferred from partial information given; here concordancing could play a role in the provision of terms for the term bank which is an essential component in these operations. Clearly, the relationships in terminology such as material, cause and function, and inheritance, have a part to play in this process.

Japan is forging ahead to link AI and CL and so provide the third generation of MT. The USA is advanced in AI techniques but shows little interest in MT, whereas in Europe, Philips in Eindhoven is probably the only enterprise engaged in long-term research; this is based on Montague grammar

> which defines a language by specifying a set of expressions and their grammatical categories, and a set of syntactic rules prescribing how these expressions may combine to form new expressions and what the grammatical category of the new expression will be.
>
> (Hutchins 1986: 287)

Research projects are delving into semantic representation using AI techniques which may be language-independent, with translation being one application, perhaps as a test of an AI system. The enormous volume of technical translation handled in such large international and multilingual organizations as the EEC illustrates the need for improved MT systems. The techniques of AI will seek to incorporate awareness and experience, or so-called 'world knowledge'. The inclusion of contrastive linguistics covering a wider range of language types than hitherto will help in the assessment of other possible forms of interlinguae used as intermediaries in MT. Parallel processing techniques and neural networks will be considered, although linguistic problems are unlikely to be solved by speed and power. Certainly a sharing of resources such as term banks and other lexical databases seems desirable.

The picture would be incomplete without mention of advances in speech synthesis; tests are being undertaken in restricted domains such as banking, where recognition of numbers can be made without the need for them to be voice specific. Other systems are AIRSPEAK and SEASPEAK and, following research by E. Johnson *et al.* at Wolfson College, Cambridge, POLICESPEAK is being developed by Kent County Constabulary and British Telecom in the UK, to cover traffic and emergencies in the

Channel Tunnel. Speech systems can also be 'trained' to recognize the voice of an individual.

Pocket-sized foreign-language translators aimed at travellers, with dictionary, thesaurus-type suggestions and pronunciation facilities, while not at present providing a useful tool for the professional translator, nevertheless have potential because of their compact size and improvements in storage capacity. A glimpse of future potential in this field is provided by a hand-held English–Japanese translating machine from Fuji-Xerox which has a vocabulary of 30,000 words and phrases, which, when stroked over English text at up to 20 cm per second, produces Japanese characters on the liquid crystal display (LCD). It is easy to envisage a number of the features mentioned being incorporated into such a convenient form which would be much easier to handle and more portable than the average dictionary. Large systems, because of cost and lack of portability, are not generally available to the freelance translator who hitherto has probably not had access to any computerized help other than a word processing package on a personal computer with a printer attached.

What advances may be envisaged to improve the lot of the translator? A workstation which will minimize the time spent on library and other searches may comprise the following: a word processor with a multi-window screen from which one or more term banks may be consulted and access given to an MT system, with the possibility of creating personal lexica; administrative and accounting facilities; style, grammar and spelling checkers for text, with the possibility of interactive prompting either on screen or via speech synthesis; desk-top publishing for the final product; and the ability to receive and transmit text through electronic mail networks or facsimile transmission.

NOTES

1 Contact British Telecom UK Sales Operation, 8th Floor, Tenter House, 45 Moorfields, London EC2Y 9TH, tel: 0800 282444, telex: 8952558 NSSAL G, fax: 071 250 8343.
2 Tel: 010 352 488 041.
3 One area in which cooperation is being achieved is work on subject classification which began in the Scandinavian countries with the development of NORDTERM. Representatives include organizations in Denmark, Finland, Iceland, Norway, Sweden, Germany and the Netherlands. The classification system is hierarchical, consisting of a

letter plus four digits, and it is hoped that it will be implemented within the next few years. Its importance lies in its effectiveness in providing small, tightly defined domains which help to clarify the exact meaning of homographs which, when appearing in more than one domain, vary semantically in each (Thomas 1988).

4   To reverse the two parts which make up a bilingual dictionary, the entry terms for the first part (for example, English, with equivalents in French) are transposed so that the translation equivalents from the first part become the entry terms for the second part (the original English entry terms then become the translation equivalents in the French–English part). The fact that the semantic fields of 'equivalents' drawn from different languages rarely (if ever) coincide exactly makes this a dubious basis for dictionary creation in anything but the most restricted domains.

5   For a comprehensive resource guide to the then available word-processing software, localized DTP, on-line multilingual term banks and dictionaries see the special insert in *LT/Electric Word*, issue 13, May/June 1989.

BIBLIOGRAPHY

Ahmad, K., Fulford, H., Holmes-Higgin, P., Rogers, M. and Thomas, P. (1990) 'The translator's workbench project', in C. Picken (ed.) *Translating and the Computer 11: Preparing for the Next Decade*, London: Aslib, 9–19.

Danzin, A., Allen, B., Coltof, H., Recoque, A., Steusloff, H. and O'Leary, M. (1990) 'Eurotra Programme Assessment Report', Commission of the European Communities, March 1990.

Fulford, H., Höge, M. and Ahmad, K. (1990) 'User requirements study', European Commission Esprit II Project no. 2315, Translator's Workbench Project, Final Report on Workpackage 3.3.

Hutchins, W.J (1986) *Machine Translation: Past, Present, Future*, Chichester: Ellis Horwood.

Hutchins, W.J. and Somers, H.L. (1992) *An Introduction to Machine Translation*, London: Academic Press.

Iljon, A. (1977) 'Scientific and technical databases in a multilingual society', in *Proceedings of Third European Congress on Information Systems*, Munich: Commission of the European Communities.

ISO 2788 (1974) 'Documentation – guidelines for the establishment and development of multilingual thesauri'.

ISO 6156 (1987) 'Magnetic tape exchange format for terminological/lexicographical records (MATER)'.

Knowles, F. (1979) 'Error analysis of Systran output: a suggested criterion for "internal" evaluation of translation quality and a possible corrective design', in B.M. Snell (ed.) (1979) *Translation and the Computer*, Amsterdam: North-Holland, 109–33.

McNaught, J. (1988) 'A survey of termbanks worldwide', in C. Picken (ed.) *Translating and the Computer 9: Potential and Practice*, London: Aslib, 112–29.

Melby, A. (forthcoming) 'MicroMATER: a proposed standard format for exchanging lexical/terminological data files', *META* (special issue).

Pogson, G. (1989) 'The LT/Electric Word multilingual wordworker's resource guide', *LT/Electric Word* 13, Amsterdam: Language Technology BV.

Skuce, D. and Meyer, I. (1990) 'Computer-assisted concept analysis: an essential component of a terminologist's workstation', in H. Czap and W. Nedobity (eds) *TKE '90: Terminology and Knowledge Engineering*, Frankfurt: INDEKS Verlag, 187–99.

Smith, D. and Tyldesley, D. (1986) 'Translation Practices Report', Reading: Digital Equipment Corporation.

'Terminological Data Banks' (1989) *TermNet News* 24, Infoterm, Vienna: 25–30.

Thomas, P. (1988) 'Analysis of an English and French LSP: some comparisons with English general text corpora', *ALSED–UNESCO Newsletter 11*, 1(26), 2–10.

Chapter 9

The translator workstation

Alan Melby

A decade ago, when Martin Kay wrote of the need to develop software for a translator workstation (Kay 1980), most translators were either still using typewriters or, in the case of dictating translators, their secretaries were using typewriters to transcribe tapes. Today, however, most translators (or their secretaries) are using word processing software, and, in addition, some translators have even added other translator workstation functions to their word processors. The 1990s promise widespread use of translator workstations on new, more powerful, yet affordable microcomputers.

PREVIEW

The functions of a translator workstation can be divided into three levels (Melby 1982) as follows:

- level one includes word processing, telecommunications, and terminology management;
- level two adds text analysis, automatic dictionary look-up, and synchronized bilingual text retrieval;
- level three provides an interface to machine translation systems.

These various functions deserve a more detailed explanation, but before elaborating, I will address the question of whether machine translation is likely to eliminate the need for multi-level translator workstations in the near future.

FULLY AUTOMATIC MACHINE TRANSLATION VERSUS TRANSLATOR WORKSTATIONS

The primary objection to investing in the development of translator workstations has always been that available resources would be better spent on the development of automatic machine translation systems. A background assumption for this objection is that machine translation will soon replace human translators altogether. This chapter will challenge that assumption. If we examine the history of machine translation since the early 1950s, we see that its success is highly dependent on the nature of the source text and the intended use of the translation.

Indicative machine translation

If the purpose is simply to obtain a rough indication of the source text content, and not a careful, finished translation by human standards, then fully automatic machine translation may be in order. Raw, low-quality output which is not intended to be edited into a high-quality translation is sometimes called 'indicative' translation.

Indicative translation has been used for many years by the US Air Force to avoid unnecessary human translation. A scientist can use an indicative translation to decide whether a foreign language document is sufficiently interesting to warrant a careful human translation. To obtain indicative translations, translator workstations are not really needed.

Translation for publication or distribution

If, however, the purpose of the translation is to produce a high-quality document for publication and distribution, then a translator workstation is useful. The case of dialogue-based machine translation (such as the translation of telephone conversations or machine translation involving on-line interaction between a human and a computer), although very interesting, will not be treated in this chapter.

There are many types of text translated for publication and distribution, the extremes being sublanguage text and literary text.

A sublanguage text is restricted in several ways, including vocabulary, syntax and universe of discourse. Perhaps the best known example of naturally occurring sublanguage text is weather bulletins. The METEO machine translation system translates Canadian weather bulletins throughout the day. In this case, human translators review the machine-translated output at a translator workstation. This workstation needs mainly level-three functions as only minor corrections to the raw machine-translated output are necessary. Any true sublanguage in which there is a large, constant flow of text is a good candidate for machine translation.

The other extreme of translation for publication and distribution is literary text. Here there are no predefined restrictions on vocabulary, syntax and universe of discourse. A literary text is often filled with creative metaphors and words used in slightly 'twisted' ways. Far from being negative factors, freedom and flexibility give life to the text and help stimulate the reader to read on. General background knowledge is drawn on implicitly to avoid ambiguity. Sometimes ambiguity is intentional, providing two levels of understanding in the same passage.

For literary texts, both prose and poetry, a translator workstation can be useful but only at levels one and two, and then only in a limited way, since literary texts are not filled with standardized terminology. Nevertheless, the word processor can be as useful as for any writer, and the terminology management function can be used to record notes about interesting expressions and solutions to their translation problems. Even the text analysis function could be used by a literary translator to look for other occurrences of an interesting expression encountered in the source text. However, it is generally accepted that current machine translation systems should not be applied to literary text.

The problem, of course, is that most texts are somewhere between the extremes of literary text and sublanguage text. We will use Snell-Hornby's terms of 'general language' and 'special language' (Snell-Hornby 1988) to describe two points along the spectrum of text types. General-language texts include newspaper articles, light fiction and advertising texts. Special-language texts, which represent the bulk of the translation done by professional translators, are a mixture of the lexical flexibility found in general texts and the precise terminology found in sublanguage texts. Special-language texts include the vast number of scientific reports and the huge volume of technical documentation written and translated every year. One could predict that machine translation applied to such texts would give mixed results, and this is indeed the case. Raw machine translation of special-language text requires so much human revision that it is often not worth post-editing for publication and distribution. Indeed, it is in the translation of special-language texts that the translator workstation comes into its own. Level-one and level-two functions are often very effective tools in the hands of human translators for producing high-quality translations of scientific or technical documents.

It would be worthwhile conducting a careful study of the worldwide translation market in terms of the types of translation discussed above. But, failing that, we can look at the results of many years of development of the SYSTRAN machine translation system in the European Community (EC). It is well known that translation represents an important portion of the EC budget and that SYSTRAN has been refined and tailored to the needs of the EC. There is a motivation to use SYSTRAN when it is more efficient than human translation; however, SYSTRAN is currently used on fewer than 5 per cent of the texts translated by the EC. This reticence reflects the increased difficulties involved in providing high-quality machine translations of special-language texts as opposed to pure sublanguage texts.

Studies of the worldwide translation market consistently estimate that the amount of money spent annually on translations to be published and distributed totals several thousands of millions of US dollars. And, assuming that most of the text translated for these vast sums of money is special-language text, as in the case of the EC, it would be reasonable to conclude that the major portion of today's translation market would benefit from increased use of translator workstations. The most important unresolved issue is whether machine translation will soon be applicable to most special-language texts to be translated, thus reducing the motivation to develop level-one and level-two functions.

The claim of this chapter is that translator workstations are not just a stopgap measure to improve translator productivity until human translators are made superfluous by fully automatic high-quality machine-translation systems. It is believed by some that such systems will eventually be produced through the refinement of current design techniques. However, research in the philosophy of language indicates that this will not be so. Recent thinking in philosophy and translation theory suggests that special-language texts draw on the following two types of semantic networks: general semantic networks, which correspond to the general and literary texts described above, and domain-specific semantic networks, which correspond to sublanguage texts or to standardized terminology in special-language texts (Melby forthcoming). Thus, special-language texts consist of a mixture of words linked to general semantic networks and terms linked to domain-specific semantic networks.

Present techniques of machine translation implicitly assume that entire texts draw solely on domain-specific networks. Both transfer approaches and 'interlingual' approaches (Hutchins 1986) are based on the assumptions of modern, mainstream generative grammar. They treat language as a formal system in which meaning is computed compositionally from the bottom up (i.e. by combining word meanings to form larger semantic units). These word meanings are drawn from lexicons containing lists of predefined, distinct word senses. For each of these senses, one literal meaning is held to be more basic, while additional, metaphorical meanings are considered to be more derivative. As Lakoff has demonstrated so well (Lakoff 1987), mainstream generative grammar is firmly based on objectivism, which is being called into question in the various branches and re-evaluations of post-modern philosophy.

It exceeds the scope of this chapter to attempt to explore current trends in the philosophy of language. But it is appropriate to point out that if Lakoff and others are right, there is no reason to assume that current 'objectivist' techniques in machine translation will ever provide an adequate solution for general texts or even for special-language texts that contain a significant incidence of general language. For predominantly general texts, entirely new techniques will have to be developed. Some theorists say that neural networks are the answer; others maintain that the simplifications made in current individual simulated neurons will lead to a dead end and will require a new start. All admit that a neural network capable of dealing with full-blown natural language is still only a distant goal. Clearly, at this time, there exists no foreseeable new formal linguistic model that will allow machines to deal with general language.

The implications of these findings with regard to the difference between the two types of semantic networks are clear. Current techniques of machine translation should only be applied to sublanguage texts and special-language texts that are predominantly based on domain networks. Instead of wasting effort applying current techniques to texts which are too heavily tied to general semantic networks, more funding should be provided for basic research in non-objectivist linguistics. How do we design machines that can do what humans do, that is, draw on an unlimited amount of context and background information to interpret new expressions, such as the phrase 'a jaw for news' (creatively based on the standard expression 'a nose for news')?

Given the relatively small amount of progress that has been made in machine translation in the past forty years, and the expanding market for high-quality translation for publication and distribution, along with the relatively modest investment required to develop effective tools for human translators, it seems entirely reasonable to expect that substantial funding should also be made available for the development of sophisticated level-one and level-two functions for translator workstations. The return on investment from such development will probably be high. Funding should be directed at both translator workstation and machine translation systems. However, neither is likely to provide an easy, total solution to the problem of translating every type of text. Experimentation will reveal which type of text is best translated with each type of system.

The complexity of natural language and the difficulty of building systems that deal with it effectively help me appreciate the wisdom of some advice I received in 1972 from David G. Hays, the father of computational linguistics. I was a 'young turk' out to solve the problem of machine translation, and he told me that no matter what syntactic–semantic model we used, a good machine translation system would still require mostly plain hard work. At the time, his comment irritated me because I was convinced that using the right formal linguistic model would make the problems melt before my eyes. Objectivism is so pervasive that we normally do not even recognize it. Now I realize that I was so wrapped up in the assumptions of objectivism that I could not see either the beauty or the implications of the impossibility of distinctly listing all the senses associated with a word of general language. A good lexicographer knows that the word senses in a general dictionary do not represent a fixed, unchanging set of all the possible meanings of a word carved into a marble pillar, but rather some of the common landing points for a free-floating butterfly.

SOME TRANSLATOR WORKSTATION FUNCTIONS

The rest of this chapter will describe level-one and level-two functions in more detail, then explain the need for a standard format to facilitate exchange of terminology files and finally situate the translator workstation in the total document creation process.

Word processing, hardware and operating environments: considerations of an 'ideal' translator workstation

The core function of a translator workstation is word processing. As more and more translators use word processing, they accept without question its superiority over typing and retyping texts on a typewriter. In addition, the use of dedicated word processors has given way to the use of word processing software on general-purpose microcomputers. The advantage of using such general-purpose microcomputers is their flexibility. A dedicated unit, because of proprietary design, normally cannot allow the user to add the other software packages required for a higher level translator workstation. Years ago, the word processing software available for use on stand-alone units provided a greater number of more powerful functions. Today, however, the word processing software available for general-purpose microcomputers is superior.

If the translator workstation is to be a practical tool for a typical real-life translator, it must be affordable. In the 1070s, when translator workstations were only a pipe dream, some of us dreamers predicted that translators would start buying translator workstations when the cost of a complete workstation, including the computer, a printer, the operating system and essential applications software, became less than the cost of a modest automobile. At that point, it was predicted, a workstation would become a truly viable choice for individual translators. In an area where many people get along using public transportation, it becomes a real alternative to owning an automobile; in an area where most people do own automobiles and many families have two, it becomes a real alternative to a second automobile. Clearly, with today's microcomputers and the increased cost of automobiles, we have arrived at that predicted day, as the cost of workstations using both IBM personal computers and compatibles (PCs), and even Macintoshes (Macs), is comparable to or less than the cost of a modest automobile.

The second important consideration for a translator workstation is the wise choice of an operating system. This choice must be based not only on the processing capabilities of the operating system and its level of user-friendliness, but also on the application software that is available under that operating system.

In 1980, the dominant operating system running on affordable microcomputers was CP/M for 8080-type microprocessors, an operating system with too many inherent limitations to become a viable foundation for translator workstation software. Xerox Corporation was already developing experimental computers using a graphical user interface, multiple windows, and a mouse, but these computers were very expensive and thus beyond the reach of the typical translator.

Then, during the 1980s, three significant events occurred in the microcomputer world.

1 The IBM PC with its PC-DOS operating system appeared; it took the microcomputer world by storm. More importantly, the open architecture of the IBM PC was accepted as a standard and gradually most other microcomputer hardware vendors began building IBM PC compatibles, bringing the price down to an affordable range and the power up to an acceptable level. There are now tens of millions of IBM PCs and PC compatibles worldwide.

2 A few years after the introduction of the PC, the Apple Macintosh brought the Xerox user-interface technology to the attention of the general public. Although the first Macintoshes suffered from memory and disk space limitations, like the first PCs, the current Mac II series hardware and operating system (system 6 and beyond) are powerful enough to support adequate translator workstation software. Unfortunately, because the closed architecture of the Macintosh has prevented clones from being made, the price of a Mac II is higher than that of a comparable PC based on an 80386-type microprocessor (or its more powerful successors).

3 A few years after the introduction of the Mac, a similar graphical interface was introduced for PCs, called MicroSoft Windows (Windows). Like many new products, it was hardly usable at first, but its later versions (version 3 and above), in conjunction with a PC, are much more usable. Currently, a Mac, operating with the standard Apple operating system, and a powerful PC, operating with DOS plus Windows, are both viable, affordable 'platforms' for a translator workstation.

An important element of this sequence of developments is that the

Mac and the PC + Windows platforms each utilize a standard user-interface style to which all application programs must conform. This is highly important to translators because of their need for a consistent user interface across the various functions of their translator workstations. For a number of years, there was no standard user interface in the world of PC-DOS text-based programs. Because of this deficiency, the only way to get a consistent user interface across a set of functions was for one software vendor to write all of them. For a while, 'integrated' packages, those which combined word processing, spreadsheet and other functions within one program, appeared to be the answer in the business software world. However, users soon realized that no one vendor could write all of the best application software. The world of translator workstation-related software development has also suffered from the lack of a standard because it is too expensive to develop a word processor from scratch that specifically meets translators' needs. So translators must use general-purpose word processors and adapt them to their needs. The various graphical user interfaces (GUIs) in use today are, fortunately, becoming more rather than less similar. This means that the translator workstation of the 1990s will probably use a GUI and compatible software components developed by various vendors.

Further hardware developments

Another hardware development trend emerging during the 1980s that affects translator work groups is the appearance of inexpensive high-capacity disk storage, the rise of local area networks, and the development of intelligent GUI Unix workstations.

If terminology and translation quality are to remain consistent across various documents translated by different humans, there needs to be some sharing of terminology throughout a work group. This can be accomplished in various ways. Shared information can be placed on each separate workstation using either a magnetic or an optical disk, or the information can be shared by connecting a workstation to a local area network or central computer. Each method has advantages and disadvantages. Until recently, being connected to a central computer was far from user-friendly. Now, however, microcomputers can be used as terminals to a central computer while retaining a GUI interface. The main progress in this regard is the development of the X-windows interface for the Unix operating system.

An important spin-off of GUI development is an increased ability to handle multiple languages on the screen at the same time. On the Mac, since characters are generated in software, there can be characters from several different alphabets on the screen at the same time. On a PC running DOS alone, it is difficult to have more than 256 different characters available at any given time, since each character is represented as one 'byte', a basic unit of information which can have only 256 different values. Extensions to this system of using one byte for each character become very specific to one piece of software. But with the standard operating system on the Mac and with Windows on the PC, extended alphabets are handled in a more global fashion.

Having established the need for translator workstations and having examined some likely hardware/software platforms for a translator workstation, I will now look at some of the individual level-one functions (word processing, telecommunications and terminology management) and level-two functions (text analysis, automatic [dictionary] look-up and synchronized [bilingual] text retrieval) of a translator workstation in more detail.

LEVEL-ONE FUNCTIONS

Improvements needed in word processing

Current word processing and desk-top publishing software is very sophisticated. The first improvement that may be suggested is in the area of spell checking. Systems that provide spell checking for languages other than English are currently limited. However, pressure from bilingual users of word-processing software will probably prompt the enhancement of this type of software.

Another needed improvement in word processing is in morphology-based search and replace. All word processors have a search-and-replace function which allows the user to find all instances of a character string. Sometimes the search and replace can be made case insensitive so that it will find a string such as 'Break' at the beginning of a sentence, even though the search string was 'break'. But what if the user wants to replace all occurrences of the verb 'break' with 'fracture'? The typical search-and-replace function will not find 'broke' because it does not know enough about morphology to identify past, plural and other forms of words. Again, translators would not be the only clients to use this feature, so it is likely that normal market pressures will eventually result in general-purpose word processors with morphology-based search-and-replace functions becoming available.

An interesting enhancement to word processing proposed by Professor Gregory Shreve (personal communication) of Kent State University is a database of prototypical texts. When translating a patent, for example, a translator would find it helpful to have ready access to a typical patent in the target language and country as well as a description of the elements of such a document. We see the beginnings of functions to support this in the style sheets available in some word processors.

Also, SGML, a very flexible mark-up language, promises to make document structure descriptions available in a universal form. Once SGML document descriptions are widely adopted, it will make it easier to transfer texts among different word processing software packages.

SGML, which stands for Standard Generalized Mark up Language, became an international standard (ISO 8879) in 1986.

The text encoding initiative (TEI) is an international effort including representatives from the Association for Computing in the Humanities and the Association for Computational Linguistics. The TEI group is producing an application of SGML which will create a standardized system of embedded format codes. Eventually, through end-user pressure, word processing software packages will include utilities to import to and export from TEI-SGML format. This will solve one of the problems with word processing for translators today: some clients want the final version of their translation returned to them containing the internal format codes for one word processor while others prefer that it contain those of another. Translators should not have to switch back and forth between different word processors to meet these requirements. However, lacking any other option, they sometimes turn to utilities, either supplied with the word processing software or by a third party, that switch between all kinds of word processing formats. However, these utilities need to be updated constantly for new releases of word processing software and thus tend to be incomplete. The final solution to this dilemma is for each word processing vendor to support the TEI-SGML format.

Telecommunications

Telecommunications is a basic need for most translators today. The apparent exception is the in-house translator who is handed a source text from someone else in the organization and who hands the translation to someone else. But even in this situation, it is likely that some text transfer using telecommunications takes place either as the document travels from the technical writers to the organization or from the translation office to an office in another country.

It seems that mail is just not fast enough for many text deliveries today. One reason for this is the crucial need for business to reduce the time lag between launching a new product in one language market and making it available in another. Corporations will probably find the problem of reducing this interval even more critical in the 1990s, particularly after 1992 in Europe.

The most common form of telecommunications used in the late 1980s was text transfer by means of a fax machine. As useful as fax has become, it is only a partial solution for the translator. Text transfer of target-language texts via fax presents two important problems: first, a fax cannot be edited using a word processor; second, a faxed copy of a text is not camera-ready. Perhaps the optimum solution to this problem would be the widespread use of file transfer by modem with automatic error detection and correction. Fortunately, there are several such error-calculating transmission protocols available, such as X-modem and Kermit.

Another important translation-related function of telecommunications is the obtaining of access to remote databases, such as bibliographic databases, for doing research. This research may relate either to single terms or to general research about the domains of the source text and would be carried out by locating related or explanatory documents.

Terminology management

Terminology management is extraordinarily important to translation of special-language texts containing many technical terms. Terminology is standardized at multiple levels. Some terms are coined by individuals working in the forefront of a branch of technology as they describe a newly invented concept. These terms may work their way 'up' to larger and larger groups of users, until they are adopted as an international standard term defining that concept. Others are imposed by a larger group and filter 'downward' to the increasingly smaller groups in the individual organizations. Of course, standardization can also take place at any point between the two extremes described. This process takes some time and different terms may be used to describe the same concept in different organizations at any one time. Translators who do work for several different requestors cannot and should not be expected to carry these differing translation standards for technical terms in their heads.

Since there is another chapter devoted specifically to terminology management, I will only mention a few enhancements that need to be made to current terminology management software over the next few years.

First, we must get away from the notion of externally defined record layouts which is nearly universal in today's sophisticated database-management packages. This notion is fine for business data processing, where you can pre-define what an employee record will look like and what fields it will have. However, in lexical and terminological data management, one record in a given electronic glossary may have five fields and another may have fifty. No one can dictate that all terms will have the same number of alternative forms and the same number of notes. Similarly, no one can dictate that all the words in a general-purpose dictionary will have the same number of definitions. Ultimately, there will need to be a new kind of data management tailored to the needs of handling many records of 'structured text' with internally defined fields. Several groups, including one at the University of Waterloo (Canada) which is pioneering work on software to access the new *Oxford English Dictionary*, are working on this problem.

Terminology-management software will also have to be able to associate several files containing different types of data. For example, a translator might define a team of files which consists of a bilingual reference, two appropriate monolingual references, and a user-annotation file. Once the system has activated all of these files, the user would type in a word or multi-word expression only once and the system would be able to access all the entries keyed to that word or expression within any of those reference files, passing automatically through hypertext cross-reference links if appropriate. Perhaps the initial search would locate the related entries corresponding to that term or expression in the language in which it was entered. A second search for user-selected correspondences in the target language could be activated either by a limited number of keystrokes or with a single mouse click. This second search would also provide information from all of the selected reference files that comprise another user-selected team.

Another important feature for terminology software is the availability of 'filters' and 'views'. A filter makes only qualifying records visible to the user, and a view makes only a selected subset of the fields in a record visible. These functions allow the user to see what is of most interest at the time and reduce the amount of scrolling that needs to be done.

Also, there should be multiple indexes on a file so that a record can be accessed rapidly in several ways. In the area of the development of indexing programs, the problem of how to deal effectively with words that appear in a file either dozens or hundreds of times has not as yet been effectively solved. Current software programs often present all of these multiple occurrences in an unstructured list, which can easily result in information overload for the user.

In working on these various enhancements, much important information can be gleaned from standard relational database systems and fourth-generation programming languages, but we must avoid using the externally defined record layouts that are usually associated with such database systems. Avoiding externally defined record layouts without sacrificing the retrieval and manipulation power of relational databases is the central challenge for terminology-management software in the 1990s: the trick is to provide additional power without compromising flexibility.

Another significant challenge is where to obtain the data to put into a bilingual terminology file. An important benefit from such work is that the translator can become knowledgeable in a particular domain more easily and more efficiently. A major source would be monolingual conceptual knowledge bases in each domain. The central obstacle to this effort is the astounding rate of creation of new knowledge in today's scientific and technological world.

Unfortunately, there is no obvious practical solution to the problem of how to codify knowledge more efficiently. The most obvious ideal solution would be for technical writers to create, as a matter of course, easily accessible concept-based terminology files containing all of the new terms they create while writing. But this change in conventions will likely occur very slowly. A particular solution may be in more sophisticated text-analysis tools, which brings us to the level-two functions of a translator workstation.

LEVEL-TWO FUNCTIONS

Level one does not assume that the source text is available in machine-readable form. The target text can be created on a word processor, various terminology files can be consulted and the translation can be sent to the requestor by electronic file transfer, all without the source text being available to the translator in a compatible electronic form. Although most translation produced in the 1980s was produced from hard copy only, this situation should change during the 1990s.

When the source text is available in compatible electronic form, three new functions can be added to the translator workstation: text analysis, automatic term look-up in electronic terminology files and synchronized retrieval of source and target texts.

The distinction between level-one functions and level-two functions is simply that level one is restricted to what can be done when the source text is only available in hard-copy form. Level two comprises all functions included in level one plus additional functions for processing the source text in various ways.

Text analysis

One basic text analysis tool is a dynamic concordance system which indexes all the words in the document and which allows the user to request all occurrences of a word or combination of words within the document. This type of analysis may assist in the translation of a long document because it allows the translator to quickly see how troublesome terms are used in various contexts throughout the document.

Several text-analysis software packages are available commercially for PCs. There are two basic types: one which searches a text 'on-the-fly' without any pre-processing; and one which requires a pre-processing pass to create an index of all the words of the text (except a few common words like 'and' and 'the', called 'stop' words). A long document is probably better studied by pre-processing it during a lunch hour or some other break and then looking up words and combinations very quickly using the index. These rapid searches could be done before starting translation, or, more likely, during translation as questions arise.

The most important addition to a dynamic concordance system would be access to various monolingual references through the terminology-management function of level one. Using some kind of dynamic data exchange between programs, the user should be able to look for the occurrences of a term in the source text and then ask the terminology-management software to find references to that term in a reference dictionary or terminology file without retyping the term. The problem, of course, is when the term does not appear in the reference and is not clearly defined in the source text. At some point, it should become the responsibility of requestors of translation to provide a terminology file with each source text that contains the definitions of new terms that appear in the text as well as how new terms fit conceptually with related terms in that domain. Until that responsibility is widely accepted, the terminologist/translator must be content with keyword searches in bibliographic databases and access to the minds of colleagues by telephone, telefax or electronic mail.

One international project that could perhaps benefit communication as much as anything else would be the creation and maintenance of a roster of experts in many (perhaps thousands of) domains in dozens of major languages. A pay-per-use service bureau would accept an unknown term with a definition and specification of domain and desired target language and consult an appropriate expert for a translation equivalent. All communication would, of course, be done by electronic mail.

Automatic lookup

Once terminology files are available and routines are in place to find the basic forms of inflected words (i.e. to perform morphological analysis), it is a straightforward matter to identify the words in a piece of source text and automatically look them up in a terminology file. Terms found in the file would be displayed on the screen along with the corresponding target-language terms, and the human translator could copy selected terms into the target text.

Synchronized retrieval

Another level-two spin-off of morphological analysis could be the automatic creation of synchronized (i.e. parallel) bilingual text files. When a document had been translated and revised, the final version, as well as its source text, would be stored in such a way that each unit of source text was linked to a corresponding unit of target text. The units would generally be sentences, except in cases where one sentence in the source text becomes two in the target text or *vice versa*. The benefits of synchronized bilingual text retrieval are manifold with appropriate software. A translator beginning a revision of a document could automatically incorporate unmodified units taken from a previous translation into the revision with a minimum of effort. Such a system has been developed and marketed by Alpnet but it requires that the text be marked and segmented by the software and then translated segment by segment. The next generation of such software would automatically synchronize source and target units 'after the fact', along the lines of several experimental software research projects.

Another benefit of synchronized bilingual retrieval would be the creation of large bilingual databases of previously translated texts. Thus, an individual requestor, service bureau or, most interestingly, a large corporation or agency, could provide to its translators a database (perhaps on CD-ROM) showing how various terms had been translated in the organization's documents over the past several years. Not only would such information be invaluable for helping the translator or terminologist choose the appropriate equivalent terms for the purposes of the current text, it would also have the added benefit of instantly allowing them to determine whether or not a particular use of a term was new.

The long-range plan

The long-range plan to use translator workstations effectively calls for requestors of translation to cooperate with terminologists, translators and publishers in organizing the knowledge of each domain and providing it in an accessible form to all of the technical writers, terminologists and translators who handle their documents from creation to publication. The translator workstation then becomes, unsurprisingly, an extended version of a technical writer workstation, and the 'extra' work involved pays off in more readable, more consistent and thus higher-quality source and target language documents. The training required to use a translator workstation effectively should pay off in increased productivity. However, it is important to introduce new technology sensitively and for a translator to train on one function at a time.

The advanced translator workstation (Shreve and Vinciquerra 1990) would give the translator access to a 'knowledge base' integrating terminological information, encyclopedic information (thesauri and bibliographic databases), textual information (such as prototype texts) and strategic information (such as source-target unit-pairs retrieved from synchronized bilingual databases).

Once the necessity for terminology work has been recognized at the highest levels, groups of requestors and ultimately all requestors of translation need to cooperate by making standardized terminology available to each other, holding back only terms proprietary to each organization. For this purpose, the Brigham Young University Translation Research Group (c/o Alan Melby, Department of Linguistics), in cooperation with the Terminology Committee of the American Translators Association (ATA), Infoterm (an international coordination organization), and the Steering Committee of the Text Encoding Initiative is developing a universal terminological data-exchange format called Micro-MATER. (MATER is the name of ISO standard 6156 for terminology exchange.) In this way, the format for terminology exchange can be standardized in a format compatible with SGML.

The translator workstation, rather than being a short-term solution, is indeed a long-term solution to international communication problems. Level-two functions (which include level-one functions) will eventually become the dominant tools used for special-language texts when high-quality translation is required. And level-three functions (which now include the submission of texts to machine translation systems) will become common for predominantly domain texts. Eventually, translator workstations will even interface with machine translation systems, providing them with terminology information in order to avoid costly duplication of effort, as machine translation systems also need constantly updated bilingual term equivalents.

BIBLIOGRAPHY

Hutchins, W.J. (1986) *Machine Translation: Past, Present, Future*, Chichester, Ellis Horwood.

Kay, M. (1980) 'The proper place of men and machines', in *Language Translation*, Research Report, Xerox Palo Alto Research Center, Palo Alto, California.

Lakoff, G. (1987) *Women, Fire, and Dangerous Things: What Categories Reveal about the Mind*, Chicago: University of Chicago Press.

Melby, A. (1982) 'Multi-level translation aids in a distributed system', in J. Horecky (ed.) *Proceedings of COLING–82*, Prague, July 1982, Amsterdam: North-Holland.

—— (forthcoming) 'Causes and effects of partial asymmetry between semantic networks tied to natural languages' (a lecture series given at the Collège de France, Paris, February, 1990), to appear in *Les Cahiers de Lexicologie*, Paris.

Shreve, G.M. and Vinciquerra, K.J. (1990) 'Hypertext knowledge-bases for computer-assisted translation: organization and structure', in A.L. Wilson (ed.) *Proceedings of the 31st Annual Conference of the American Translators Association*, New Orleans, October 1990: Learned Information, Inc.

Snell-Hornby, M. (1988) *Translation Studies: An Integrated Approach*, Amsterdam: John Benjamins.

Chapter 10

SYSTRAN: it obviously works but how much can it be improved?

Yorick Wilks

INTRODUCTION

To this day the SYSTRAN system (Toma 1976) remains the existence proof of machine translation (MT). When people argue (as they sometimes still do) that usable MT (of a quality that benefits a large class of consumers) does not exist, one can simply point to the existence of SYSTRAN and, in particular, to its twenty-year history at the Foreign Technology Division (FTD) in Dayton, Ohio, where it translates large numbers of Russian scientific and engineering theses every month.

At the present time, there is a resurgence of MT research based only on text statistics at IBM, New York, a revived technique (Brown *et al.* 1990) that has attracted both interest and funding. Their claim that MT can and should be done on the basis of correlations of English and foreign words, established between very large bilingual corpora, assumes that 'symbolic,' non-quantitative, MT cannot do the job. The quick answer to them is again SYSTRAN, which IBM's 'proportion of sentences correct' percentage (40 per cent versus SYSTRAN's 60–70 percent success rate) lags far behind, with no evidence beyond hope, energy and application of ever closing the gap. IBM's argument simply ignores what constitutes a refutation of their claims, namely, SYSTRAN.

A more detached observer might say of this clash of opinion that, while SYSTRAN has twenty years of work to its name, the IBM results would *still* be important even if all they could do was reach the same levels of accuracy as SYSTRAN, simply because the IBM procedures would be wholly automatic, requiring no linguistics, translations, text marking, rules, dictionaries or even foreign-language speakers.

However, the fallacy here is that it ignores SYSTRAN's long

history of tackling the most obvious language pairs (English–French, English–Japanese, etc.). The purported economic gain for statistical methods would have to be found in less common language pairs (in terms of translation volume): but these are, almost by definition, the very pairs for which the very large bilingual corpora the IBM method requires will not be available. So the assumption, even if true, will not yield much.

The IBM researchers would like to claim that their method will eventually outperform SYSTRAN but as it is not obvious that their method is as yet incrementally improvable as SYSTRAN has been (and that is the core subject of this chapter), there is no reason to believe their claims. It may well be that the IBM statistical techniques have already done all they can, and that their success rate (46 percent) of correctly translated sentences is simply inadequate, remarkable though it may be given their non-standard assumptions.

I do not wish to suggest that the only challenge to SYSTRAN in MT comes from the use of statistical techniques. On the contrary, a number of researchers in linguistics and artificial intelligence (AI) continue to claim that advances in linguistics, semantics and knowledge representation during the past decades now permit the construction of a wholly new MT system that will be able to break through the quality ceiling of about 65–70 percent correctly translated sentences established by SYSTRAN. I am of that school of thought, as well as being a participant in a new, large-scale, effort (Wilks *et al.* 1990) to achieve just that result with a co-operative alliance of three American university laboratories.

The last effort to surpass SYSTRAN on a substantial scale was EUROTRA (Johnson *et al.* 1985). While one must admit that its results after ten years have been undistinguished, this can be largely attributed to failures in the management of an overly large-scale international cooperative venture, and to the inappropriateness of using classical linguistic methods, as opposed to AI or knowledge-based methods. But as with everything else, time will tell whether those efforts will bear fruit or not.

The purpose of this pocket history of MT is to emphasize SYSTRAN's central role, and to establish it as *the* point of reference. Twenty years after its inception, SYSTRAN is still in the running to become the European Community's rough translator of memoranda: it is being used in Luxembourg to some degree, while EUROTRA is not. In spite of all its advantages, however,

SYSTRAN's methods and nature are both in dispute, as is the quality of its repeated performance evaluations. This shadow of doubt has many sources, including the suspicious nature of many early MT demonstrations; some doubt clings to any system, like SYSTRAN, whose origins go back to those days.

Yet since that time, there have been many evaluations of SYSTRAN, in the course of which it has performed well, and it is one of these (which I carried out for the US Air Force in 1979–80) that I wish to describe in this chapter, since I believe it to have been of considerable importance (I have received repeated requests for it over the years). This was not only because of continuing interest in SYSTRAN but also because it was an evaluation that *assumed a priori* that SYSTRAN performed MT at a level suitable for some classes of customers, and sought further to investigate the issue of how far revisions to the system done for a new type of text (in this case, political texts as opposed to the scientific Russian texts upon which the SYSTRAN Russian–English system had been built) transferred to more (unseen) texts of that type.

This test answered what is to me the key question about MT systems: how improvable are they, and what are their optimization ceilings, when new errors introduced by revisions to the lexicon or grammar equal or outweigh their benefits (i.e. sentences worsened versus those improved)? In other words, it demonstrated that, while all MT systems are certain to fail in many cases, what counts is their flexibility and improvability. In this and other ways, I believe, SYSTRAN has discovered answers while evolving methods more familiar to AI than to linguistics proper. This may sound to some an absurd remark since, by conventional standards, SYSTRAN has neither conventional linguistic–syntactic rules, nor any explicit representation of world knowledge of the kind found in many AI systems. This is because, as I argued elsewhere (Wilks 1990), SYSTRAN confirms two 'principles' of MT:

a any theory (however absurd) can be the basis of an MT system; and
b MT systems, if they have substantial coverage, normally do not operate by means of their stated principles.

While SYSTRAN translates to a reasonably high degree of proficiency, it has no underlying theory that a theoretical linguist would acknowledge as such: hence we have (a) above. SYSTRAN has been the subject of few published descriptions (though see

Toma 1976), most of which have described it in terms of multiple passes through texts and the extraction of phrases and clauses by a 'partial parser.' But, in fact, there is good reason to believe that SYSTRAN's original Russian–English performance is as good as it is because of the very large number of long word-collocations in Russian (about 300,000, together with a 300,000-word stem vocabulary): hence we have principle (b) above.

One can view this as an early application of what in AI is now called 'case-based techniques': the storage of very large numbers of individual cases of usage. Again, partial parsing is a technique that is constantly being rediscovered in AI (e.g. Jacobs *et al.* 1991), as are techniques for controlling and keeping in use large bodies of usable but antique software whose internal structure is no longer modifiable. In the case of SYSTRAN, of course, it is its core routines that are no longer modifiable but which are simply imported *en bloc* when a new language pair is started. It is for this reason (the reusability of blocks of analysis and generation software, even if they have little function in reality) that SYSTRAN has been described by its owners as a *transfer* rather than a direct system, even though, in fact, it has no true separable transfer lexicon for a language pair.

In conclusion, the power of SYSTRAN lies in its well-established and relentless system of lexicon modification and augmentation in the face of bad translation results. It is these cycles that yield its subsequently high performance levels; the role of the following experiments was to see how far the process could go when SYSTRAN's capabilities were applied to a totally new subject area.

BACKGROUND: ASSESSMENT OF THE FTD/MT SYSTEMS

What follows is different from previous assessments of the SYSTRAN system in two ways:

1 the subject matter tested (political articles and books) differs greatly from the scientific areas for which the SYSTRAN FTD/MT system was originally designed;
2 the methodology of the present study differs from all existing

studies with the exception of the Battelle Memorial Institute report (1977), henceforth referred to as BR.

The present project's goals in evaluating the US Foreign Technology Division's (FTD) version of SYSTRAN committed it to the BR methodology, at the core of which is an important and valuable point (I shall touch on some of BR's shortcomings later). Given a realistic and developing system like SYSTRAN, a sensible questionnaire would not require an evaluator to assign an arbitrary value to a translated sentence (such as six or seven on a scale of ten) but rather would reduce evaluator judgments to the form:

Sentence X is better than sentence Y in terms of quality Z

where Z might be translation accuracy or some other wholly internal quality of the target language material, such as intelligibility or naturalness of the language.

Such a method is appropriate to a system like FTD's SYSTRAN which is constantly being updated and improved in the face of new requirements (i.e. new Russian language usages). According to BR, it is reasonable to ask an evaluator: 'Is version X better than version Y in terms of quality Z?' where X and Y are two different target-language translations of the same source language string (English, we shall assume here, translated from Russian) and Y was produced after the correction of errors found in a body of sentences that may or may not have included X. If the corpus whose errors were corrected did include X, then the improvement of Y over X is to be expected. If X was *not* in the corpus update but Y improved anyway, then that would be very interesting to us indeed, and this is the heart of the BR method.

Our testing method had two such corpora: texts that were updated with corrections after a 'first run', and whose corrections were fed into the system's dictionaries and rules, and those whose improvement was *not* examined after the first run but after the second run only. This latter was the *control text*, the most significant for our study: if great translation improvements were subsequently achieved in this non-updated corpus, that would indicate that a continually expanding and updating MT system may be economically viable.

Restricting oneself to this form of qualitative assessment, as the BR method does, rules out the use of some of the more original methods of MT assessment, such as Carroll's, in which an evaluator judged whether a translation from FTD was informative by comparing it to a normative (correct) translation (Carroll 1966). The assumption here was that if the translation was informative (compared to the original) it must be, to that degree, wrong. Monolinguals could perform that function, and bilinguals could compare the machine translation to the original source text as well. Carroll's method was only appropriate for relatively small text samples for which high-quality normative translations could be given, however. And, more importantly, his methodology also assumed that the question, 'How well does the FTD/MT system translate?' had been answered elsewhere. The present study assumes that too and, that having satisfactorily answered that question, we are free to discover how far updating improves the translation of unseen sentences.

A key element in the BR methodology was the prominence given to monolinguals. The origin of such an emphasis can be found in the following passages from the ALPAC report.

> The results from the ratings by bilinguals contribute nothing more to the differentiation of the translations than is obtainable with the monolinguals' ratings . . . one is inclined to give more credence to the results from the monolinguals because monolinguals are more representative of potential users of translations and are not influenced by knowledge of the source language.
>
> (ALPAC 1966: 72)

This passage will undoubtedly elicit conflicting reactions in readers: on the one hand, given that a high correlation between fidelity and intelligibility is well established with regard to translation, the above seems reasonable enough. And, as we shall see, some of the bilinguals' odd behavior in the present study can only be explained if we, too, assume that they are adversely influenced by their knowledge of the source text when making certain judgments. On the other hand, it is quite risky to base one's judgment of MT largely on the performance of monolinguals, if only because sentences may be intelligible and coherent without being faithful translations, something a monolingual would have no way of spotting.

In this study, we used three monolinguals and six bilinguals and, despite the discrepancies among the former group's judgments, all agreed on the improvements of the control text sentences. It turned out that our results relied more heavily than we expected upon the evidence provided by the bilingual evaluators. It also should be noted that nothing in our study challenged the hypothesized correlation between fidelity and intelligibility: the statistics for the present study were not analyzed in such a way as to allow that to be tested for individual sentences.

THE BATTELLE REPORT: ITS METHODOLOGY AND SHORTCOMINGS

The BR had two objectives: it surveyed existing methods of machine translation evaluation, and then applied a version of the updating methodology sketched above to a sample of scientific texts. In this section I will examine discussions of monolingual evaluation and its relation to categories such as intelligibility.

The arguments for monolingual evaluation in the BR survey of evaluation methods were twofold: first, that estimates of the fidelity (correctness) of a translation strongly correlate to estimates of its quality in monolingual judgments of the output. And, second, that a monolingual expert can be expected to judge the overall coherence of an output text since, as a text lengthens, the chances of its being both coherent and incorrect approach zero.

BR counted as distinct the following three concepts that it completely failed to distinguish: intelligibility, comprehensibility and readability (Battelle 1977: 10–11). At first glance, it might seem that the difference between these categories is one of scale (with only *comprehensibility* applying to entire texts) but the intelligibility test is also applied by it to long sequences of output. Likewise, readability which 'measures the appropriate overall contextual cohesivness' of a text (Battelle 1977: 14) has little obvious contrast to the previous two categories. Indeed, the three separate tests given (one rating output on a 'clarity scale', the second asking questions about the content of the output and the third 'Cloze technique' requiring a subject to fill in word gaps left at regular intervals in the output) could be applied equally to any of the three concepts with no change in the results. What is actually being discussed here are three different methods of measuring *coherence*, nothing more.

Battelle also seems to miss the significance of its essentially monolingual tests when it asserts:

Although results obtained from these methods may correlate well with quality of translation [*monolingual quality assessment: YW*], many of them do not really test the correctness of translation, the basic purpose of both an MT system and an evaluation method.

(Battelle 1977: 23)

This completely contradicts its earlier remark that, in a significant class of cases, monolingually judged quality and correctness of translation correlate strongly.

Despite these ambiguities, Battelle's survey of monolingual tests gives us a useful notion of test coherence that can be assessed by experts ignorant of the source language. Moreover, we can be confident that the results of such tests may well continue to correlate strongly with bilingually assessed translation correctness, which brings us to our adaptation of its experimental design.

METHODOLOGY OF THE PRESENT TEST

The test had the following stages:

i   Text materials containing one-and-a-half million Russian words were sent from FTD to LATSEC, the SYSTRAN company in California.
ii   Of these, 150,000 were chosen by a random procedure and divided into two roughly equal groups of documents: the object or update text (O) and the control text (C).
iii Both texts were keypunched and the object text translated by an existing copy of the FTD/MT Russian–English MT system.
iv   The control text was left unexamined and untouched, while errors in the translation of the object text were analyzed at LATSEC, and dictionary and program corrections implemented for them. This process took four-and-a-half months, during which 2,750 stem dictionary entries and 2,800 expression dictionary entries were updated.
v   With the update system inserted, a second version of the MT program was created which was then run on both object and control texts.
vi   The first copy of the MT system (without the updating) was then run on the control text, thus creating four sets of output: first runs of object and control texts and second runs of both.
vii A comparator program took the first and second runs of each

text and listed only those sentences that were changed between runs.

viii The two outputs of the comparator program (one object, one control) were each divided into three parts.

ix Evaluators were chosen at three sites as follows:

A at Essex University, two bilinguals familiar with Russian–English translation but not with MT, plus one monolingual with qualifications in political science, were named A1, A2, A3, respectively;

B at FTD, three bilinguals familiar with MT were named B1, B2, B3, respectively;

C at LATSEC, the inverse of (A) was done: one non-MT bilingual plus two monolinguals familiar with the subject matter were chosen, called C3, C1, C2, respectively.

Each evaluator with a given digit in their name code received that same one-third of the change object and control text.

x Each evaluator received the same instructions and questionnaire (see below). The sentences came to them in the form of a Russian sentence, a first-run English sentence or a second-run English sentence. These last two sentences were randomly ordered, so as to avoid any assumption that the second was 'better'. For each of three questions the evaluator was asked to choose one of the four answers A, B, C, or D. Their choice was indicated by circling one of the letters on a computer form containing the number of the sentence and the letters A to D. Answer sheets were mailed directly back to LATSEC.

xi A totalizator program compiled the results from each evaluator for each set of texts, plus monolingual and bilingual totals and these in turn were subjected to statistical analysis.

xii The evaluators were asked to give their reactions to the test and questionnaire, and some were asked to review sample sentences, answering with different choice orders, and to count the Russian words that survived translation (for the significance of this, see questionnaire below).

Precautions taken against bias and to ensure security of the data

For anyone, especially those who are sceptical about MT or the FTD/MT system in particular, it is critical to be sure that none of the updatings were performed on the control text, for the 'unplanned' improvement of the control text (or carry-over effect) is at the very heart of the study. And, while no methodology is foolproof, we believe that ours took all reasonable precautions against obvious sources of bias in its results, and against any criticisms that must inevitably arise about the security of the control text.

Test selection

A keypuncher at LATSEC prepared a card for each document in the one-and-a-half million word Russian corpus. On each card was punched the number of one of the documents and a random number (these being taken from the standard library copy of a random number table, starting on the first page with the first number, and continuing in order from that page). The pack of cards prepared for all the documents in the corpus went to Teledyne Ryan who ran it through a standard program that sorts random numbers in ascending order. LATSEC then keypunched the Russian documents by taking their numbers from the ordered list provided by Teledyne Ryan (taking the document numbers in turn which corresponded one-to-one in that they were on the same card) to the random numbers, now in numerical sequence.

For security, the original card pack was then sent to FTD so that the whole procedure could be verified later with any standard sorting program. We believe this procedure gave a random selection of 150,000 Russian words by LATSEC keypunching down the list until that total was reached (the first 75,000 becoming the object text so that translation and updating could start immediately, and the second 75,000 becoming the control text). While this method was perhaps overly detailed, it yielded a significant sample of the corpus by any normal statistical criteria, one which compared very well in terms of sample size with experiments referred to in other surveys.

Anonymity and spread of evaluators

The nine evaluators were marked on the totalized output by their code names only (A1, . . . C3). They communicated directly with LATSEC, and their identities were not divulged to the project director. As previously noted, the evaluators were not only of three types but were from three sites: six out of nine had no previous connection with LATSEC.

Order of A, B, C, D choices and 1, 2, 3 questions

To prevent the order of questions, and answer types within questions, influencing the evaluators (such as the suggestion that both translations might be too poor to assess their relationship), the evaluators at FTD answered the questions in the orders 2 1 3, 3 2 1, 3 2 1, while all other evaluators used orders 1 2 3; Essex evaluators further redid a sample of their answers to the questions with the choices re-ordered as BCDA.

Order of presentation of the English translations

An obvious source of bias would have been the ordering of first- and second-run English translations in regular patterns, creating an order bias in quality assessment. To avoid such a bias, the two translations were presented in random order on the data sheets, and the input answers corrected for this by the totalizator program question by question.

Security of the control text

The first-run MT program was copied and sent to FTD so that it could be tested later to ensure that it was in fact the program that ran on the control text. More substantially, each sheet used by LATSEC in updating the object text (like all the originals, these were sent to FTD at the end of the project) was labeled with the text and sentence number that gave rise to update for later reference.

Finally, FTD was sent a copy of all the updates made during the project for incorporation into its system, so that it could run the following smallscale check: taking a number of updates from the whole set, it traced back (via the hand-marked sheets and the texts) to ensure that they did indeed arise from a text in the object sample rather than the control text.

RESULTS OF THE STUDY AND THEIR SIGNIFICANCE

Let us begin by asking the main question: has this procedure improved translation quality as judged by bilinguals?

Question 1: fidelity of translation as judged by FTD and non-FTD bilinguals

Of 3,655 sentences analyzed by both FTD and non-FTD bilinguals, the standard application of confidence intervals around any of the percentages for responses A through D shows them to be statistically significant, due to the large sample size of the texts (see the appendix for the A, B, C, D codes). Using the orthodox formula for confidence intervals yielded a maximum error (at the 95 percent confidence level) of less than 2 percent either way for any of these categories. It was thus established that the technique did improve the translation, with an improvement rate of 47 ± 2 percent.

The pattern and significance levels were the same for both FTD and non-FTD evaluators, with a large variance within both sets of results. The percentage of C codes given varies inside both teams by around 14per cent. The FTD team had a high of 53per cent improvement by one evaluator, while the non-FTD team went from 51 percent to 38 percent accuracy, a difference that cannot be accounted for by the varying difficulty of the text batches (the batch which for B2 improved by 38 percent caused A2 to find 47 percent improvement).

These differences of proportion (Z test = 5.89) are statistically significant at any known level. As the frequency of B code judgments also varied (though not as much), the most obvious measure of success (percentage improved minus percentage made worse) fluctuated considerably. The table below shows this:

Evaluator	C code %	B code %	Balance of improvement = C–B%
A1	53	11	42
A2	47	10	37
C3	41	6	35
B1	45	7	38
B2	38	15	23
B3	51	13	38

The average, it should be noted, was for a net improvement rate of 36 per cent. We now turn to the control text results for the carry-over effect on question 1.

Once more, the basic table shows us the consistency between the aggregate results of the two teams, how the results demonstrated a statistically significant improvement and that the A/D distinction was an unreliable one, although the combined A + D response categories were nearly constant between the two teams (a matter I shall return to below).

Non-FTD team

Answer codes	A %	B %	C %	D %
	44	10	29	17

Total sentences analyzed: 3,127

FTD team

Answer codes	A %	B %	C %	D %
	42	13	31	14

Total sentences analyzed: 3,127

Note: Some sets of figures do not add up to 100 because of rounding errors. The margin of error for any of these percentages was again less than ± 2 per cent.

The fluctuation range was much the same over evaluators as before, though its net impact is less important. The table below gives the balance, and, of course, displays the range of fluctuation:

Evaluator	B code %	C code %	Balance of improvement = C − B%
A1	21	42	21
A2	9	30	21
C3	41	6	−35
B1	14	35	21
B2	12	25	13
B3	13	38	25

Note: Some sets of figures do not add up to 100 because of rounding errors.

Question 2: intelligibility

The results may be summarized as follows:

Team	Object text Codes A %	B %	C %	D %	Control text Codes A %	B %	C %	D %
Non-FTD	32	8	46	14	37	9	31	23
FTD	27	11	51	11	21	18	44	17
Mono	10	13	48	29	12	11	28	50

Note: Some sets of figures do not add up to 100 because of rounding errors. All percentages accurate to ± 1%.

These results generally confirm that for both object (O) and control (C) texts, there was a significant improvement in the second translation. For the O text, this should be assessed as 44 percent to 53 percent improvement. (All C code percentages have a margin of error of no more than 2 percent.) Little attention should be paid to the monolingual value (especially where it differs in the C text), as the three monolinguals disagreed with each other sharply. The overall result for the bilinguals can be seen by pooling the FTD and non-FTD teams as follows:

O Text = 6,304 judgments

A %	B %	C %	D %
29	10	50	11

C Text = 5,003 judgments

A %	B %	C %	D %
25	16	40	19

Note: Some sets of figures do not add up to 100 because of rounding errors. All percentages accurate to ± 1%.

This shows us an average improvement (C − B%) of 40 percent for the object text and 24 percent for the control text, subject to the limits shown.

Question 3: naturalness of the English

In some ways, these were the most interesting results, in that they clearly showed the difference between monolinguals and bilinguals. The table below gives the percentages for the two bilingual teams and the monolinguals separately:

	O Text				C Text			
	A %	B %	C %	D %	A %	B %	C %	D %
Non-FTD	61	4	22	13	65	5	18	12
FTD	71	5	20	4	88	3	7	2
C1	4	15	57	23	3	23	49	24
C2 mono	3	16	59	23	9	18	46	27
A3	23	9	32	37	18	9	33	40

Note: Some sets of figures do not add up to 100 because of rounding errors. All percentages accurate to ± 2%.

(All percentages in this table have a statistical margin of error of less than 5 percent.) Here we see that bilinguals were unprepared to treat the sentences as good enough to make judgments about them on this dimension, although they did judge there to be a significant improvement (20 percent). The monolinguals, on the other hand, found the judgement relatively easy to make, and found nearly 50 percent improvement for the O text, reduced to just under 40 percent for the C text (I shall return to this contrast later).

To summarize the results in one great table (see Appendix for the questions asked):

Proportion of improvement (i.e., column C responses, not improvement balance C–B)

Group	Update (object) text			Control text		
	Qu1 %	Qu2 %	Qu3 %	Qu1 %	Qu2 %	Qu3 %
Non-FTD	48* (3,655)	46 (3,655)	22* (3,655)	29* (3,127)	31 (3,127)	18 (3,127)
FTD	45 (3,654)	51 (3,654)	20* (3,654)	31* (3,127)	44 (3,127)	72 (3,127)
Mono	—	48 (2,645)	52 (2,645)	—	28 (1,876)	37 (1,876)
All	—	45	30	—	34 (9,381)	21 (9,381)

Note: All these figures were subject to very small error margins (1.5–2.5 per cent), and are statistically significant. The slots followed by an asterisk are those in which the FTD/non-FTD differences are insignificant.

The effect of question and choice order

The complete results show us that inter-evaluator disagreement was high and that question order might have been one cause of this, as the FTD bilinguals answered not in order 1 2 3 but 2 1 3, 3 2 1 and 3 2 1, respectively. While question order as one possible cause of the variance cannot be ruled out, I do not believe it explains much of it. The table below demonstrates that there is no significant difference between improvement percentages among any of the orderings in question 1.

Group and ordering	A %	B %	C %	D %
A1, A2 and C3 (1 2 3)	31	9	47	13
B1 (2 1 3)	41	7	45	7
B2 and 3 (3 2 1)	34	14	45	8

Note: Some sets of figures do not add up to 100 because of rounding errors. All percentages accurate to ± 1%.

One might argue that the difference in question 3's results was dependent on ordering: those who answered it last (non-FTD and B1 at FTD) were less likely to find improvement (only 18 percent of the cases), while B2 and 3 (at FTD), who answered it fiirst, found a 28 percent improvement. But if we look further, we find that there was actually more disagreement within this order group (B2 = 19 percent, B3 = 33 percent) than between the two groups! Furthermore, A3 (non-FTD) found as high an improvement score (32 per cent) as did B3 (FTD), while C3 (non-FTD) found an even higher one (38 percent).

To investigate the effect of choice order, the Essex (A) group re-did a large sample of their data sheets in the choice order B C D A. The average difference they found was around 4 per cent: most likely an insignificant figure.

Evaluator variance

As already noted, a striking feature of the results is the high level of evaluator variance. The standard deviation of the twenty-four individual judgments made by nine evaluators on three questions (monos did not answer the first question) is very high: 17.2 percent (19.4 percent for the control text) for the proportion deemed judgeable (the sum of B+C percent). While this is unfortunate, it is compensated for by the much lower standard deviation for those judgments that were made, around 4.8–4.9 percent. In other words, we should attach little importance to the figures when a sentence translation pair (i.e. first run, second run) could not be judged as different, but considerable reliability to the 70–80 percent figure for improvement when a decision could be made.

Thus while the average unjudgeable (A+D) proportion was 50 percent for O text and 60 percent for C text, the range within which the true figure lies is much greater, for the margin of error was +7 percent. But for the actual judgments, we can confidently state that the error range was less than 2 percent. This is reassuring because had the reverse result occurred (i.e. had the evaluations of improvement varied greatly in a subjective way), we would have had cause to doubt our entire methodology of evaluation.

Further confirmation of our method came from examining correlations between evaluations of O and C texts. Reassuringly, the correlation coefficient over the 25 judgements made on each text is not significantly different from zero. On the other hand, the tendency to deem sentences unjudgeable was shown to arise from evaluators' individual differences in outlook; the correlation between each evaluator's unjudgeability evaluations for each question between O and C text was amazingly high (0.913). As this clearly did not represent any actual link between such evaluation items (the texts having been drawn at random), the average level and the variance of these decisions should not concern us.

SHORTCOMINGS OF THE PRESENT STUDY

After the completion of their task, the evaluators were invited to comment on the questionnaire and the entire study in which they had taken part. Their comments are distilled in the following discussion of a number of interconnected problems:

The A/D choice

Even for the bilinguals, the distinction between codes A and D seemed unreliable (monolinguals had no way of expressing their preference for a D-choice sentence, as the bilinguals could by choosing A, for instance). The FTD team found 7 percent more sentences to be unjudgeable because of translation errors (choice A), and 7 percent fewer sentences undifferentiable (choice D). This pattern was further highlighted by the individual evaluator's distinctions: there was a high negative correlation (−0.715) between categories A and D. The ambiguity follows from the fact that the choices Code A (either i: both English sentences are so bad as translations that no choice can be made between them; or ii: both English sentences contain Russian words) or Code D (iii: no preference) are subjective. Of these, (ii) is an objective assessment, while (i) and (iii) are not mutually exclusive. Our assumption was that choice D applied to two equally acceptable translations, and choice A to two equally unacceptable translations but, unfortunately, the evaluators appear not to have acted according to our assumption.

The basic error here was not a lack of strict definition for the categories (as some monolinguals felt) but asymmetry between mono and bilinguals. This may have contributed to the wide variance (and hence downgrading) of the monolinguals' evidence. To compensate for this effect, we simply combined choices A and D into an 'unjudgeable' category, leaving us with three possibilities: worsened, improved and unjudgeable translations.

The 'question 3 effect'

Certainly, the strong negative correlation between choices A and D cannot be explained away by a mistaken blurring of the two categories (as can be seen by the strikingly different A/D behavior of the mono and bilinguals between questions 2 and 3). As I remarked earlier, in responding to question 3 the bilinguals simply declined to judge the naturalness of the English, and often took refuge in choice A, even though they were quite prepared to accept these same translations in question 2 on the basis of intelligibility (A choices for question 2 for the two bilingual groups were 37 percent and 21 percent versus 65 percent and 88 percent for question 3), while the monolinguals had no problem making the choice, a fact that confirms the value of monolingual judgments.

The original sampling of O and C texts

Our process standardized the total number of words in the documents but not the number of documents in each sample. Thus, if document length varied greatly, word samples drawn from a smaller number of long texts would be chosen alongside word samples drawn from a large number of short texts, which creates a problem if there is, in fact, a relationship between the length of a text and the nature of its language. By making the documents sampled units, a random selection could have represented them proportionately to the frequency with which different text lengths co-occurred in the corpus. But happily, no such problem arose.

The 'Russian word problem'

Part of the A choices refer to the presence of Russian words in the output but, as we saw with B1, an evaluator may be tempted to interpret this loosely (considering the word's meaning obvious, or unimportant), or deeming a Cyrillic misspelling not a Russian word. On the other hand, some monolinguals can guess the meaning of a Russian word, especially if it is close to the Latin spelling, as in N'YUSDEY ('Newsday' in 78054/177). Furthermore, the questionnaire forces the monolingual to choose the sentence without Russian words as more natural English. Finally, there were many sentences where the program translated a proper name into English, also creating confusion in the mind of the monolinguals, who might well believe that (wholly) English sentences contained Russian words.

In summary, what it meant for a sentence to contain a Russian word was not made totally clear, presenting a genuine difficulty for clarity. As fewer than 10 percent of the sentences contained Russian words, this had a negligible effect on our results. In future tests, the problem could be avoided by removing untranslated items in the sentences from the data seen by the evaluators.

Monolingual expertise

It is generally accepted that the value of monolingual evaluation in scientific subjets depends on monolingual subject expertise. While our monolingual evaluators all had some expertise in the field of political science, this simply did not transfer from Russian to English in the way that a universally understood area like physics would. To some degree, this explains the high variance among the monolinguals, and their consequently diminished role compared to the BR study of scientific texts.

CONCLUSION: SUMMARY OF FINDINGS

1 While the Battelle Report was poorly argued and statistically flawed, it provided us with the methodological basis for a new study.

2 The most significant finding was the 20 percent carry-over effect from updated to control text (balance of improvement: 30 percent of sentences improved minus 10 percent worsened) in a very different subject area from the one for which the system was originally developed.

3 There was a very high variance among evaluators, especially monolinguals. This was reduced to a significant result by distinguishing between sentences deemed judgeable and, of those judgeable, taking those deemed improved. While variance as to what was judgeable remained high, in the vital category of which judgeables were improved, variance was minimal: a strong, indirect confirmation of our methodology.

4 Since the question of naturalness of English output produced an odd response in the bilinguals, it is better ignored, especially as this notion is of little importance to the ultimate monolingual user, in any case.

APPENDIX

Notes for evaluators

It is most important that you study these notes and the questionnaire before reading the data.

In the body of the data you will find sets of three items: a Russian sentence followed by two English sentences. If you do not know any Russian, you should simply ignore the former, and concentrate on the latter. The English sentences which contain items that are not really in English (those that contain numbers, for instance) are easily spotted, and will be referred to in the questions as Russian words, even though they are written mostly in the English alphabet.

When looking at the English sentences you should ignore all questions of stylistic nicety, such as differences between British and

American English, and think only in terms of what is natural English for you.

When looking at both the Russian and the English, you should be careful not to assume that the sets of sentences form coherent, continuous texts; rather, you should treat each triplet individually. Also, do not assume that the second English sentence is better than the first: the order of the sentence pairs is entirely random.

The difference between 'understandable' and 'natural' can be illustrated as follows: the sentences 'To John gave I the apple' and 'I want you go now' are both understandable but not natural English.

Questionnaire

Each line on the form corresponds to one sentence triplet (one Russian and two English) by number. Each numbered section below corresponds to a column on the answer form. You should circle one and only one letter (A, B, C or D) for each question and then do that for each sentence triplet in the data.

1 (enter in column 1 for each triplet)
  Look at the set of three sentences and consider (if you can) whether the English sentences are accurate translations of the Russian one.

Circle

A if you do not speak Russian, OR if you speak Russian and consider both English sentences to be such bad translations that no choice can be made between them, OR if you speak Russian and can see that BOTH English sentences contain Russian words

B if you prefer the first sentence as an accurate translation

C if you prefer the second sentence

D if you have no preference

2 (enter in column 2 for each triplet)
  Now look at only the English sentences in the triplet, and ask yourself if you can comprehend them as such, accounting for your knowledge of the subject matter.

Circle

A if you speak Rusian, but consider both texts to be such bad translations that you decline to form a judgment, OR if both

English sentences contain Russian words (this option is available to non-Russian speakers, as well)

B if you prefer the first sentence for its understandability
C if you prefer the second sentence
D if you have no preference

3 (enter in column 3 for each triplet)
Consider the English sentences alone once more, and judge their naturalness of language (word order, word choice and so forth).

Circle

A if you speak Russian and consider both sentences such bad translations of the Russian that you decline to make this judgment, OR if both English sentences contain Russian words (once again, you can select this if you do not speak Russian but should NOT do so if only one of the English sentences contains Russian words)
B if you prefer the first sentence for the naturalness of its English
C if you prefer the second sentence
D if you have no preference

BIBLIOGRAPHY

ALPAC (1966) *Language and Machines: Computers in Translation and Linguistics* (Report by the Automatic Language Processing Advisory Committee, Division of Behavioral Sciences, National Research Council), Washington, DC: National Academy of Sciences.

Battelle Columbus Laboratories (1977) 'The evaluation and systems analysis of the SYSTRAN machine translation system', RADC–TR–76–399 Technical Report.

Brown, P.F., Cocke, J., Della Pietra, S.A., Della Pietra, V.J., Jelinek, F., Lafferty, J.D., Mercer, R.L. and Roossin, P.S. (1990) 'A statistical approach to machine translation', *Computational Linguistics* 16: 79–85.

Carroll, J.B. (1966) 'An experiment in evaluating the quality of translations', *Mechanical Translation and Computational Linguistics* 9 (3 & 4): 55–66.

Jacobs, P., Krupka, G. and Rau, L. (1991) 'Lexico-semantic pattern matching as a companion to parsing in text understanding', in *Proceedings of the DARPA Speech and Natural Language Workshop*, Monterey, California.

Johnson, R., King, M. and des Tombe, L. (1985) 'EUROTRA: a multilingual system under development', in *Computational Linguistics* 11 (2–3): 155–69.

Toma, P. (1976) 'An operational machine translation system', in R.W.

Brislin (ed.) *Translation: Applications and Research*, New York: Gardner, 247–59.

Wilks, Y. (1990) 'Form and content in semantics', in *Synthèse* 82: 329–51.

Wilks, Y., Carbonell, J., Farwell, D., Hovy, E. and Nirenburg, S. (1990) 'Machine translation again?', in *Proceedings of the DARPA Speech and Natural Language Workshop*, Monterey, California.

Chapter 11

Current research in machine translation

Harold L. Somers

INTRODUCTION

The purpose of this chapter is to give a view of current research in machine translation (MT). It is written on the assumption that readers are, in fact, more or less familiar with most of the well-known current MT projects, or else can find out more about them by following up the references given. The research described here will be divided into two sets: the members of the first set have in common a direct line of descent from the classical 'second generation' design. The second set forms a significantly different set and heterogeneous group of current MT research projects — mostly rather less well known — having in common only the feature that they in some sense reject the conventional orthodoxy that typifies the first group.

Part of the background to this division is the feeling that basic *research* within the second-generation paradigm has reached its limits: for example, it could be said that in the twenty-six years since the ALPAC report of 1966, the second-generation architecture has led to only slightly better results than the architecture it replaced; so from a research point of view it is timely to question *all* the assumptions that have been accepted unequivocally in that period, *just to see what would happen*. I will return to this view later.

PROBLEMS WITH THE CLASSICAL SECOND-GENERATION ARCHITECTURE

Let me start by considering the classical second-generation architecture. Examples would be GETA's ARIANE system (Boitet and Nedobejkine 1981; Vauquois 1985; Vauquois and Boitet 1985), TAUM's METEO (Chevalier *et al.* 1981; Lehrberger and

Bourbeau 1988), the European Commission's EUROTRA (Raw *et al.* 1988, 1989; Steiner (ed.) 1991) and several other systems which incorporate most of the typical design features. These include the well-known notions of linguistic rule-writing formalisms with software implemented independently of the linguistic procedures, stratificational analysis and generation, and an intermediate linguistically motivated representation which may or may not involve the direct application of contrastive linguistic knowledge. The key unifying feature is *modularity*, both 'horizontal' and 'vertical': the linguistic formalisms are supposed to be declarative, so that linguistic and computational issues are separated; and the whole process is divided up into computationally and/or linguistically convenient modules.

While these are admirable design features, at least insofar as they seem to address the perceived problems of MT system design pre-ALPAC, they also lead to several general or specific deficiencies in design.

In general, they reflect the preferred computational and linguistic techniques of the late 1960s and early 1970s, which have to a great extent been superseded. There are now several viable alternatives to the procedural algorithmic strictly typed programming style; while in linguistics the transformational–generative paradigm and its associated stratificational view of linguistic processing (morphology – surface syntax – deep syntax) has become somewhat old-fashioned.

A serious problem with the stratificational approach is the extent to which it encourages an approach to translation which I have called 'structure-preserving translation as first choice' (Somers *et al.* 1988: 5). This stems from the commitment to compositionality in translation, i.e. that the translation of the whole is some not too complex function over the translations of the parts. This leads to a strategy which embodies the motto, 'Let's produce translations that are as literal as we can get away with' (Somers 1986: 84). Notice that this is in direct contrast to the human translator's view, which is roughly 'structure-preserving translation as a last resort'. This attitude can be seen again in discussions of the need to limit 'structural transfer' and to build systems which are essentially interlingual systems with lexical transfer. But we know very well the difficulties of designing an interlingua, even if we remove the burden of a 'conceptual lexicon'.

I must admit that I do not have a ready solution here. But it seems to me important to recognize the limitations and pitfalls of the now traditional stratified linguistic approach to both processing and representation, so that even the apparently well-established technique should not necessarily be assumed as a 'given' in MT system design.

I will end this section by making one other observation. This is that all MT systems so far have been designed with the assumption that the source text contains enough information to permit translation. This is obviously true of non-interactive systems; but it is also true even of the few systems which interact with a user *during processing* in order to disambiguate the source text or to make decisions (usually regarding lexical choice) about the target text. Notice, by the way, that I want to distinguish here between truly interactive systems, and those which merely incorporate some sort of interactive post-editing. In fact, very few research systems are truly interactive in this sense (e.g. Ntran – see below). However, the point I want to make concerns how MT researchers view this problem: it is seen as a deficiency of the system – that is to say, either the linguistic theory used, or its implementation – rather than of the text. Consequently, the solutions offered almost inevitably involve trying to enhance the performance of the part of the system seen to be at fault: incorporating a better semantic theory, dealing with translation units bigger than single sentences, trying to take account of contextual or real-word knowledge. Of course, these are all worthy research aims but I think the extent to which they will address the problems they are supposed to solve is generally exaggerated.

CURRENT RESEARCH DIRECTLY DESCENDED FROM THAT ARCHITECTURE

I want to look now at current research projects which I take to be directly descended from the second-generation architecture, and which, therefore, in a sense can be said to be subject to the same criticisms. The research projects in this group can be divided into subgroups according to which specific part of the problem of MT, as traditionally viewed, they try to address. So we have projects which address the problem of insufficient contextual and real-world knowledge; projects which seek a more elegant linguistic or computational linguistic framework; and projects where translation quality is enhanced by constraining the input.

For a while now it has been the conventional wisdom that the next advance in MT design – the 'third generation' – would involve the incorporation of techniques from AI. In his instant classic, Hutchins is typical in this respect:

> The difficulties and past 'failures' of linguistics-oriented MT point to the need for AI semantics-based approaches: semantic parsers, preference semantics, knowledge databases, inference routines, expert systems, and the rest of the AI techniques.
>
> (Hutchins 1986: 327)

He goes on to say:

> There is no denying the basic AI argument that at some stage translation involves the 'understanding' of a [source language] text in order to convey its 'meaning' in a [target language] text.
>
> (*idem*)

In fact, this assertion has been questioned by several commentators (Johnson 1983: 37; Slocum 1985: 16), as Hutchins himself notes.

Incorporating AI techniques

Returning to the question of AI-oriented 'third-generation' MT systems, it is probably fair to say that the most notable example of this approach is at the Center for Machine Translation at Carnegie Mellon University (CMU), where a significantly sized research team was expressly set up to pursue the question of 'knowledge-based MT' (KBMT) (Carbonell and Tomita 1987). Similar work on the Japanese ATR project has recently been reported (Kudo 1990). What then are the 'AI techniques' which the CMU team has incorporated into its MT system, and how do we judge them?

In the Nirenburg and Carbonell description of KBMT, the emphasis seems to be on the need to integrate discourse pragmatics in order to get pronouns and anaphora right (Nirenburg and Carbonell 1987). This requires texts to be mapped onto a corresponding knowledge representation in the form of a frame-based conceptual interlingua. More recent descriptions of the project (Nirenburg 1989; Nirenburg and Levin 1989) stress the use of domain knowledge. In Kudo's case, local 'cohesive' knowledge (in a dialogue) is stressed. These are well-respected techniques in the general field of AI, and we cannot gainsay their application to MT. But as twenty years of AI research has shown, the step up from a prototype 'toy' implementation to a more fully practical implementation is a huge one. And there still remain doubts as to whether the improvement of quality achieved by these AI techniques is commensurate with the additional computation they involve.

Better linguistic theories

It is normally said that a major design advance from the first to the second generation of MT systems was the incorporation of better linguistic theories, and there is certainly a group of current research projects which can be said to be focusing on this aspect. This is especially true if we extend the term 'linguistic' to include 'computational linguistic' theories. The scientific significance of the biggest of all the MT research projects – EUROTRA – can be seen as primarily in its development of existing linguistic models, and notable innovations include the work on the representation of tense (van Eynde 1988), work on homogeneous representation of heterogeneous linguistic phenomena (especially through the idea of 'featurization of purely surface syntactic elements, and a coherent theory of 'canonical form' (Durand et al. 1991), as well as, in some cases, the first ever wide-coverage formal (i.e. computational) descriptions of several European languages. As much as anything else, EUROTRA has shown the possibilities of an openly eclectic approach to computational linguistic engineering. Nevertheless, 'Eurotrians' will be the first to admit that the list of remaining problems is longer than the list of problems solved or even half solved. 'Lexical gaps', usually illustrated by the well-worn example of *like/gern*, modality and determination are just a few more or less purely linguistic problems that remain, before we even think of anaphora resolution, use of contextual and real-world knowledge and so on, already discussed.

Several research projects have taken a more doctrinaire view of linguistics in that they have explicitly set out to use MT as a testing ground for some computational linguistic theory. Most notable of these is Rosetta (Landsbergen 1987a,b) based on Montague grammar but we could also mention Ntran (Whitelock et al. 1986; Wood and Chandler 1988), which uses a combination of Lexical Functional Grammar (LFG) and Generalized Phrase Structure Grammar (GPSG) in analysis, and Categorial Grammar for generation. There are several other research projects based on specific linguistic theories, notably LFG (Rohrer 1986; Alam 1986; Kudo and Nomura 1986; Kaplan *et al.* 1989; Sadler *et al.* 1990; Zajac 1990) but also GPSG (Hauenschild 1986), Head-driven Phrase Structure Grammar (HPSG) (van Noord *et al.* 1990), Government and Binding (Wehrli 1990), Systemic functional Grammar (Bateman 1990), Tree-adjoining Grammars (Abeillé *et al.* 1990), categorial grammar (Beaven and Whitelock 1988), Functional Grammar (van der Korst 1989), Situation semantics (Rupp 1989), and, although it may be regarded as more of a programming technique than a linguistic 'theory' as such, Logic Grammar (Dymetman and Isabelle 1988; Farwell and Wilks 1989; McCord 1989). Given the right theory and programming environment it is possible to develop very quickly a reasonable state-of-the-art toy system: for example, Amores Carredano was able, in only three man-months, to build an LFG-based system programmed in PROLOG with a coverage comparable to early systems which took many man-years to develop (Amores Carredano 1990). But this says as much about our expectations of MT systems as it does about the suitability of LFG or PROLOG. In all these cases, I think it is fair to say that under the stress of use in a real practical application, the linguistic models, whose original developers were more interested in a general approach than in working out all the fine details, inevitably crack.

Sublanguage

Obviously, the most successful MT story of all is that of the METEO system, which translates daily more than 30,000 words of weather bulletins from English into French at a cost of less than 0.5 ¢ (Canadian) per word, with an accuracy rate of 95 per cent (Chandioux 1987/9: 169). The system performs a translation task too boring for any human doing it to last for more than a few months, yet sufficiently constrained to allow an MT system to be devised which only makes mistakes when the input is ill formed. Some research groups have looked for similarly constrained domains. Alternatively, the idea of *imposing* constraints on authors has a long history of association with MT. At the 1978 Aslib conference, Elliston showed how at Rank Xerox acceptable output could be got out of SYSTRAN by forcing technical writers to write in a style that would not catch the system out (Elliston 1979). It is interesting to see much the same experience reported again ten years later, at the same forum, but this time using Weidner's

MicroCat (Pym 1990). This rather haphazard activity has fortunately been 'legitimized' by its association with research in the field of language for special purposes (LSP), and the word 'sublanguage' is starting to be widely used in MT circles (e.g. Kosaka *et al.* 1988; Luckhardt 1991). In fact, I see this as a positive move, as long as 'sublanguage' is not just used as a convenient term to camouflage the same old MT design but with simplified grammar and a reduced lexicon.

Studies of sublanguage (e.g. Kittredge and Lehrberger 1982) remind us that the topic is much more complex than that: should a sublanguage be defined prescriptively (or even *pro*scriptively) as in the Elliston and Pym examples, or *de*scriptively, on the basis of some corpus judged to be a homogeneous example of the sublanguage in question? And note that even the term 'sublanguage' itself can be misleading: in most of the literature on the subject, the term is taken to mean 'special language of a particular domain' as in 'the sublanguage (of) meteorology'. Yet a more intuitive interpretation of the term, especially from the point of view of MT system designers, would be something like 'the grammar, lexicon, etc. of a particular *text-type* in a particular domain', as in 'the sublanguage of meteorological reports as given on the radio', which might share some of the lexis of, say, 'the sublanguage of scientific papers on meteorology', although clearly not (all) the grammar. By the same token, scientific papers on various subjects might share a common grammar, while differing in lexicon. Furthermore, there is the question of whether the notion of a 'core' grammar or lexicon is useful or even practical. Some of these questions are being addressed as part of one of the MT projects started in 1990 at UMIST (Manchester), concerning the design of an architecture for a system which interacts with various types of experts to 'generate' a sublanguage MT system: I will begin my final section with a brief description of this research.

SOME ALTERNATIVE AVENUES OF RESEARCH

In this final section, I would like to mention some research projects which have come to my attention which, I think, have in common that they reject, at least partially, the orthodoxy of the 'second-generation and derivative' design, or in some other way incorporate some ideas which I think significantly broaden the scope of MT research.

Sublanguage plus

One system recently proposed at UMIST is a sublanguage MT system for the Matsushita company (Ananiadou *et al.* 1990). The design is for a system with which individual sublanguage MT systems can be created, on the basis of a bilingual corpus of 'typical' texts. The system therefore has two components: a core MT engine, which is to a certain extent not unlike a typical second-generation MT system, with explicitly separate linguistic and computational components; and a set of expert systems which interact with humans in order to extract from the corpus of texts the grammar and lexicon that the linguistic part of the MT system will use. The expertise of the expert systems and the human users is divided between domain expertise and linguistic expertise, corresponding to the separate domain knowledge and linguistic knowledge (i.e. of grammars, lexicons and contrastive knowledge). Using various statistical methods (see below), the linguistic expert system will attempt to infer the grammar and lexicon of the sublanguage, on the assumption that the corpus is fully representative (and approaches closure). From our observation of other statistics-based approaches to MT, we concluded that the statistical methods needed to be 'primed' with linguistic knowledge, for example, concerning the nature of linguistic categories, morphological processes and so on. We have investigated the extent to which this can be done without going as far as to posit a core grammar, as we are uneasy about the idea that a sublanguage be defined in terms of deviation from some standard. The system will make hypotheses about the grammar and lexicon, to be confirmed by a human user, who must clearly be a linguist rather than, say, the end user. In the same way, the contrastive linguistic knowledge is extracted from the corpus, to be confirmed by interaction with a (probably different) human. Again, some 'priming' is almost always necessary.

Automatic grammar updating

A research project which I find particularly appealing concerns an MT system which revises its own grammars in response to having its output post-edited (Nishida *et al.* 1988; Nishida and Takamatsu 1990). A common complaint from post-editors is that post-editing MT output is frustrating, not least because the same errors are repeated time and time again (e.g. Green 1982). The idea that such errors can somehow be corrected by feedback from post-editors is obviously one worth pursuing vigorously.

The idea is roughly as follows: there is a fairly traditional second-generation type English–Japanese MT system (MAPTRAN) whose output is post-edited interactively. The post-editing system PECOF (*P*ost-*E*ditor's *CO*rrection *F*eedback) asks post-editors to identify which of the basic post-editing operations (replacement, insertion, deletion, movement and exchange) each correction involves, with optionally a reason expressed in terms of other words in the text, or some primitive linguistic features, e.g. 'replace *n1* by "*new word sequence*" where *n1* conflicts with *n2* in terms of *feature*'. What PECOF does with such a correction is try to locate the linguistic rule in the MT system responsible for the error, and then propose a revision of it (typically an extension to the general rule to cover the particular instance identified), which must be confirmed by the post-editor.

The way it locates the error is also of interest. Translation errors are assumed, given the architecture of MAPTRAN, to come from errors in analysis, lexical transfer or structural transfer. In order to locate which of these modules is responsible, the corrected text is subjected to reverse translation back into English using an MT system which is an exact mirror image of MAPTRAN, i.e. structural transfer precedes lexical transfer. The intermediate representations at each stage are compared with the corresponding original representations, and in this way the discrepancy is highlighted. Then, the appropriate rule can be located, and amended.

I believe that research on this system is still at an early stage, and it is obvious that only a certain category of translation error can be dealt with in this way. But it seems to be a useful way of extending the grammar and lexicon of the system to account for 'special cases' on the basis of experience, rather than relying on linguists to somehow predict things. If PECOF can also interact with the post-editor to see how generalizable a given correction is, then this is clearly an excellent way of developing a large-scale MT system.

Dialogue MT

A recent research direction to emerge is an MT system aimed at a user who is the original author of a text to be composed in a foreign language. Two such systems are Ntran, mentioned above, and

Huang's system (Huang 1990), both for use by a *monolingual* writer of the source language, which embeds this idea in a fairly standard interactive MT environment, where interaction with the machine is aimed at disambiguating the input text. An alternative scenario is one where the interaction takes place *before* text is input, in the form of a dialogue between the system and the user, in which the text to be translated is worked out, taking into account the user's communicative goals and the system's translation ability.

The idea of automatic composition of foreign language texts was suggested by Saito and Tomita (1986), and is the basis of work done at UMIST for British Telecom (Jones and Tsujii 1990). In this system, the user collaborates with the machine to produce high-quality 'translations' of business correspondence on the basis of pre-translated fragments of stereotypical texts with slots in them which are filled in by interaction. The advantage is that the system only translates what it 'knows' it can translate accurately, with the result that the system shows what MT *can* do, rather than what it cannot, as in traditional MT. Obviously, though, this strength is also a weakness in the sense of the severe limitation on what the system can be used for.

However, we can extend the idea to make it more flexible, and conceive of a system which has more scope concerning the range of things it can translate, with corresponding degrees of confidence about translation quality. This is the case in our dialogue-MT system (Somers *et al.* 1990) which we are working on in collaboration with the Japanese ATR research organization: we are constructing a system which will act as a bilingual intermediary for the user in a dialogue with a conference office, where the user wants to get information about a forthcoming conference. It is thus a 'dialogue-MT system' both in the sense that it enters into a dialogue with the user about the translation (see Boitet 1989), *and* in that the object of the translation is the user's contribution to a dialogue. Dialogue is a particularly good example of the problem, inherent in MT, that the translation of the text depends to a greater or lesser extent on the surrounding context (Tsujii and Nagao 1988). In other words, the source text alone does not carry sufficient information to ensure a good translation. We envisage a sort of MT 'expert system' which can play the role of an 'intelligent secretary with knowledge of the foreign language', gathering the information necessary to formulate the target text by asking the user questions, pushing the user towards a formulation of the 'source' text that the system can be confident of translating correctly, on the basis of some existing partial 'model translations' which have been supplied by a human expert beforehand.

The fact that the object of translation is also part of a dialogue (with another user) adds another dimension of complexity to the project described in Somers *et al.* (1990) but the idea of dialogue MT in general is an interesting development away from the current situation where the MT system makes the best of what it is given (and cannot really be sure whether or not its translation is good) towards a situation where quality can be assured by the fact that the system knows what it can do and will steer the user to the safe ground within those limitations.

Corpus-based MT

The approaches to be described in this final section have in common the idea that a pre-existing large corpus of already translated text could be used in some way to construct an MT system. They can be divided into three types, called 'memory-based', 'example-based' and 'statistics-based' translation.

Memory-based translation

The most 'linguistic' of the corpus-based approaches is 'memory-based translation' (Sato and Nagao 1990): here, example translations are used as the basis of new translations. The idea – first suggested by Nagao (1984) – is that translation is achieved by imitating the translation of a similar example in a database. The task becomes one of matching new input to the appropriate stored translation. In this connection, a secondary problem is the question of the most appropriate means of *storing* the examples. As they believe that combining fragments of sentences is an essential feature, it is natural for Sato and Nagao to think in terms of storing *linguistic* objects – notably partial syntactic trees (in their case, dependency trees). An element of statistical manipulation is introduced by the need for a scoring mechanism to choose between competing candidates. Advantages of this system are ease of modification – notably by changing or adding to the examples – and the high quality of translation seen here again, as above, as a result of translations being established *a priori* rather than compositionally (although there *is* an element of compositionality in Sato and Nagao's approach). The major disadvantage is the great deal of computation involved, especially in matching partial dependency trees.

Example-based translation

A similar approach which overcomes this major demerit has been developed quite independently by two groups of researchers at ATR in Japan (Sumita *et al.* 1990), and at UMIST in Manchester (Carroll 1990). In both cases, the central point of interest is the development of 'distance' or 'similarity' measures for sentences or parts of sentences, which permit the input sentence to be translated to be matched rapidly against a large corpus of existing translations. In Carroll's case, the measure can be 'programmed' to take account of grammatical function words and punctuation, which has the effect of making the algorithm apparently sensitive to syntactic structure without actually parsing the input as such. While Sumita *et al.*'s intention is to provide a single correct translation by this approach, Carroll's measure is used in an interactive environment as a translator's aid, selecting a *set* of apparently similar sentences from the corpus, to guide the translator in the choice of the appropriate translation. For this reason, spurious or inappropriate selections of examples can be tolerated as long as the correct selections are also made at the same time.

Statistics-based approaches

Other corpus-based approaches have been more overtly statistical or mathematical. The most notable of these is the work at IBM (Brown *et al.* 1988a,b, 1990). These researchers, encouraged by the success of statistics-based approaches to speech recognition and parsing, decided to apply similar methods to translation. Taking a huge corpus of bilingual text available in machine-readable form (3 million sentences selected from the Canadian *Hansard*), the probability that any one word in a sentence in one language corresponds to zero, one or two words in the translation is calculated. The glossary of word equivalences so established consists of lists of translation possibilities for every word, each with a corresponding probability. For example, *the* translates as *le* with a probability of 0.610, as *la* with probability 0.178, and so on.

These probabilities can be combined in various ways, and the highest-scoring combination will determine the words which will make up the target text. An algorithm to get the target words in the right order is now needed. This can be calculated using rather well-known statistical methods for measuring the probabilities of word–pairs–triples, etc.

The results of this experiment are certainly interesting. Translations which were either the same as or preserved the meaning of the official translations were achieved in about 48 per cent of the cases. Although at first glance this level of success would not seem to make this method viable as it stands, it is to be noted that not many commercial MT systems achieve a significantly better quality. More interesting is to consider the near-miss cases in the IBM experiment: incorrect translations were often the result of the fact that the system contains no linguistic 'knowledge' at all. Brown *et al.* admit that serious problems arise when the translation of one word depends on the translation of others, and suggest (Brown *et al.* 1988a: 11–12) that some simple morphological and/or syntactic analysis, also based on probabilistic methods, would greatly improve the quality of the translation.

As part of sublanguage MT research at UMIST, Arad (Arad 1991) investigated the possibility of using statistical methods to derive morphological and syntactic grammars and mono- and bilingual lexica from bilingual corpora. A similar goal is reported by Kay and Röscheisen (1988). That the text type is restricted permits Arad to work with lower thresholds of statistical significance, and hence smaller corpora. In the future she intends to prime the system with a certain amount of *a priori* linguistic knowledge of a very basic kind, for example, what sort of morphological processes are likely? (e.g. for English mainly non-agglutinative suffixes, stems should contain a vowel and be longer than their affixes), typical characteristics of phrase structure (notions of open- and closed-class words, headedness and so on). Arad has resisted the idea of priming the system with a core grammar but recognizes that this may prove to be a necessary step.

CONCLUSIONS

In this chapter I have given a view – at times personal – of current research in MT. Of course, there are probably numerous research projects that I have omitted to mention, generally because I have not been able to get information about them, or simply because they have not come to my notice or have emerged while this book was in press. I am conscious that some readers of this chapter will be relative newcomers to the field, and so I should stress that my coverage of the subject here has been from my own viewpoint rather than as a neutral reporter. For those readers, let me end by indicating some possible future sources of information on MT research.

The conference series 'Theoretical and Methodological Issues in Machine Translation of Natural Languages', which recently held its fourth meeting in Montreal in 1992, is rapidly becoming an established event for MT researchers. To a lesser extent, the International Conference on Computational Linguistics (COLING) and meetings of the ACL likewise provide a much-appreciated forum for publicizing ongoing research. There are typically one or two MT-related events in Japan every year, which generally repay the effort (and expense) of attending them; the annual Aslib Translating and the computer conference in London views MT from the translator's point of view. Finally, there are two specialist quarterly journals, *Machine Translation*, and *Applied Computer Translation*, published by Sigma Press, which, as their names suggest, carry articles of direct relevance.

BIBLIOGRAPHY

Abeillé, A., Schabes, Y. and Joshi, A.K. (1990) 'Using lexicalized tags for machine translation', in H. Karlgren (ed.) *COLING–90: Papers Presented to the 13th International Conference on Computational Linguistics*, Helsinki: Yliopistopaino, vol. 3: 1–6.

Alam, Y.S. (1986) 'A lexical-functional approach to Japanese for the purpose of machine translation', *Computers and Translation* 1: 199–214.

ALPAC (1966) *Language and Machines: Computers in Translation and Linguistics* (Report by the Automatic Language Processing Advisory Committee, Division of Behavioral Sciences, National Research Council), Washington, DC: National Academy of Sciences.

Amores Carredano, J.G. (1990) 'An LFG machine translation system in DCG-PROLOG', unpublished MSc dissertation, UMIST, Manchester.

Ananiadou, S., Carroll, J.J. and Phillips, J.D. (1990) 'Methodologies for development of sublanguage MT systems', CCL Report 90/10, Centre for Computational Linguistics, UMIST, Manchester.

Arad, I. (1991) 'A quasi-statistical approach to automatic generation of linguistic knowledge, PhD thesis, UMIST, Machnester.

Bateman, J.A. (1990) 'Finding translation equivalents: an application of grammatical metaphor', in H. Karlgren (ed.) *COLING–90: Papers Presented to the 13th International Conference on Computational Linguistics*, Helsinki: Yliopistopaino, vol. 3: 13–18.

Beaven, J.L. and Whitelock, P. (1988) 'Machine translation using isomorphic UCGs', in D. Vargha (ed.) *COLING Budapest: Proceedings of the 12th International Conference on Computational Linguistics*, Budapest: John von Neumann Society for Computing Sciences, 32–5.

Boitet, Ch. (1989) 'Speech synthesis and dialogue based machine translation', in *ATR Symposium on Basic Research for Telephone Interpretation*, Kyoto, Japan, Proceedings, 6/5/1–9.

Boitet, Ch. and Nedobejkine, N. (1981) 'Recent developments in Russian–French machine translation at Grenoble', *Linguistics* 19: 199–271.

Brown, P.F., Cocke, J., Della Pietra, S.A., Della Pietra, V.J., Jelinek, J., Lafferty, J.D., Mercer, R.L. and Roossin, P.S. (1990) 'A statistical approach to machine translation', *Computational Linguistics* 16: 79–85.

Brown, P.F., Cocke, J., Della Pietra, S.A., Della Pietra, V.J., Jelinek, J., Mercer, R.L. and Roossin, P.S. (1988a) 'A statistical approach to French/English translation', *Proceedings, Second International Conference on Theoretical and Methodological Issues in Machine Translation of Natural Languages*, Carnegie Mellon University, Pittsburgh, Pennsylvania.

—— (1988b) 'A statistical approach to language translation', in D. Vargha (ed.) *COLING Budapest: Proceedings of the 12th International Conference on Computational Linguistics*, Budapest: John von Neumann Society for Computing Sciences, 71–6.

Carbonell, J.G. and Tomita, M. (1987) 'Knowledge-based machine translation, the CMU approach', in S. Nirenburg (ed.) *Machine Translation: Theoretical and Methodological Issues*, Cambridge: Cambridge University Press, 68–89.

Carroll, J.J. (1990) 'Repetitions processing using a metric space and the angle of similarity', CCL Report 90/3, Centre for Computational Linguistics, UMIST, Manchester.

Chandioux, J. (1987/9) '10 ans de METEO (MD)' (texte présenté lors du Congrès du Conseil des traducteurs et interprètes du Canada, octobre 1987) reprinted in A. Abbou (ed.) *La Traduction Assistée par Ordinateur: Perspectives technologiques, industrielles et économiques envisageables à l'horizon 1990: l'offre, la demande, les marchés et les évolutions en cours*, Actes du séminaire international (Paris, March 1988), Paris: DAICADIF, 169–73.

Chevalier, M., Isabelle, P., Labelle, F. and Lainé, C. (1981) 'La traductologie appliquée à la traduction automatique', *Meta* 26: 35–47.

Durand, J., Bennett, P., Allegranza, V., van Eynde, F., Humphreys, L., Schmidt, P. and Steiner, E. (1991) 'The Eurotra linguistic specifications: an overview', *Machine Translation*, 6: 103–47.

Dymetman, M. and Isabelle, P. (1988) 'Reversible logic grammars for machine translation', *Proceedings, Second International Conference on Theoretical and Methodological Issues in Machine Translation of Natural Langauges*, Carnegie Mellon University, Pittsburgh, Pennsylvania.

Elliston, J.S.G. (1979) 'Computer-aided translation: a business viewpoint', in B.M. Snell (ed.) *Translating and the Computer*, Amsterdam: North-Holland, 149–58.

Farwell, D. and Wilks, Y. (1989) 'Ultra: a multilingual machine translator', Research Report, Computing Research Laboratory, New Mexico State University, Las Cruces, New Mexico.

Green, R. (1982) 'The MT errors which cause most trouble to posteditors', in V. Lawson (ed.) *Practical Experience of Machine Translation*, Amsterdam: North-Holland, 101–4.

Hauenschild, C. (1986) 'KIT/NASEV oder die Problematik des Transfers bei der maschinellen Übersetzung', in I. Bátori and H.J. Weber (eds) *Neue Ansätze in Maschineller Sprachübersetzung: Wissensrepräsentation und Textbezug*, Tübingen: Niemeyer Verlag, 167–95.

Huang, X. (1990) 'Machine translation in a monolingual environment', in *Third International Conference on Theoretical and Methodological Issues in Machine Translation of Natural Languages*, Austin, Texas, 33–41.

Hutchins, W.J. (1986) *Machine Translation: Past, Present, Future*, Chichester: Ellis Horwood.

Johnson, R.L. (1983) 'Parsing – an MT perspective', in K. Sparck Jones and Y. Wilks (eds) *Automatic Natural Language Parsing*, Chichester: Ellis Horwood, 32–8.

Jones, D. and Tsujii, J. (1990) 'Interactive high-quality machine translation for monolinguals', in *Third International Conference on Theoretical and Methodological Issues in Machine Translation of Natural Languages*, Austin, Texas, 43–46.

Kaplan, R.M., Netter, K., Wederkind, J. and Zaenen, A. (1989) 'Translation by structural correspondences', Fourth Conference of the European Chapter of the Association for Computational Linguistics, Manchester, Proceedings, 272–81.

Karlgren, H. (ed.) (1990) *COLING–90: Papers Presented to the 13th International Conference on Computational Linguistics*, Helsinki: Yliopistopaino.

Kay, M. and Röscheisen, M. (1988) 'Text-translation alignment', Research Memo, Xerox Palo Alto Research Center, Palo Alto, California.

Kittredge, R. and Lehrberger, J. (1982) *Sublanguage: Studies of Language in Restricted Semantic Domains*, Berlin: de Gruyter.

Kosaka, M., Teller, V. and Grishman, R. (1988) 'A sublanguage approach to Japanese–English machine translation', in D. Maxwell, K. Schubert and T. Witkam (eds) *New Directions in Machine Translation*, Dordrecht: Foris, 109–20.

Kudo, I. (1990) 'Local cohesive knowledge for a dialogue–machine translation system', in H. Karlgren (ed.) *COLING–90: Papers presented to the 13th International Conference on Computational Linguistics*, Helsinki: Yliopistopaino, vol. 3: 391–3.

Kudo, I. and Nomura, H. (1986) 'Lexical-functional transfer: a transfer framework in a machine translation system based on LFG', *11th International Conference on Computational Linguistics*, Proceedings of COLING–86, Bonn: 112–14.

Landsbergen, J. (1987a) 'Isomorphic grammars and their use in the ROSETTA translation system', in M. King (ed.) *Machine Translation Today: the State of the Art*, Edinburgh: Edinburgh University Press, 351–72.

—— (1987b) 'Montague grammar and machine translation', in P. Whitelock, M.MacG. Wood, H.L. Somers, R. Johnson and P. Bennett (eds) *Linguistic Theory and Computer Applications*, London: Academic Press, 113–47.

Lehrberger, J. and Bourbeau, L. (1988) *Machine Translation: Linguistic Characteristics of MT Systems and General Methodology of Evaluation*, Amsterdam: John Benjamins.

Luckhardt, H.D. (1991) 'Sublanguages in machine translation', Fifth conference of the European chapter of the Association for Computational Linguistics, Berlin, Proceedings 306–8.

McCord, M.C. (1989) 'Design of LMT: a Prolog-based machine translation system', *Computational Linguistics* 15: 33–52.

Nagao, M. (1984) 'A framework of a mechanical translation between Japanese and English by analogy principle', in A. Elithorn and R. Banerji (eds) *Artificial and Human Intelligence*, Amsterdam, North-Holland, 172–80.

Nirenburg, S. (ed.) (1987) *Machine Translation: Theoretical and Methodological Issues*, Cambridge: Cambridge University Press.

—— (1989) 'Knowledge-based machine translation', *Machine Translation* 4: 5–24.

Nirenburg, S. and Carbonell, J.G. (1987) 'Integrating discourse pragmatics and propositional knowledge for multilingual natural language processing', *Computers and Translation* 2: 105–16.

Nirenburg, S. and Levin, L. (1989) 'Knowledge representation support', *Machine Translation* 4: 25–52.

Nishida, F. and Takamatsu, S. (1990) 'Automated procedures for the improvement of a machine translation system by feedback from postediting', *Machine Translation* 5: 223–46.

Nishida, F., Takamatsu, S., Tani, T. and Doi, T. (1988) 'Feedback of correcting information in postediting to a machine translation system', in D. Vargha (ed.) *COLING Budapest: Proceedings of the 12th International Conference on Computational Linguistics*, Budapest: John von Neumann Society for Computing Sciences, 476–81.

Pym, P.J. (1990) 'Pre-editing and the use of simplified writing for MT: an engineer's experience of operating an MT system', in P. Mayorcas (ed.) *Translating and the Computer 10: The Translation Environment 10 Years On*, London: Aslib, 80–96.

Raw, A., Vandecapelle, B. and van Eynde, F. (1988) 'Eurotra: an overview', *Interface* 3: 5–32.

Raw, A., van Eynde, F., ten Hacken, P., Hoekstra, H. and Vandecapelle, B. (1989) 'An introduction to the Eurotra machine translation system', Working Papers in Natural Language Processing 1, TAAL Technologie, Utrecht and Katholieke Universiteit Leuven.

Rohrer, C. (1986) 'Maschinelle Übersetzung mit Unifikationsgrammatiken', in I. Bátori and H.J. Weber (eds) *Neue Ansätze in Maschineller Sprachübersetzung: Wissensrepräsentation und Textbezug*, Tübingen: Niemeyer Verlag, 75–99.

Rupp, C.J. (1989) 'Situation semantics and machine translation', Fourth Conference of the European Chapter of the Association for Computational Linguistics, Manchester, Proceedings, 308–18.

Sadler, L., Crookston, I., Arnold, D. and Way, A. (1990) 'LFG and translation', in *Third International Conference on Theoretical and Methodological Issues in Machine Translation of Natural Languages*, Austin, Texas, 121–30.

Saito, H. and Tomita, M. (1986) 'On automatic composition of stereotypic documents in foreign languages', presented at 1st International Conference on Applications of Artificial Intelligence to Engineering Problems, Southampton, April 1986; Research Report CMU–CS–86–107, Department of Computer Science, Carnegie Mellon University.

Sato, S. and Nagao, M. (1990) 'Toward memory-based translation', in H. Karlgren (ed.) *COLING–90: Papers presented to the 13th International Conference on Computational Linguistics*, Helsinki: Yliopistopaino, vol. 3: 247–52.

Slocum, J. (1985) 'A survey of machine translation: its history, current status, and future prospects', *Computational Linguistics* 11: 1–17.

Somers, H.L. (1986) 'Some thoughts on interface structure(s)', in W. Wilss and K.-D. Schmitz (eds) *Maschinelle Übersetzung – Methoden und Werkzeuge*, Tübingen: Max Niemeyer Verlag, 81–99.

Somers, H.[L.], Hirakawa, H., Miike, S. and Amano, S. (1988) 'The treatment of complex English nominalizations in machine translation', *Computers and Translation* 3: 3–21.

Somers, H.L., Tsujii, J. and Jones, D. (1990) 'Machine translation without a source text', in H. Karlgren (ed.) *COLING–90: Papers Presented to the 13th International Conference on Computational Linguistics*, Helsinki: Yliopistopaino, vol. 3: 271–6.

Steiner, E. (ed.) (1991) Special issue on EUROTRA, *Machine Translation*, 6: 2–3.

Sumita, E., Iida, H. and Kohyama, H. (1990) 'Translating with examples: a new approach to machine translation', *Third International Conference on Theoretical and Methodological Issues in Machine Translation of Natural Languages*, Austin, Texas, 203–12.

Tsujii, J. and Nagao, M. (1988) 'Dialogue translation vs text translation – Interpretation based approach', in D. Vargha (ed.) (1988) *COLING Budapest: Proceedings of the 12th International Conference on Computational Linguistics*, Budapest: John von Neumann Society for Computing Sciences, 688–93.

van der Korst, B. (1989) 'Functional grammar and machine translation', in J.H. Connolly and S.C. Dik (eds) *Functional Grammar and the Computer*, Dordrecht: Foris, 289–316.

van Eynde, F. (1988) 'The analysis of tense and aspect in Eurotra', in D. Vargha (ed.) *COLING Budapest: Proceedings of the 12th International Conference on Computational Linguistics*, Budapest: John von Neumann Society for Computing Sciences, 699–704.

van Noord, G., Dorrepaal, J., van der Eijk, P., Florenza, M. and des Tombe, L. (1990) 'The MiMo2 research system', *Third International Conference on Theoretical and Methodological Issues in Machine Translation of Natural Languages*, Austin, Texas, 213–33.

Vargha, D. (ed.) (1988) *COLING Budapest: Proceedings of the 12th International Conference on Computational Linguistics*, Budapest: John von Neumann Society for Computing Sciences.

Vauquois, B. (1985) 'The approach of Geta to automatic translation: comparison with some other methods', paper presented at International Symposium on Machine Translation, Riyadh; in Ch. Boitet (ed.) (1988) *Bernard Vauquois et la TAO: vingt-cinq ans de traduction automatique – Analectes*, Grenoble: Association Champollion, 631–86.

Vauquois, B. and Boitet, Ch. (1985) 'Automated translation at Grenoble University', *Computational Linguistics* 11: 28–36.

Wehrli, E. (1990) 'STS: an experimental sentence translation system', in H. Karlgren (ed.) *COLING–90: Papers Presented to the 13th International Conference on Computational Linguistics*, Helsinki: Yliopistopaino, vol. 1: 76–8.

Whitelock, P.J., Wood, M.MacG., Chandler, B.J., Holden, N. and Horsfall, H.J. (1986) 'Strategies for interactive machine translation: the experience and implications of the UMIST Japanese project', *11th International Conference on Computational Linguistics*, Proceedings of COLING–86, Bonn: 329–34.

Wood, M.M. and Chandler, B.J. (1988) 'Machine translation for monolinguals', in D. Vargha (ed.) *COLING Budapest: Proceedings of the 12th International Conference on Computational Linguistics*, Budapest: John von Neumann Society for Computing Science, 760–63.

Zajac, R. (1990) 'A relational approach to translation', *Third International Conference on Theoretical and Methodological Issues in Machine Translation of Natural Languages*, Austin, Texas, 235–54.

Bibliography

Abbou, A. (ed.) (1989) *Traduction Assistée par Ordinateur: Perspectives technologiques, industrielles et économiques envisageables à l'horizon 1990: l'offre, la demande, les marchés et les évolutions en cours*, Actes du Séminaire international (Paris, March 1988), Paris: DAICADIF.

Abeillé, A., Schabes, Y. and Joshi, A.K. (1990) 'Using lexicalized tags for machine translation', in H. Karlgren (ed.) *COLING–90: Papers Presented to the 13th International Conference on Computational Linguistics*, Helsinki: Yliopistopaino, vol. 3: 1–6.

Ahmad, K., Fulford, H., Holmes-Higgin, P., Rogers, M. and Thomas, P. (1990) 'The translator's workbench project', in C. Picken (ed.) *Translating and the Computer 11: Preparing for the Next Decade*, London: ASLIB, 9–19.

Aitchison, J. (1978) *Teach Yourself Linguistics*, Sevenoaks: Hodder and Stoughton.

Alam, Y.S. (1986) 'A lexical-functional approach to Japanese for the purpose of machine translation', *Computers and Translation* 1: 199–214.

ALPAC (1966) *Language and Machines: Computers in Translation and Linguistics* (Report by the Automatic Language Processing Advisory Committee, Division of Behavioral Sciences, National Research Council), Washington, DC: National Academy of Sciences.

Amores Carredano, J.G. (1990) 'An LFG machine translation system in DCG-PROLOG', unpublished MSc dissertation, UMIST, Manchester.

Ananiadou, S., Carroll, J.J. and Phillips, J.D. (1990) 'Methodologies for development of sublanguage MT systems', CCL Report 90/10, Centre for Computational Linguistics, UMIST, Manchester.

Arad, I (1991) A quasi-statistical approach to automatic generation of linguistic knowledge, PhD thesis, UMIST, Manchester.

Bar-Hillel, Y. (1951) 'The state of machine translation in 1951', *American Documentation* 2: 229–37.

Bateman, J.A. (1990) 'Finding translation equivalents: an application of grammatical metaphor', in H. Karlgren (ed.) *COLING–90: Papers Presented to the 13th International Conference on Computational Linguistics*, Helsinki: Yliopistopaino, vol. 3: 13–18.

Bátori, I. and Weber, H.J. (eds) (1986) *Neue Ansätze in Maschineller Sprachübersetzung: Wissensrepräsentation und Textbezug*, Tübingen: Niemeyer Verlag.

Battelle Columbus Laboratories (1977) 'The evaluation and systems analysis of the SYSTRAN machine translation system', RADC–TR–76–399 Technical Report.

Beaven, J.L. and Whitelock, P. (1988) 'Machine translation using isomorphic UCGs', in D. Vargha (ed.) *COLING Budapest: Proceedings of the 12th International Conference on Computational Linguistics*, Budapest: John von Neumann Society for Computing Sciences, 32–5.

Ben-Avi, S. (1977) 'An investigation into the use of Esperanto as an intermediate language in a machine translation project', PhD thesis, Manchester.

Bennett, W.S. and Slocum, J. (1985) 'The LRC machine translation system', in *Computational Linguistics* 11: 111–21; reprinted in J. Slocum (ed.) *Machine Translation Systems*, Cambridge: Cambridge University Press, 1988, 111–40.

Blanke, D. (1985) *Internationale Plansprachen*, Berlin: Akademic-Verlag.

Bloomfield, L. (1933) *Language*, New York: Holt, Rinehart & Winston (reprinted in great part in 1984, University of Chicago).

—— (1944) 'Secondary and tertiary responses to language', in *Language* 20: 45–55 and in C.F. Hockett (ed.) (1970) *A Leonard Bloomfield Anthology*, Chicago: University of Chicago Press.

Boitet, Ch. (1989) 'Speech synthesis and dialogue based machine translation', in *ATR Symposium on Basic Research for Telephone Interpretation*, Kyoto, Japan, Proceedings, 6/5–1/9.

—— (1990) 'Towards personal MT: general design, dialogue structure, potential role of speech', in H. Karlgren (ed.) *COLING–90: Papers presented to the 13th International Conference on Computational Linguistics*, Helsinki: Yliopistopaino, vol. 3, 30–35.

Boitet, Ch. and Nedobejkine, N. (1981) 'Recent developments in Russian–French machine translation at Grenoble', *Linguistics* 19: 199–271.

Booth, A.D. (ed.) (1967) *Machine Translation*, Amsterdam: North Holland.

Briem, S. (1990) 'Maskinoversaettelse fra esperanto til islandsk', in J. Pind and E. Rögnvaldsson (eds) *Papers from the Seventh Scandinavian Conference of Computational Linguistics (Reykjavík 1989)*, Reykjavík: Institute of Lexicography/Institute of Linguistics, 138–45.

Brower, R.A. (ed.) (1959) *On Translation*, Cambridge, Mass.: Harvard University Press.

Brown, P.F., Cocke, J., Della Pietra, S.A., Della Pietra, V.J., Jelinek, F., Lafferty, J.D., Mercer, R.L. and Roossin, P.S. (1990) 'A statistical approach to machine translation', *Computational Linguistics* 16: 79–85.

Brown, P.F., Cocke, J., Della Pietra, S.A., Della Pietra, V.J., Jelinek, J., Mercer, R.L. and Roossin, P.S. (1988a) 'A statistical approach to French/English translation', *Proceedings, Second International Conference on Theoretical and Methodological Issues in Machine Translation of Natural Languages*, Carnegie Mellon University, Pittsburgh, Pennsylvania.

—— (1988b) 'A statistical approach to language translation', in D. Vargha (ed.) *COLING Budapest: Proceedings of the 12th International Conference on Computational Linguistics*, Budapest: John von Neumann Society for Computing Sciences, 71–6.

Carbonell, J.G. (1990) 'Machine translation technology: status and recommendations', in T. Valentine (1990) 'Status of machine translation (MT) technology: Hearing before the Subcommittee on

Science, Research and Technology of the Committee on Science, Space and Technology, US House of Representatives, 101st Congress, Second Session, September 11, 1990', [no. 153], Chairman: Rep. T. Valentine, Washington: US Government Printing Office, 119–31.

Carbonell, J.G. and Tomita, M. (1987) 'Knowledge-based machine translation, the CMU approach', in S. Nirenburg (1987) *Machine Translation: Theoretical and Methodological Issues*, Cambridge: Cambridge University Press, 68–9.

Carroll, J.B. (1966) 'An experiment in evaluating the quality of translations', *Mechanical Translation and Computational Linguistics* 9 (3 & 4): 55–66.

Carroll, J.J. (1990) 'Repetitions processing using a metric space and the angle of similarity', CCL Report 90/3, Centre for Computational Linguistics, UMIST, Manchester.

Celt, S. and Gross, A. (1987) 'The challenge of translating Chinese medicine', *Language Monthly* 43: 19–21.

Chandioux, J. (1987/9) '10 ans de METEO (MD)' (texte présenté lors du Congrès du Conseil des traducteurs et interprètes du Canada, octobre 1987) reprinted in A. Abbou (ed.) *La Traduction Assistée par Ordinateur: Perspectives technologiques, industrielles et économiques envisageables à l'horizon 1990: l'offre, la demande, les marchés et les évolutions en cours*, Actes du Séminaire international (Paris, March 1988), Paris: DAICADIF, 169–73.

—— (1989) 'METEO: 100 million words later', in ATA conference proceedings, 449–53.

Chevalier, M., Isabelle, P., Labelle, F. and Lainé, C. (1981) 'La traductologie appliquée à la traduction automatique', *Meta* 26: 35–47.

Chisholm, S. Jr. (1981) *Elements of English Linguistics*, London: Longman.

Chomsky, N. (1957) *Syntactic Structures*, The Hague: Mouton.

—— (1965) *Aspects of the Theory of Syntax*, Cambridge, Mass.: MIT Press.

—— (1975) *The Logical Structure of Linguistic Theory*, Chicago: University of Chicago Press.

Coughlin, J. (1988) 'Artificial intelligence and machine translation: present developments and future prospects', in *Babel* 34: 1, 1–9.

Cruz, E. and Ortiz y Ortiz, R. (1981) *Translation Strategies/Estrategias para Traducción*, London: Macmillan.

Crystal, D. (1985) *Linguistics*, Harmondsworth: Penguin Books Limited.

Danzin, A., Allén, S., Coltof, H., Recoque, A., Steusloff, H. and O'Leary, M. (1990) 'Eurotra Programme Assessment Report', Commission of the European Communities, March 1990.

Datta, J. (1988) 'MT in large organizations: revolution in the workplace', in M. Vasconcellos (ed.) *Technology as Translation Strategy* (American Translators Association Scholarly Monograph Series, vol. II), Binghamton, New York: State University of New York, 167–83.

Denisov, P.N. (1965) *Principy modelirovanija jazyka (na materiale vspomogatel'nych jazykov dlja avtomatičeskogo poiska i perevoda)*, Moscow: Moskovskij Universitet.

Dietze, J. (1986) 'Projekt der rechnergestützten Erarbeitung eines Wörterbuchs von Esperantowurzeln', *Wissenschaftliche Zeitschrift der Universität Halle*, 35 [G, 5]: 90–1.

Drexler, E.K. (1986) *Engines of Creation*, New York: Anchor Press.

Duličenko, A.D. (1989) 'Ethnic language and planned language, and its place in language science', in K. Schubert (ed.) *Interlinguistics. Aspects of the Science of Planned Languages*, Berlin/New York: Mouton de Gruyter, 47–61.

Durand, J., Bennett, P., Allegranza, V., van Eynde, F., Humphreys, L., Schmidt, P. and Steiner, E. (1991) 'The Eurotra linguistic specifications: an overview', *Machine Translation*, 6: 103–47.

Dymetman, M. and Isabelle, P. (1988) 'Reversible logic grammars for machine translation', *Proceedings, Second International Conference on Theoretical and Methodological Issues in Machine Translation of Natural Languages*, Carnegie Mellon University, Pittsburgh, Pennsylvania.

EEC (1990) 'Council Decision of 26 November 1990 adopting a specific programme concerning the preparation of the development of an operational Eurotra system', *Official Journal of the European Communities*, no. L 358/84, EEC/664/90, 21.12.90.

Elliston, J.S.G. (1979) 'Computer-aided translation: a business viewpoint', in B.M. Snell (ed.) *Translating and the Computer*, Amsterdam: North-Holland, 149–58.

Farwell, D. and Wilks, Y. (1989) 'Ultra: a multilingual machine translator', Research Report, Computing Research Laboratory, New Mexico State University, Las Cruces, New Mexico.

Fodor, J.A. and Katz, J.J. (1964) *The Structure of Language*, New York: Prentice-Hall.

Forster, P.G. (1987) 'Some social sources of resistance to Esperanto', in José-Luis Melena Jiménez *et al.* (eds) *Serta gratvlatoria in honorem Juan Régulo*, vol. 2: *Esperantismo*, La Laguna: Universidad, 203–11.

Fulford, H., Höge, M. and Ahmad, K. (1990) 'User requirements study', European Commission Esprit II Project no. 2315, Translator's Workbench Project, Final Report on Workpackage 3.3.

García Yebra, V. (1984) *Teoría y Práctica de la Traducción* 2nd edn, Madrid: Editorial Gredos.

Godel, K. (1931) 'Über formal unentscheidbare Sätze der Principia Mathematica und verwandte Systeme I', *Monatshefte für Mathematik und Physik* 38: 173–98.

Gordos, G. (1985) 'Parol-sintezo kun limigita vortaro', in I. Koutny (ed.) *Perkomputila tekstoprilaboro*, Budapest: Scienca Eldona Centro, 11–29.

Green, R. (1982) 'The MT errors which cause most trouble to posteditors', in V. Lawson (ed.) *Practical Experience of Machine Translation*, Amsterdam: North-Holland, 101–4.

Greenberg, J. (1963) *Universals of Language*, Cambridge, Mass.: MIT Press.

Grimes, J.E. (1975) *The Thread of Discourse*, The Hague: Mouton.

Grosjean, F. (1982) *Life with Two Languages: an Introduction to Bilingualism*, Cambridge, Mass.: Harvard University Press.

Guzmán de Rojas, I. (1985) 'Logical and linguistic problems of social communication with the Aymara people', Ottawa: The International Development Research Center.

Halliday, M.A.K. (1967) 'Notes on transitivity and theme in English', part 2, *Journal of Linguistics* 3: 199–244.

Harel, D. (ed.) (1987) *Algorithmics: The Spirit of Computing*, Wokingham: Addison-Wesley.

Harris, Z. (1951) *Structural Linguistics*, Chicago: University of Chicago Press.

Hartmann, R.R.K and Stork, F.C. (1976) *Dictionary and Language and Linguistics*, New York: Wiley.

Hauenschild, C. (1986) 'KIT/NASEV oder die Problematik des Transfers bei der maschinellen Übersetzung', in I. Bátori and H.J. Weber (eds) *Neue Ansätze in Maschineller Sprachübersetzung: Wissenrepräsentation und Textbezug*, Tübingen: Niemeyer Verlag, 167–95.

Hjelmslev, L. (1961) *Prolegomena to a Theory of Language*, Madison: University of Wisconsin Press.

—— (1963) *Sproget*, 2nd edn, Copenhagen: Berlingske forlag.

Hockett, C.F. (1968) *The State of the Art*, The Hague: Mouton.

—— (ed.) (1987) *A Leonard Bloomfield Anthology*, Chicago: University of Chicago Press.

Hodges, A. (ed.) (1985) *Alan Turing: The Enigma of Intelligence*, London: Unwin Paperbacks.

Huang, X. (1990) 'Machine translation in a monolingual environment', in *Third International Conference on Theoretical and Methodological Issues in Machine Translation of Natural Languages*, Austin, Texas.

Hunn, E.S. (1977) *Tzeltal Folk Zoology: The Classification of Discontinuities in Nature*, New York: Academic Press.

Hutchins, W.J. (1982) 'The evolution of machine translation systems', in V. Lawson (ed.) *Practical Experience of Machine Translation*, Amsterdam: North-Holland, 21–37.

—— (1986) *Machine Translation: Past, Present, Future*, Chichester: Ellis Horwood.

—— (1988) 'Future perspectives in translation technologies', in M. Vasconcellos (ed.) *Technology as Translation Strategy* (American Translators Association, Scholarly Monograph Series, vol. II, Binghamton, New York: State University of New York, 223–40.

Hutchins, J. and Somers, H. (1992) *An Introduction to Machine Translation*, London: Academic Press.

Iida, H. (1989) 'Advanced dialogue translation techniques: plan-based, memory-based and parallel approaches', in *ATR Symposium on Basic Research for Telephone Interpretation*, Kyoto, Japan, Proceedings 8/7–8/8.

Iljon, A. (1977) 'Scientific and technical databases in a multilingual society', in *Proceedings of Third European Congress on Information Systems*, Munich: Commission of the European Communities.

Isabelle, P. (1989) 'Bilan et perspectives de la traduction assistée par ordinateur au Canada', in A. Abbou (ed.) *Traduction Assistée par Ordinateur: Perspectives technologiques, industrielles et économiques envisageables à l'horizon 1990: l'offre, la demande, les marchés et les évolutions en cours*, Actes du séminaire international (Paris, March 1988), Paris: DAICADIF, 153–8.

ISO 2788 (1974) 'Documentation – guidelines for the establishment and development of multilingual thesauri'.

ISO 6156 (1987) 'Magnetic tape exchange format for terminological/ lexicographical records (MATER)'.

Jacobs, P., Krupka, G. and Rau, L. (1991) 'Lexico-semantic pattern matching as a companion to parsing in text understanding', in *Proceedings of the DARPA Speech and Natural Language Workshop*, Monterey, California.

Jakobson, R. (1959) 'On linguistic aspects of translation', in R.A. Brower (ed.) *On Translation*, Cambridge, Mass.: Harvard University Press.

Janot-Giorgetti, M.T. (1985) 'Parol-rekono kun limigita vortaro, ĝia apliko en la lernado de parolataj lingvoj', in I. Koutny (ed.) *Perkomputila tekstoprilaboro*, Budapest: Scienca Eldona Centro, 57–68.

JEIDA (1989) 'A Japanese view of machine translation in light of the considerations and recommendations reported by ALPAC, USA', Tokyo: JEIDA.

Johnson, R.L. (1983) 'Parsing – an MT perspective', in K. Sparck Jones and Y. Wilks (eds) *Automatic Natural Language Parsing*, Chichester: Ellis Horwood, 32–8.

Johnson, R., King, M. and des Tombe, L. (1985) 'EUROTRA: a multilingual system under development', in *Computational Linguistics* 11 (2–3): 155–69.

Jones, D. and Tsujii, J. (1990) 'High quality machine-driven text translation', in *Third International Conference on Theoretical and Methodological Issues in Machine Translation of Natural Languages*, Austin, Texas.

Kaplan, R.M., Netter, K., Wederkind, J. and Zaenen, A. (1989) 'Translation by structural correspondences', Fourth Conference of the European Chapter of the Association for Computational Linguistics, Manchester, Proceedings, 272–81.

Karlgren, H. (ed.) (1990) *COLING–90: Papers Presented to the 13th International Conference on Computational Linguistics*, Helsinki: Yliopistopaino.

Kat, J.O. de (1985) 'Traduko el la internacia lingvo al naciaj', in I. Koutny (ed.) *Perkomputila tekstoprilaboro*, Budapest: Scienca Eldona Centro, 259–66.

Katumori, H. and Hukuda, M. (1984) 'Esuperanto o tyûkai-gengo to suru kikai-hoṅyaku no kokoromi', *WGNL meeting 1984-7-26*.

Kay, M. (1980) 'The proper place of men and machines', in *Language Translation*, Research Report, Xerox Palo Alto Research Center, Palo Alto, California.

—— (1982) 'Machine translation', *American Journal of Computational Linguistics*, April–June, 74–8.

Kay, M. and Röscheisen, M. (1988) 'Text-translation alignment', Research Memo, Xerox Palo Alto Research Center, Palo Alto, California.

Kelly, I.D.K. (1978) 'How Esperanto can aid machine translation', *Computer Weekly* 19 January 1978.

King, M. (ed.) (1987) *Machine Translation Today: the State of the Art*, Edinburgh: Edinburgh University Press.

—— (1989) 'Perspectives, recherches, besoins, marchés et projets en Suisse', in A. Abbou (ed.) *Traduction Assistée par Ordinateur: Perspectives technologiques, industrielles et économiques envisageables à l'horizon 1990: l'offre, la demande, les marchés et les évolutions en cours*, Actes du Séminaire international (Paris, March 1988), Paris: DAICADIF, 177–9.

Kingscott, G. (1990) 'SITE buys B'Vital: relaunch of French national MT project', *Language International*, April.

Kittredge, R. and Lehrberger, J. (1982) *Sublanguage: Studies of Language in Restricted Semantic Domains*, Berlin: de Gruyter.

Klein, F. (1988) 'Factors in the evaluation of MT: a pragmatic approach', in M. Vasconcellos (ed.) *Technology as Translation Strategy* (American Translators Association Scholarly Monograph Series, vol. II), Binghamton, New York: State University of New York.

Knowles, F. (1979) 'Error analysis of Systran output: a suggested criterion for "internal" evaluation of translation quality and a possible corrective design', in B.M. Snell (ed.) *Translation and the Computer*, Amsterdam: North-Holland, 109–33.

Kosaka, M., Teller, V. and Grishman, R. (1988) 'A sublanguage approach to Japanese–English machine translation', in D. Maxwell, K. Schubert and T. Witkam (eds) *New Directions in Machine Translation*, Dordrecht: Foris, 109–20.

Koutny, I., Olaszy, G. and Kisfaludy, K. (1988) 'Esperanto speech synthesis and its application in language learning', in T. Szende (ed.) *From Phonology to Applied Phonetics*, Magyar Fonetikai Füzutek//Hungarian Papers in Phonetics, 19, Budapest: Linguistics Institute of the Hungarian Academy of Sciences, 47–54.

Kudo, I. (1990) 'Local cohesive knowledge for a dialogue–machine translation system', in H. Karlgren (ed.) *COLING–90: Papers presented to the 13th International Conference on Computational Linguistics*, Helsinki: Yliopistopaino, vol. 3: 391–3.

Kudo, I. and Nomura, H. (1986) 'Lexical-functional transfer: a transfer framework in a machine translation system based on LFG', *11th International Conference on Computational Linguistics*, Proceedings of COLING–86, Bonn: 112–14.

Laffling, J.D. (1990) 'Machine disambiguation and translation of polysemous nouns', PhD thesis, (CNAA) Wolverhampton Polytechnic.

Lakoff, G. (1987) *Women, Fire, and Dangerous Things: What Categories Reveal about the Mind*, Chicago: University of Chicago Press.

Landsbergen, J. (1987a) 'Isomorphic grammars and their use in the ROSETTA translation system', in M. King (ed.) *Machine Translation Today: the State of the Art*, Edinburgh: Edinburgh University Press, 351–72.

—— (1987b) 'Montague grammar and machine translation', in P. Whitelock, M.MacG. Wood, H.L. Somers, R. Johnson and P. Bennett (eds) *Linguistic Theory and Computer Applications*, London: Academic Press, 113–47.

Lawson, V. (ed.) (1982) *Practical Experience of Machine Translation*, Amsterdam: North-Holland.

Lehmann, W.P. (1987) 'The context of machine translation', *Computers and Translation* 2.

Lehrberger, J. and Bourbeau, L. (1988) *Machine Translation: Linguistic Characteristics of MT Systems and General Methodology of Evaluation*, Amsterdam: John Benjamins.

León, M. and Schwartz, L.A. (1986) 'Integrated development of English–Spanish machine translation: from pilot to full operational capability: technical report of Grant DPE–5543–G–SS–3048–00 from the US Agency for International Development', co-ordinated by M. Vasconcellos, Washington, DC: Pan American Health Organization.

Lewis, D. (1985) 'The development and progress of machine translation systems, *ALLC Journal* 5: 40–52.

Li Wei (1986) 'Aŭtomata tradukado el la internacia en la ĉinan kaj anglan lingvojn (Esperanta–angla/ĉina maŝintraduka sistemo)', *Grundlagenstudien aus Kybernetik und Geisteswissenschaft/Humankybernetik* 27: 147–52.

Luckhardt, H.-D. (1991) 'Sublanguages in machine translation; Proceedings of the Fifth Conference of the European Chapter of the Association for Computational Linguistics. Berlin: 306–8.

Maas, H.D. (1982) 'Aŭtomata tradukado en kaj el Esperanto', in H.F. Yashovardhan and B. Frank-Böhringer (eds) *Lingvokibernetiko kaj aliaj internacilingvaj aktoj de la IX-a Internacia Kongreso de Kibernetiko//Sprachkybernetik und andere internationalsprachige Akten vom IX. Internationalen Kybernetikerkongreß*, Tübingen: Narr, 75–81.

—— (1985) 'Pri kelkaj strategioj por fraz-analizo', in I. Koutny (ed.) *Perkomputila tekstoprilaboro*, Budapest: Scienca Eldona Centro, 175–205.

—— (1987a) 'The MT system SUSY', in M. King (ed.) *Machine Translation Today: the State of the Art*, Edinburgh: Edinburgh University Press, 209–46, 392–435.

—— (1987b) 'The Saarbrücken automatic translation system (SUSY)', in *Overcoming the language barrier*, Commission of the European Communities, Munich: Verlag Dokumentation, vol. 1: 585–92.

McCord, M.C. (1989) 'Design of LMT: a Prolog-based machine translation system', *Computational Linguistics* 15: 33–52.

McElhaney, T. and Vasconcellos, M. (1988) 'The translator and the postediting experience', in M. Vasconcellos (ed.) *Technology as Translation Strategy* (American Translators Association Scholarly Monograph Series, vol. II), Binghamton, New York: State University of New York

McNaught, J. (1988) 'A survey of termbanks worldwide', in C. Picken (ed.) *Translating and the Computer 9: Potential and Practice*, London: Aslib, 112–29.

Makino, S., Hirata, M. and Katumori, H. (1986) 'Esuperanto o tyûkaigengo to suru kikai hon'yaku', *WGNL meeting 1986-3-28*.

Malmberg, B. (1967) 'Los nuevos caminos de la lingüística', *Siglo Veintiuno*, Mexico: 154–74.

Mehta, V. (1971) *John is easy to please*, New York: Ferrar, Straus & Giroux.

Melby, A. (1982) 'Multi-level translation aids in a distributed system', in J. Horecky (ed.) *Proceedings of COLING-82*, Prague, July 1982, Amsterdam: North-Holland.

—— (forthcoming) 'Causes and effects of partial asymmetry between semantic networks tied to natural languages' (a lecture series given at the Collège de France, Paris, February, 1990), to appear in *Les Cahiers de Lexicologie*, Paris.

—— (forthcoming) 'MicroMATER: a proposed standard format for exchanging lexical/terminological data files', *META* (special issue).

Minsky, M. (1986) *The Society of Mind*, New York: Simon & Schuster.

Mohai, L. (1986) 'Komputila tradukprogramo el Esperanto hungaren', in P. Broczkó, I. Koutny and A. Lukács (eds) *Language Cybernetics, Educational Cybernetics//Lingvokibernetiko, pedagogia kibernetiko//Cybernétique de la langue, cybernétique de l'éducation*, Budapest: Neumann Society, 47–51.

Nagao, M. (1984) 'A framework of a mechanical translation between Japanese and English by analogy principle', in A. Elithorn and R. Banerji (eds) *Artificial and Human Intelligence*, Amsterdam, North-Holland, 172–80.

Nagao, M., Tsujii, J. and Nakamura, J. (1985) 'The Japanese government project for machine translation', *Computational Linguistics* 11: 91–110.

Nagel, E. and Newman, J.R. (eds) (1990) *Godel's Proof*, London: Routledge.

Newman, P.E. (1988) 'Information-only machine translation: a feasibility study', in M. Vasconcellos (ed.) *Technology as Translation Strategy* (American Translators Association Scholarly Monograph Series, vol. II), Binghamton, New York: State University of New York, 178–89.

Newton, J. (1987) 'An insider's view of machine translation', in *The Linguist*, vol. 26, no. 1: 21–3.

—— (1988) 'Translating software for the national language', in R. Sharpe (ed.) *Information Technology Manufacturing – Europe 1988*, London: Sterling Publishing Group, 302–4. Reprinted in *The Linguist*, vol. 27, no. 3: 102–4.

—— (1989) 'The terminology database in the translation department', *The Linguist*, vol. 28, no. 2: 46–8.

Nirenburg, S. (ed.) (1987) *Machine Translation: Theoretical and Methodological Issues*, Cambridge: Cambridge University Press.

—— (1989) 'Knowledge-based machine translation', *Machine Translation*, 4: 5–24.

Nirenburg, S. and Carbonell, J.G. (1987) 'Integrating discourse pragmatics and propositional knowledge for multilingual natural language processing', *Computers and Translation* 2: 105–16.

Nirenburg, S. and Levin, L. (1989) 'Knowledge representation support', *Machine Translation* 4: 25–52.

Nishida, F. and Takamatsu, S. (forthcoming) 'Automated procedures for the improvement of a machine translation system by feedback from postediting', to appear in *Machine Translation*.

Nishida, F., Takamatsu, S., Tani, T. and Doi, T. (1988) 'Feedback of correcting information in postediting to a machine translation system', in D. Vargha (ed.) *COLING Budapest: Proceedings of the 12th International Conference on Computational Linguistics*, Budapest: John von Neumann Society for Computing Sciences, 476–81.

Pappegaaij, B.C., Sadler, V. and Witkam, A.P.M. (eds) (1986) *Word Expert Semantics: an Interlingual Knowledge-based Approach*, (Distributed Language Translation 1), Dordrecht: Foris.

Paulos, J.A. (1989) *Innumeracy, Mathematical Illiteracy and its Consequences*, New York: Hill & Wang.

Picken, C. (1986) *Translating and the Computer 7*, London: Aslib.

—— (ed.) (1989) *The Translator's Handbook*, revised edition. London: Aslib.

Piron, C. (1987) 'Esperanto: l'immagine e la realità', in A. Chiti-Batelli (ed.) *La comunicazione internazionale tra politica e glottodidattica*, Milan: Marzorati, 68–116.

Pogson, G. (1989) 'The LT/Electric Word multilingual wordworker's resource guide', *LT/Electric Word* 13, Amsterdam: Language Technology BV.

Pym, P.J. (1990) 'Pre-editing and the use of simplified writing for MT: an engineer's experience of operating an MT system', in P. Mayorcas (ed.) *Translating and the Computer 10: The Translation Environment 10 Years On*, London: Aslib, 80–96.

Raw, A., Vandecapelle, B. and van Eynde, F. (1988) 'Eurotra: an overview', *Interface* 3: 5–32.

Raw, A., van Eynde, F., ten Hacken, P., Hoekstra, H. and Vandecapelle, B. (1989) 'An introduction to the Eurotra machine translation system', Working Papers in Natural Language Processing 1, TAAL Technologie, Utrecht and Katholieke Universiteit Leuven.

Riesbeck, C.K. (1975) 'Conceptual analysis', in R.C. Shank (ed.) *Conceptual Information Processing*, Amsterdam: North-Holland, 83–156.

Rohrer, C. (1986) 'Maschinelle Übersetzung mit Unifikationsgrammatiken', in I. Bátori and H.J. Weber (eds) *Neue Ansätze in Maschineller Sprachübersetzung: Wissenrepräsentation und Textbezug*, Tübingen: Niemeyer Verlag, 75–99.

Rumelhart, D.E. and McClelland, J.L. (1987) *Parallel Distributed Processing*, Cambridge, Mass.: MIT Press.

Rupp, C.J. (1989) 'Situation semantics and machine translation', Fourth Conference of the European Chapter of the Association for Computational Linguistics, Manchester, Proceedings, 308–18.

Sadler, L., Crookston, I., Arnold, D. and Way, A. (1990) 'LFG and translation', in *Third International Conference on Theoretical and Methodological Issues in Machine Translation of Natural Languages*, Austin, Texas.

Sadler, V. (1989) *Working with Analogical Semantics. Disambiguation Techniques in DLT*, Dordrecht/Providence: Foris.

—— (forthcoming) 'Machine translation project reaches watershed', *Language Problems and Language Planning* 15.

Saito, H. and Tomita, M. (1986) 'On automatic composition of stereotypic documents in foreign languages', presented at 1st International Conference on Applications of Artificial Intelligence to Engineering Problems, Southampton, April 1986; Research Report CMU–CS–86–107, Department of Computer Science, Carnegie Mellon University.

Santangelo, S. (1988) 'Making an MT system work: perspective of a translator', in M. Vasconcellos (ed.) *Technology as Translation Strategy* (American Translators Association Scholarly Monograph Series, vol. II), Binghamton, New York: State University of New York.

Sapir, E. (1921) *Language: An Introduction to the Study of Speech*, New York: Harcourt, Brace & World.

Sato, S. (1989) 'Phonetic form generation in a semantics-to-speech system of Japanese', Sendai: Dissertation, Tohoku University.

Sato, S. and Kasuya, H. (1987) 'Automatic translation/speech synthesis of Japanese from written Esperanto incorporating a linguistic knowledge base editor', in J. Laver and M.A. Jack (eds) *European Conference in Speech Technology (Edinburgh 1987)*, vol. 2, Edinburgh: CEP, 414–17.

Sato, S. and Nagao, M. (1990) 'Toward memory-based translation', in H. Karlgren (ed.) *COLING–90: Papers presented to the 13th International Conference on Computational Linguistics*, Helsinki: Yliopistopaino, vol. 3: 247–52.

Saussure, F. de (1916) *Cours de linguistique générale*, Paris: Payot.

Schubert, K. (1986) 'Linguistic and extra-linguistic knowledge', *Computers and Translation* 1: 125–52.

—— (1987) *Metataxis. Contrastive Dependency Syntax for Machine Translation*, Dordrecht/Providence: Foris.

—— (1988) 'Ausdruckskraft und Regelmäßigkeit. Was Esperanto für automatische Übersetzung geeignet macht', *Language Problems and Language Planning* 12: 130–47.

—— (ed.) (1989a) *Interlinguistics. Aspects of the Science of Planned Languages*, Berlin/New York: Mouton de Gruyter.

—— (1989b) 'Interlinguistics – its aims, its achievements, and its place in language science', in K. Schubert (ed.) *Interlinguistics. Aspects of the Science of Planned Languages*, Berlin/New York: Mouton de Gruyter, 7–44.

—— (1989c) 'An unplanned development in planned languages. A study of word grammar', in K. Schubert (ed.) *Interlinguistics. Aspects of the Science of Planned Languages*, Berlin/New York: Mouton de Gruyter, 249–74.

—— (1990) 'Kunskap om världen eller kunskap om texten? En metod för korpusstödd maskinöversättning', in J. Pind and E. Rögnvaldsson (eds) *Papers from the Seventh Scandinavian Conference of Computational Linguistics (Reykjavík 1989)*, Reykjavik: Institute of Lexicography/Institute of Linguistics, 218–28.

Scott, B.E. (1989) 'The Logos System', paper presented at *MT Summit II*, Munich.

Shanker, S.G. (ed.) (1987) *Godel's Theorum in Focus*, London: Croom Helm.

Sherwood, B.A. (1978) 'Fast text-to-speech algorithms for Esperanto, Spanish, Italian, Russian and English', *International Journal of Man–Machine Studies* 10: 669–92.

—— (1982) 'Raporto pri sintezo de Esperanta parolado', in I. Koutny (ed.) *Homa lingvo kaj komputilo*, Budapest: NJSzT//Societo Neumann, 64–75.

—— (1985) 'Komputila tradukado de esperanta teksto', in I. Koutny (ed.) *Perkomputila tekstoprilaboro*, Budapest: Scienca Eldona Centro, 153–60.

Sherwood, J.N. and Sherwood, B.A. (1982) 'Computer voices and ears furnish novel teaching options', *Speech Technology* [1982]: 46–51.

Shreve, G.M. and Vinciquerra, K.J. (1990) 'Hypertext knowledge-bases for computer-assisted translation: organization and structure', in A.L. Wilson (ed.) *Proceedings of the 31st Annual Conference of the American Translators Association*, New Orleans, October 1990: Learned Information, Inc.

Sjögren, S. (1970) *En syntax för datamaskinell analys av esperanto*, FOA P rapport C 8264–11(64), Stockholm: Försvarets forskningsanstalt.

Skuce, D. and Meyer, I. (1990) 'Computer-assisted concept analysis: an essential component of a terminologist's workstation', in H. Czap and W. Nedobity (eds) *TKE '90: Terminology and Knowledge Engineering*, Frankfurt: INDEKS Verlag, 187–99.

Slocum, J. (1984) 'Machine translation: its history, current status, and future prospects', in *10th International Conference on Computational Linguistics*, Proceedings of COLING–84, Stanford, California, 546–61.

—— (1985) 'A survey of machine translation: its history, current status, and future prospects', *Computational Linguistics* 11: 1–17.

—— (ed.) (1988) *Machine Translation Systems*, Cambridge: Cambridge University Press.

Smith, D. and Tyldesley, D. (1986) 'Translation Practices Report', Reading: Digital Equipment Corporation.

Snell, B.M. (ed.) (1979) *Translating and the Computer*, Amsterdam: North-Holland.

Snell, B.M. (ed.) (1983) *Term Banks for Tomorrow's World*, London: Aslib.

Snell-Hornby, M. (1988) *Translation Studies: An Integrated Approach*, Amsterdam: John Benjamins.

Somers, H.L. (1986) 'Some thoughts on interface structure(s)', in W. Wilss and K.-D. Schmitz (eds) *Maschinelle Übersetzung – Methoden und Werkzeuge*, Tübingen: Max Niemeyer Verlag, 81–9.

Somers, H.L., Hirakawa, H., Miike, S. and Amano, S. (1988) 'The treatment of complex English nominalizations in machine translation', *Computers and Translation* 3: 3–21.

Somers, H.L., Tsujii, J. and Jones, D. (1990) 'Machine translation without a source text', in H. Karlgren (ed.) *COLING–90: Papers Presented to the 13th International Conference on Computational Linguistics*, Helsinki: Yliopistopaino, vol. 3: 271–6.

Steer, M.G. and Stentiford, F.W.M. (1989) 'Speech language translation', in J. Peckham (ed.) *Recent Developments and Applications of Natural Language Processing*, London: Kogan Page, 129–40.

Steiner, E. (ed.) (1991) Special issue on Eurotra, *Machine Translation*, 6: 2–3.

Sumita, E., Iida, H. and Kohyama, H. (1990) 'Translating with examples: a new approach to machine translation', *Third International Conference on Theoretical and Methodological Issues in Machine Translation of Natural Languages*, Austin, Texas.

Tarski, A. (1943–4) 'The semantic conception of truth', *Philosophy and Phenomenological Research IV*: 347.

Taylor, P.J. and Cronin, B. (eds) (1983) *Information Management Research in Europe*, London: Aslib.

'Terminological Data Banks' (1989) *TermNet News* 24, Infoterm, Vienna: 25–30.

Tesnière, L. (1959) *Eléments de syntaxe structurale*, 2nd edn, 4th print. 1982, Paris: Klincksieck.

Thomas, P. (1988) 'Analysis of an English and French LSP: some comparisons with English general text corpora', *ALSED–UNESCO Newsletter 11*, 1(26), 2–10.

Thurmair, G. (1990) 'Complex lexical transfer in METAL', *Third International Conference on Theoretical and Methodological Issues in Machine Translation of Natural Languages*, Austin, Texas, 91–107.

Toma, P. (1976) 'An operational machine translation system', in R.W. Brislin (ed.) *Translation: Applications and Research*, New York: Gardner, 247–59.

Trabulsi, S. (1989) 'Le système Systran', in A. Abbou (ed.) *Traduction Assistée par Ordinateur: Perspectives technologiques, industrielles et économiques envisageables à l'horizon 1990: l'offre, la demande, les marchés et les évolutions en cours*, Actes du Séminaire international (Paris, March 1988), Paris: DAICADIF, 15–27.

Tsujii, J. (1989) 'Machine translation with Japan's neighboring countries', in M. Nagao (ed.) *Machine Translation Summit*, Tokyo: Ohmsha, 50–3.

Tsujii, J. and Nagao, M. (1988) 'Dialogue translation vs text translation – Interpretation based approach', in O. Vargha (ed.) *COLING Budapest: Proceedings of the 12th International Conference on Computational Linguistics*, Budapest: John von Neumann Society for Computing Sciences, 688–93.

Uchida, H. and Kakizaki, T. (1989) 'Electronic dictionary project', in M. Nagao (ed.) *Machine Translation Summit*, Tokyo: Ohmsha, 83–7.

Valentine, T. (1990) 'Status of machine translation (MT) technology: Hearing before the Subcommittee on Science, Research and Technology of the Committee on Science, Space and Technology, US House of Representatives, 101st Congress, Second Session, September 11, 1990 [no. 153], Chairman: Rep. T. Valentine. Washington: US Government Printing Office.

van der Korst, B. (1989) 'Functional grammar and machine translation', in J.H. Connolly and S.C. Dik (eds) *Functional Grammar and the Computer*, Dordrecht: Foris, 289–316.

van Eynde, F. (1988) 'The analysis of tense and aspect in Eurotra', in D. Vargha (ed.) *COLING Budapest: Proceedings of the 12th International Conference on Computational Linguistics*, Budapest: John von Neumann Society for Computing Sciences, 699–704.

van Noord, G., Dorrepaal, J., van der Eijk, P., Florenza, M. and des Tombe, L. (1990) 'The MiMo2 research system', *Third International Conference on Theoretical and Methodological Issues in Machine Translation of Natural Languages*, Austin, Texas.

Vargha, D. (ed.) (1988) *COLING Budapest: Proceedings of the 12th International Conference on Computational Linguistics*, Budapest: John von Neumann Society for Computing Sciences.

Vasconcellos, M. (1984) 'Machine translation at the Pan American Health Organization: a review of highlights and insights', *Newsletter*, British Computer Society Natural Language Translation Specialist Group.

—— (1985) 'Theme and focus: cross-language comparison vis translations from extended discourse', unpublished PhD dissertation, Georgetown University, Washington, DC.

—— (1986) 'Functional considerations in the postediting of MT output: dealing with V(S)O versus SVO', *Computers and Translation* 1, 1: 21–38.

—— (1987a) 'Postediting on-screen: machine translation from Spanish into English', in C. Picken (ed.) *A Profession on the Move: Proceedings of Translating and the Computer 8*, London: Aslib.

—— (1987b) 'A comparison of MT postediting and traditional revision', in K. Kummer (ed.) *Proceedings of the 28th Annual Conference of the American Translators Association*, Medford, New Jersey: Learned Information.

—— (1988) 'Factors in the evaluation of MT: formal vs functional approaches', in M. Vasconcellos (ed.) *Technology and Translation Strategy* (American Translators' Association Scholarly Monograph Series, vol. II), Binghamton, New York: State University of New York.

—— (ed.) (1988) *Technology as Translation Strategy* (American Translators Association Scholarly Monograph Series, vol. II), Binghamton, New York: State University of New York.

—— (1989a) 'Cohesion and coherence in the presentation of machine translation products', in *Georgetown University Round Table on Languages and Linguistics 1989*, Washington, DC: Georgetown University Press.

—— (1989b) 'Long-term data for an MT policy', *Literary and Linguistic Computing* 4, 3: 203–13.

Vasconcellos, M. and León, M. (1988) 'SPANAM and ENGSPAN: machine translation at the Pan American Health Organization', in J. Slocum (ed.) *Machine Translation Systems*, Cambridge: Cambridge University Press.

Vauquois, B. (1985) 'The approach of Geta to automatic translation: comparison with some other methods', paper presented at International Symposium on Machine Translation, Riyadh; in Ch. Boitet (ed.) (1988) *Bernard Vauquois et la TAO: vingt-cinq ans de traduction automatique – Analectes*, Grenoble: Association Champollion, 631–86.

Vauquois, B. and Boitet, Ch. (1985) 'Automated translation at Grenoble University', *Computational Linguistics* 11: 28–36.

Vinay, J.-P. and Darbelnet, J. (1977) *Stylistique comparée du français et de l'anglais*, Paris: Didier.

Weaver, W. (1955) 'Translation', in W.N. Locke and A.D. Booth (eds) *Machine Translation of Languages*, New York: Wiley, 15–23.

Wehrli, E. (1990) 'STS: an experimental sentence translation system', in H. Karlgren (ed.) *COLING–90: Papers Presented to the 13th International Conference on Computational Linguistics*, Helsinki: Yliopistopaino, vol. 1: 76–8.

Whitelock, P.J., Wood, M.M., Chandler, B.J., Holden, N. and Horsfall, H.J. (1986) 'Strategies for interactive machine translation: the experience and implications of the UMIST Japanese project', *11th International Conference on Computational Linguistics*, Proceedings of COLING–86, Bonn, 329–34.

Whitfield, F. (1969) 'Glossematics', in A.A. Hill (ed.) *Linguistics*, Voice of America Forum Lectures.

Whorf, B.L. (1956) *Language, Thought and Reality* (collected papers), Cambridge, Mass.: MIT Press.

Wilks, Y. (1972) *Grammar, Meaning and the Machine Analysis of Language*, London: Routledge & Keegan Paul.

—— (1984a) 'Machine translation and the artificial intelligence paradigm of language processes', *Computers in Language Research* 2.

—— (1984b) 'Artificial intelligence and machine translation', in S. and W. Sedelon (eds) *Current Trends in the Language Sciences*, Amsterdam: North Holland.

—— (1990) 'Form and content in semantics', in *Synthèse* 82: 329–51.

Wilks, Y., Carbonell, J., Farwell, D., Hovy, E. and Nirenburg, S. (1990) 'Machine translation again?', in *Proceedings of the DARPA Speech and Natural Language Workshop*, Monterey, California.

Witkam, A.P.M. (1983) *Distributed Language Translation. Feasibility study of a multilingual facility for videotex information networks*, Utrecht: BSO.

Wood, M.M. and Chandler, B.J. (1988) 'Machine translation for monolinguals', in D. Vargha (ed.) *COLING Budapest: Proceedings of the 12th International Conference on Computational Linguistics*, Budapest: John von Neumann Society for Computing Sciences, 760–3.

Zajac, R. (1990) 'A relational approach to translation', *Third International Conference on Theoretical and Methodological Issues in Machine Translation of Natural Languages*, Austin, Texas.

Zeidenberg, M. (1987) 'Modeling the Brain', *Byte*, vol. 12, no. 14: 237–46, New York: McGraw-Hill.

Glossary of terms

Anaphora The use of a word (e.g. a pronoun) to refer to a preceding word or group of words (e.g. in *Peter entered the room. He was wearing a blue overcoat.*, The pronoun *he* is an example of anaphora).

Automatic look-up A function provided in some software packages that allows the user direct access to a dictionary or glossary from a text file (i.e. via a window).

Back translation A translation into the original source language of a text which is itself a translation. This procedure may be used to verify the accuracy of the original translation.

Batch processing A mode in which a number of files are processed sequentially by the computer without intervention from the user.

Bit A binary digit, 0 or 1. The minimum element of computer coding information.

Bottom up processing An approach in which meaning is computed compositionally from the bottom up (i.e. by combining word meanings to form larger semantic units). These word meanings are drawn from lexica containing lists of predefined, distinct word senses. For each of these senses, one literal meaning is held to be more basic, while additional, metaphorical meanings are considered to be more derivative.

Byte A group of bits (usually 8) used to represent individual letters and symbols of a defined alphabet.

Central processing unit (CPU) The essential part of a computer that performs all the arithmetical and logical operations.

Clone A microcomputer which is a near replica, in appearance, configuration and function, of a machine produced by a major manufacturer.

Coherence The underlying links that establish connectedness within the communication act.

Cohesion The overt structural links by means of which the elements in discourse can be decoded in relation to each other.

Computational linguistics The branch of computer science concerned with natural-language processing.

Controlled language A circumscribed range of vocabulary and syntax. May be used to optimize MT performance.

Corpus 1. A collection or body of texts on a specific topic or within a specific domain. 2. The finite collection of grammatical sentences that is used as a basis for the descriptive analysis of a language.

Data bank A large store of information in a form that can be processed by a computer.

Data base, Database The data accessible to a computer.

Dictionary The component of an MT system or translation tools package within which source and target language lexical items and data relating thereto are stored. In MT, a dictionary will typically comprise an indexed file of records corresponding to individual entries, usually each consisting of a word to be matched against the source text, plus a series of codes (syntactic, semantic, etc.) and a pointer to a translation gloss, also accompanied by a series of codes.

Domain-specific language A sublanguage restricted to the vocabulary and syntax of a specific domain.

Electronic mail The transmission of documents from one computer terminal to another.

Ellipsis The omission of words that are understood in context but which would need to be supplied to make a structure grammatically complete (e.g. *the tools that I use* may be reduced by ellipsis to *the tools I use*).

Esperanto An artificial international language based largely on words common to the main European languages, invented in 1887 by Dr L.L. Zamenhof.

Flag 1. A character used to signal a condition or characteristic. 2. An element of data used as an indicator.

General language Unrestricted and non-specialized language.

Gloss 1. A brief explanation of a word or expression. 2. A word or phrase used as a translational equivalent, traditionally written between single quotes.

Grammar The branch of linguistics that deals with syntax and morphology.

Homograph 1. A written form functional as two or more parts of speech and/or representing two or more words. 2. Sometimes used in MT to describe lexical items which, in their base or inflected forms, can function as distinct parts of speech or as distinct words.

Human translation (HT) Translation as performed by a human.

Idiolect A variety of a language peculiar to a specific user.

Idiom   1. A group of words the meaning of which cannot be deduced from the meanings of the individual words. 2. Sometimes used in MT parlance to indicate any dictionary entry that consists of more than one word. Also referred to as a multiple-word entry.

Inflection   The change of form that words undergo depending on their function.

Inflection rules   Rules applied in MT through flagging to determine how a target language word will inflect.

Information-only translation   Translation not intended for publication, produced quickly and cheaply for a specified (and usually specialist) readership. When generated using MT, minimal post-editing will normally suffice, as style is not an important consideration.

Interactive system   A system which allows the user to interact with the computer by means of dialogue. This term is used to distinguish MT systems which solicit information from the user *during the translation process* from those which process translations in batch mode. Batch-processing MT systems usually have interactive modes for functions such as dictionary updating.

Interlingua   Any artificial language used in an MT system to represent the meaning of natural language.

Look-up   *see* **Automatic look-up**.

Machine translation (MT)   Translation as performed by a computer, with or without human assistance.

Microcomputer   A small computer, typically intended for a single user, in which the central processing unit is contained in one or more silicon chips.

Microprocessor   A single integrated circuit that functions as the central processing unit of a microcomputer.

Morpheme   A meaningful linguistic unit that cannot be subdivided into further such units.

Morphology   The study of the structure of words and their inflectional, derivational and combinational patterns.

Natural language   1. A naturally evolved language that is the native speech of a people. 2. Languages of this kind viewed collectively.

Natural language processing   The branch of computer science concerned with the machine processing of natural language(s).

Neural network   A computing configuration in which a large number of processing units operating in parallel (parallel processing units) are interconnected in a complex manner thought to resemble the connections between brain cells.

Output   *see* **Raw translation**.

Page   In the United States it is frequently considered that the translation *page* is equivalent to 250 words.

Parse   To assign constituent structure to a sentence and ascertain the grammatical relationships that exist between its component words.

Parser   A computer program which parses sentences. In the case of MT, the parser is the engine that drives the analysis component.

Parsing   *see* **Parse**.

Paste-in, Pasting-in   The copying of data directly into an open text file from a database via a window.

Personal computer (PC)   *see* **Microcomputer**.

Platform   A computer and operating system regarded as the fundamental components of a more complex whole such as a translator workstation.

Postediting, Post-editing, Post editing   Editing performed for the purpose of improving the quality and acceptability of raw MT output.

Posteditor, Post-editor, Post editor   A person who undertakes the task of post-editing.

Post-modern philosophy   Wittgenstein [later works], Heidegger, Husserl, Levinas.

Pre-analysis   The process in MT during which the computer breaks the source text down into the smallest units it can analyse.

Pre-editing   The editing of a source text prior to its submission to MT. The pre-editor seeks to eliminate ambiguity and confusion through structural and lexical modifications, thereby optimizing the system's performance. A pre-edited English-language source text will typically contain more prepositions and conjunctions and have shorter sentences than the unedited original; this is intended to assist the computer's analysis.

Pre-editor   A person who undertakes the task of pre-editing.

Raw translation   The raw, unedited output of an MT system.

Register   A form of a language associated with a particular situation, set of circumstances, subject matter or purpose.

Restricted language   *see* **Controlled language**.

Reverse translation   *see* **Back translation**.

Semantic network   A collection of points, called nodes, each of which represents a concept. Each node has a name (e.g. fair-haired girl, black dog) which is connected by a directed arc (or arrow), called a relation, to another node. The relation has a label.

Semantics   The branch of linguistics concerned with meaning.

Source language   The language in which a text is originally written and from which a translation is to be or has been produced.

Source text   The source language text from which a translation is to be or has been produced.

Special language   Special language has features in common with both general language and sublanguage. It combines relative structural freedom with specialized vocabulary. Scientific reports and technical documentation fall into this category.

Split-screen editing   A post-editing mode of MT that allows the user to view and edit a segment of raw translation whilst viewing the corresponding segment of the source text.

Staging   Point of departure for the clause, sentence, paragraph, episode or discourse.

Standard Generalized Markup Language (SGML)   A highly flexible mark-up language devised to make document structure descriptions available in a universal format. Wide adoption of SGML document descriptions will facilitate the transfer of texts between different word processing formats. SGML became an international standard (ISO 8879) in 1986.

Sublanguage   A variety of a language having restricted grammar and vocabulary, such as would facilitate MT analysis.

Syntax   A set of rules governing sentence construction and the grammatical arrangement of words.

Target language   The language into which a translation is to be or has been produced.

Target text   The target language text which is to be or has been produced through translation.

Term   A word or expression used to designate a specific object, action or process, particularly in a specialized field of knowledge.

Term bank   *see* **Terminology data base, Terminology database**.

Terminology   The body of specialized words and terms relating to a particular domain; *also* the study of such words and terms.

Terminology data base, Terminology database   A database dedicated to the storage and retrieval of terminology.

Terminology management   The act of maintaining and updating a terminology database.

Text encoding initiative   The goal of the TEI is to develop and disseminate a clearly defined format for the interchange of machine-readable texts among researchers so as to allow easier and more efficient sharing of resources for textual computing and natural-language processing. The interchange format is intended to specify how texts should be encoded or marked so that they can be shared by different research projects for different purposes. The use of specific delimiter characters and specific tabs to express specific information are all prescribed by this interchange format, based on the international standard ISO 8879, Standard Generalized Markup Language (SGML).

Translation 1. A rendering of a text from one language into another. 2. The product of such a rendering.

Translation tools Software packages which are designed to assist translators in their work but which do not perform translation. The main constituents of a translation tools package are a text analyser (parser) and a user-updatable dictionary. The text analyser is used to identify lexical items for dictionary entry. Such products usually allow translation equivalents to be pasted directly into a text file via a window during dictionary look-up.

Translator's workbench *see* **Translator workstation**.

Translator workstation A custom-built, ergonomically designed unit having a computer as its main platform, incorporating translation tools and supporting a potentially wide range of software utilities and peripheral devices. Translator workstations offer various levels of computer assistance up to and including MT. They can also incorporate fax, electronic mail and desk-top publishing facilities, and offer remote access to terminology databases.

Vocabulary 1. A listing, selective or exhaustive, of the lexical items of a language or used by a group or individual or within a specialized field of knowledge, with definitions or translation equivalents. 2. The aggregate of lexical items used or understood by a specified group, class, profession, etc.

Vocabulary search A function of MT and translation tools packages in which the system compares the words in a text with those that figure in a specified dictionary or sequence of dictionaries and copies *unfound* words into a file which can later be used as a basis for dictionary updating.

Window A feature of certain software packages that allows the user to access utilities from within a text file.

Wordage The number of words contained in a text.

Word count, Wordcount *see* **Wordage**.

Index